The Official
PUNK ROCK
BOOK OF LISTS

The Official
PUNK ROCK
BOOK OF LISTS

AMY WALLACE
&
HANDSOME DICK MANITOBA

Backbeat
Books

An Imprint of Hal Leonard Corporation

New York

Published in 2007 by Backbeat Books
An Imprint of Hal Leonard Corporation
19 West 21st Street, New York, NY 10010

Printed in the United States of America

Book design by Stephen Ramirez

Illustrations by Cliff Mott

Library of Congress Cataloging-in-Publication Data

Wallace, Amy.
 The official punk rock book of lists / Amy Wallace and "Handsome" Dick Manitoba.—1st ed.
    p. cm.
 Includes bibliographical references (p.   ).
 ISBN 978-0-87930-919-0
 1. Punk rock music—Miscellanea. I. Manitoba, Dick, 1954–
 II. Title.
 ML3534.W287 2007
 781.66—dc22
                         2007036593

www.backbeatbooks.com

Dedicated to my boyfriend, Scott Bradley, and our generation gap. On an early date I told him that the Pogues were one of my favorite bands, and he cheerily replied, "Oh, yeah, I love Joe Strummer!" And to Hank and Bella, who purred their way through *End of the Century* and *The Filth and the Fury*.

—A.W.

To my family—my wife, Zoe, and my son, Jake Koufax Manitoba. To my pal, boss, and guardian angel, Little Steven Van Zandt. To my mom, Sylvia . . . to the memories of my "brother," Steve Boone ("Boonie"), and my dad, Morris "Bill" Blum.

—H.D.M.

"In punk, everything happened late at night, among children."

—Judy Nylon

53. Joey Shithead (D.O.A.)

54. John Doe (X)

55. Johnny Moped

56. Johnny Rotten (Sex Pistols, Public Image Ltd.)

57. Johnny Thunders (New York Dolls, the Heartbreakers)

58. Kid Congo Powers (the Cramps, the Gun Club

59. Klaus Fluoride (Dead Kennedys)

60. Lee Ving (Fear)

61. Lorna Doom (the Germs)

62. Lux Interior (previously Vip Vop, the Cramps)

63. Lydia Lunch

64. Metal Mike (Angry Samoans)

65. Monoman (DMZ, Lyres)

66. Nasty Suicide (Hanoi Rocks)

67. Nick Knox (the Cramps)

68. Nikki Sudden (Swell Maps)

69. Pat Smear (the Germs, Nirvana)

70. Paul Bearer (Sheer Terror)

71. Paul Cripple (Reagan Youth)

72. Penny Rimbaud (Crass)

73. Pig Champion (Poison Idea)

74. Plastic Bertrand (Hubble Bubble)

75. Poison Ivy Rorschach (the Cramps)

76. Poly Styrene (X-ray Spex)

77. Pushead (artist, Septic Death)

78. Randy Rampage (D.O.A.)

79. Rat Scabies (the Damned)

80. Raybeez (Warzone)

81. Richard Hell (Richard Hell & the Voidoids, etc.)

82. Rik L Rik (F-Word)

83. Rodney Anonymous (Dead Milkmen)

84. Sickie Wifebeater (Mentors)

85. Sid Vicious (Sex Pistols)

86. Siouxsie Sioux (Siouxsie & the Banshees)

87. Spit Stix (Fear)

88. Spot (Black Flag producer)

89. Steve Ignorant (Crass)
90. Stinky Turner (Cockney Rejects)
91. Stiv Bators (Dead Boys)
92. Sue Catwoman (London scenester)
93. Suggs (Madness)
94. Sylvain Sylvain (New York Dolls)
95. Tesco Vee (the Meatmen)
96. Tom Verlaine (Television)
97. Tomata Du Plenty (Screamers)
98. Useless (Subhumans)
99. Vinnie Stigma (Agnostic Front)
100. Will Shatter (Flipper)
101. Wimpy (the Queers, the Jabbers)

List compiled by the Backbeat Punk Rock All-Stars.

HOW 20 PUNKS GOT THEIR NAMES

1. Bob Vermeulen, a.k.a. Tesco Vee (the Meatmen)

Vermuellen adopted this name after seeing a photo of Throbbing Gristle posing in front of Tesco, the ubiquitous British supermarket chain.

2. John Lydon, a.k.a. Johnny Rotten (Sex Pistols, PiL)

Lydon got his name when guitarist Steve Jones said the singer's teeth were "fucking rotten," in addition to which, Lydon picked at them.

3. Erick Lee Purkhiser, a.k.a. Vip Vop and Lux Interior (the Cramps)

Before Lux was Lux, he spent a year as Vip Vop. The name is taken from the title of a track by 1950s R&B stars Marvin

Phillips and Johnny "Emory" Perry. "Lux Interior" came from a '50s ad for a fine car.

4. Greg Beckerleg, a.k.a. Bryan Gregory (the Cramps)

Beckerleg chose the name Bryan Gregory because it "sounded like a movie star."

5. Brian Tristan, a.k.a. Kid Congo Powers (the Cramps, the Gun Club)

According to Dick Porter's biography, *The Cramps*, when Tristan joined the band, the name Brian Gris Gris was suggested and then dropped, because the first Bryan had been enough trouble. Other suggestions were "Mr. Tristan" and "Thing." Finally Ivy and Lux invented "Congo Powers" as an homage to their beloved Santeria voodoo candles, on which were printed, "When you light this candle, powers will be revealed to you." Tristan added "Kid" because it sounded like a boxer or a pirate. Lux saw it as a tribute to blues harp player Kid Thomas.

6. Arthur Harold Kane Jr., a.k.a. Arthur "Killer" Kane (New York Dolls)

Like Sid Vicious, Arthur Kane got his ominous name because he was anything but ominous. A high school friend of Kane's said, "He was called Killer because he was just the opposite. He was a gentle giant who would never harm anyone."

7. Steve Bailey, a.k.a. Steve Severin (Siouxsie & the Banshees)

The bassist named himself after the slave Severin in Leopold von Sacher-Masoch's S&M novel *Venus in Furs*.

8. Steve Nason, a.k.a. Steve Nieve (Elvis Costello & the Attractions)

Nason got his name after wondering aloud what a groupie was. "The first few tours we did, I was just out of school," he said. According to the Costello bio *Complicated Shadows*, by the band's second U.S. tour Steve was making up for lost time. Said journalist Charles Shaar Murray, "He was knocking down enough pussy these last six weeks to make Warren Beatty and Phil Lynott feel inadequate."

9. Brody Armstrong, a.k.a. Brody Dalle (the Distillers)

When the singer divorced Tim Armstrong, she chose her last name as an homage to Beatrice Dalle, the French star of the suffering-female film *Betty Blue*.

10. Jimmy Giorsetti, a.k.a. Don Bolles (the Germs)

Drummer Giorsetti named himself after a murdered Arizona journalist.

11. Ray Burns, a.k.a. Captain Sensible (the Damned)

In *England's Dreaming*, Burns explains that he got his name on a bus tour through France: "I got this shirt with epaulettes. I was pretending to be the pilot, and shouting, 'It's all right! It's all right! Everything's under control! It's on autopilot!' I could have passed for a pilot and people were getting upset. And someone said, 'Oh, it's fucking Captain Sensible.' . . . I thought it would last five minutes: I didn't know I would still be called Captain Sensible at 35."

12. James Osterberg, a.k.a. Iggy Pop (the Stooges)

Iggy's first name came from playing in a band called the Iguanas. In *Please Kill Me*, Scott Ashton explains where "Pop" was derived from: "Iggy had shaved off his eyebrows. We had a friend named James Pop who had a disease that robbed him of all his facial hair. So when Iggy shaved his eyebrows we started calling him Pop."

13. Marian Elliot, a.k.a. Poly Styrene (X-ray Spex)

Said Ms. Styrene, "I thought it would be a laugh to call myself a product. I think all pop stars are products."

14. Chris Miller, a.k.a. Rat Scabies (the Damned)

When Miller auditioned for the Damned, the tryout took place in a rat-infested basement, where he scratched at his skin condition. He once wore a rat as an earring.

15–18. Jeffrey Hyman, a.k.a. Joey Ramone; John Cummings, a.k.a. Johnny Ramone; Tommy Erdelyi, a.k.a. Tommy Ramone; Douglas Colvin, a.k.a. Dee Dee Ramone (Ramones)

Joey went through a glam period before becoming a Ramone, during which he wore glitter and platform boots and called himself Jeff Starship. The Ramones were taken from the name Paul Ramon, which Paul McCartney used in the early days of the Beatles' fame to check into hotels when he wanted some privacy. Also, the guys thought "Ramones" sounded like a gang name.

When Tommy Ramone left the band to work as a producer, he reverted to his original name, Tommy Erdelyi. When Dee Dee left the band and began his short-lived career as a rapper, he went by Dee Dee King. When the Ramones were inducted into the Rock 'n' Roll Hall of Fame, Dee Dee wore a sharp suit rather than the Ramones' leather-jacket, torn-jeans uniform, to indicate that he had grown beyond the Ramones.

19. John Beverly, a.k.a. Sid Vicious (Sex Pistols)

John Lydon gave Vicious his first name after his family's pet hamster, Sidney, an old animal so safe and sweet and cuddly "it couldn't hurt anybody," said Lydon. "It had no teeth and was the least dangerous thing you could imagine—just like Sid." "Vicious" was added when John's father was playing with the hamster and it took a bite out of his hand. Sid (the person) disliked his name.

20. Paul Hudson, a.k.a. HR (Bad Brains)

Darryl Jenifer of Bad Brains expatiated on how bandmate Hudson became HR: "Do you know how rich people are called by their initials? The whole concept of being 'HR' was as if he was a rich man." It was also recalled as an in-joke, "Hunting Rod" referring to his impressive masculinity. Finally, HR used the initials to stand for "Human Rights."

7 PUNK NAMES

Courtesy of Don Bolles of the Germs

1. Dinah Cancer
2. Sharon Needles
3. Cat Scandal (Don's girlfriend)
4. Dick Pearson, a modern primitive
5. Shelby Eaton, a British cannibal researcher
6 & 7. Eva Destruction and Dave Reckoning, a postapocalyptic couple

Don Bolles is the drummer for L.A. punk legends the Germs.

HOW 33 PUNK ROCK BANDS GOT THEIR NAMES

1. The Misfits
Named after Marilyn Monroe's final film.

2. The Meatmen
Tesco Vee told author Steve Blush, "'Meatmen' came from B.F., the other half of *Touch & Go* magazine—another former good friend who I've left strewn behind me on the trash pile of life. I'd pick him up—he was living with his folks—and every time he'd let out a big belch, I could guess which meat he'd had for dinner. So I said, 'You are the meat man!' That's why I called the band the Meatmen."

3. Fugazi
Ian MacKaye found the word "fugazi" in *Nam*, a collection of Vietnam vet war stories edited by Mark Baker. "Fugazi" is military slang for "a fucked-up situation." MacKaye says it reflects how the band "views the world."

4. The Cramps
Guitarist Poison Ivy suggested "the Cramps," saying, "We decided to call ourselves the Cramps because it's a painful, violent affliction that's hard to get rid of, and we thought it was in the same vein as the Kinks—one of our favorite bands."

5. Minor Threat
Says Ian MacKaye in *Our Band Could Be Your Life*, "We were minors—underage—and also just diminutive." (MacKaye is 5'7".) "Just a small threat, nothing to worry about."

6. Bad Brains
"Bad" of course, means "good," and "brains" has to do with being thought-provoking.

7. The Damned

Rat Scabies and Brian James named their band after two of their favorite films: Visconti's *The Damned*, and *Midwich Cuckoo*, which was originally filmed as *Village of the Damned*. Said Mr. Scabies, "We really liked the idea of being the band that came from Midwich," adding, "Brian was quite into the Nazi decadence thing."

8. New York Dolls

Syl Sylvain worked near the New York Doll Hospital. Rick Rivets remembers suggesting the band should go there and take photos of themselves with pieces of broken dolls—like the famous Beatles "butcher cover." Said Rivets, "It never panned out because we were probably too stoned to leave the car." David Johansen, who is known to embellish his tales, claimed that "Sylvain came up with this name, the Dolls, and I tagged on the 'New York.'" Another time, David Jo said it was the name of a Staten Island gang he belonged to. In 1973 he told *Record Mirror* that he met bass player Arthur Kane at a screening of *Beyond the Valley of the Dolls*—"We were both into dolls, I suppose." Arthur said the name was invented to sound like something from a 1930s musical. Johansen said the band was named after Barbie and Ken dolls. In 2005, Rick Rivets said that Kane added "New York" to Syl's "Dolls" in order to acquire an instant local following, "like the New York Yankees." Of all the stories, the doll hospital one is the most oft repeated.

9. The Heartbreakers

When the New York Dolls broke up, members Johnny Thunders and Jerry Nolan quickly formed a new band. Bassist Richard Hell had just left Television, and he teamed up with the lads to form the Heartbreakers. Johnny explained their name: "It's like kids that never did anything right, everyone they touch goes out of their minds—like someone who comes along and burns down your house—that's breaking your heart."

10. Butthole Surfers

The group began playing in San Antonio, Texas, in 1981, and changed its name for every show. Some of their monikers were Ashtray Babyheads, Nine Inch Worm Makes Own Food, Vodka Family Winstons, and the Inalienable Right to Eat Fred Astaire's Asshole. All that changed the night the guy introducing them forgot what they were called and used the name of one of their songs—"The Butthole Surfers"—to announce them. That was the band's first paying show, so they decided to keep the name. For years they were referred to as "B.H. Surfers" in advertisements.

11. Richard Hell & the Voidoids

Hell named his band after an unfinished novel he wrote in 1973. Alternative names under consideration were the Savage Statues, the Junkyard, the Morons, the Dogbites, and the Beauticians.

12. Dead Boys

These Cleveland rockers had originally been Rocket from the Tombs. One of their best songs, "Down in Flames," had the line "Dead boy, running scared," which inspired the name Dead Boys.

13. Blink 182

The band named themselves after the number of times Al Pacino said "fuck" in *Scarface*.

14. Devo

Their name is an abbreviation of "devolution," which is what the band members thought was happening to the world in the 1970s. It probably still is.

15. The Hugh Beaumont Experience

Some of the members would later form the Butthole Surfers. The band was named after the actor who played the dad on *Leave It to Beaver*.

16. Hüsker Dü

The band is named after a board game that was popular in the '50s. It's Swedish for "do you remember?"

17. Jane's Addiction

Jane was a prostitute acquainted with all the band members.

18. The Jesus and Mary Chain

The band was inspired by an offer on a breakfast cereal packet to send away for a gold Jesus and Mary chain.

19. Ramones

Paul McCartney's younger brother was in a band called Scaffold. To give himself an identity apart from his famous sibling, he went by the name of Mike McGear. When Paul appeared on Scaffold's records, he used the name Paul Ramon. Paul also used the name to check into hotels, in an effort to preserve his privacy. As huge Beatles fans, the Ramones chose this moniker. They also liked it because it made them sound like a gang.

20. The Pogues

Shortened from "Pogue Mahone," a distorted version of "pog ma hon," which is Gaelic for "kiss my ass."

21. Iggy Pop & the Stooges

Iggy got his name from his membership in a band called the Iguanas. The Stooges were originally the Psychedelic Stooges, combining their fondness for drugs with a liking for *The Three Stooges*. When hippies appropriated the word "psychedelic," the Stooges dropped it. Mr. Pop has been quoted as saying he hates the name Stooges.

22. The Replacements

The common belief is that the group played when another band failed to show up. When asked who they were, Paul Westerberg said, "We're the Replacements."

According to one version of the story, guitarist Chris Mars came up with the Substitutes, immediately followed by Westerberg's Replacements. Another tale has it that they played their first show at a former church, which at the time functioned as a halfway house for alkies. They played under the name the Impediments. After the show, they were told that they were so awful they would never play again. Thus, they decided on the Replacements. Once, when Westerberg was asked who they were replacing, he declared, "Everything."

23. The Residents

Hardy Fox, one of the bands' managers, said, "The first audition tape that the Residents ever sent to a record company was to Warner Bros., and they didn't have a name, they didn't use a name, they didn't even believe in names. So they sent it in, and when it was returned as a rejection, it was just addressed to 'the Residents' at the address."

24. Sonic Youth

They named themselves as a tribute to the MC5's iconic Fred "Sonic" Smith and to reggae star Big Youth.

25. The Velvet Underground

One of the band members found a copy of a book by this title on the sidewalk in New York City. The book, published in 1963, is an analysis of sexual perversion.

26. Violent Femmes

This is Milwaukee-area slang for "wimps."

27. Radio Birdman

The first Australian punk band (1974) took their name from a misheard lyric in a Stooges song: the actual lyric is "radio burnin'."

28. Pere Ubu

David Thomas named his band after French Dadaist Alfred Jarry's bizarre king, Father Ubu, because "it would be an added texture of absolute grotesqueness . . . a darkness over everything."

29. Television

An early incarnation, the Neon Boys, was finished. The group considered Goo Goo & the Liberteens but rejected it. When Richard Meyers suggested Television, the rest of the group were all for it. Said Richard Lloyd, "We wanted something that was really tinkly and mechanical and had a car radio . . . something that blared out, it's always there. It's so there that you lose your consciousness about it. 'Television' just seemed to fit that bill 'cause it's something that's in every home in America. It's so obtrusive, it's unobtrusive."

30. Pearl Jam

Contrary to popular rumor, Pearl Jam is not a term for sperm, nor is it peyote jam made by Eddie Vedder's great-grandmother. The truth is rather more mundane. The band liked the word "pearl" for its various connotations: it's surfer slang for submerging the nose of your board; it's the title of a Janis Joplin album; and it's the nickname of basketball great Earl Monroe. Vedder actually had a beloved great-grandmother named Pearl, but she didn't monkey around with hallucinogens. Vedder likes to think of "Pearl Jam" as that creative conflict which hones a grain of sand in an oyster into an exquisite pearl.

31. The Gun Club

This band was originally known as Creeping Ritual. At the time, singer Jeffrey Lee Pierce was rooming with Keith Morris, then the lead singer for Black Flag. Pierce's band did a wild show at L.A.'s Madame Wong's (the Chinese restaurant/punk club) and was worried that they would be blackballed from the scene-central club. The band considered changing their name, solving two problems at once by losing the goth vibe attached to Creeping Ritual.

Keith Morris suggested the Gun Club, and started his own new band: the Circle Jerks. Pierce gave Morris the lyrics to "Group Sex," which became the title track for the Circle Jerks' first album.

32. Foo Fighters

Dave Grohl liked this old term for UFOs that caught on with a comic strip popular during WWII, whose main character made jokes out of the word "foo." Though Grohl says "the UFO stuff is all overblown," he did name his label Roswell Records—Roswell is the famed site where UFOs supposedly landed in the '50s and where the American military had been working on a stringent cover-up about the alien landings.

33. Flipper

Richie Williams, who was in an early version of the band, gave it the name. Williams had a large menagerie of pets in his apartment and was so strung out he named the fish, the cats, the dogs, the lizards, etc. all "Flipper"—so he wouldn't forget their names.

ORIGINAL NAMES OF 9 PUNK ROCK BANDS

1. Dogbreath—the Replacements
2. Angel & the Snakes—Blondie
3. The Falling Spikes—the Velvet Underground
4. The Swankers—Sex Pistols
5. Kid Galahad & the Eternals—the Saints
6. The Psychotic Negatives, the Weak Heartdrops . . . then, after a Big Youth lyric, Paul Simonon thought of the Clash
7. Fabulous Moolah—the Dictators
8. Twisted Kites—R.E.M.
9. Mookie Blaylock—Pearl Jam

45 PUNKS' SECRET REAL NAMES

1. Henry Rollins (Black Flag)—Henry Garfield
2. Darby Crash (the Germs), who did time as Bobby Pyn and Richie Dagger—Jan Paul Beahm
3. Pat Smear (the Germs)—George Ruthenberg
4. El Duce (the Mentors)—Eldon Hoke
5. Terri Ryan (the Germs)—Lorna Doom
6. Kristy Wallace (the Cramps)—Poison Ivy Rorshach
7. Ray Burns (the Damned)—Captain Sensible
8. Becky Thatcher (the Germs)—Donna Rhia
9. Nick Knox (the Cramps)—Nicholas Stephanoff
10. Dottie Danger (the Germs)—later Belinda Carlisle of the Go-Go's
11. Tav Falco (Tav Falco's Panther Burns)—Gustavo Nelson
12. Adam Ant (Adam & the Ants)—Stuart Goddard
13. Joe Strummer (the Clash)—John Mellor
14. Richard Hell (Television, Richard Hell & the Voidoids)—Richard Meyers
15. Dee Generate (Eater)—Roger Bullen
16. Rat Scabies (the Damned)—Chris Miller
17. Ray Burns (the Damned)—Captain Sensible
18. Sylvain Sylvain (New York Dolls)—Ronald Mizrahi
19. Daniel Rey (producer)—Daniel Rabinowitz
20. Tom Verlaine (Televison)—Tom Miller
21. Handsome Dick Manitoba (the Dictators)—Richard Blum
22. Ross "the Boss" Funicello (the Dictators)—Ross Friedman
23. Alan Vega (Suicide)—Alan Bermowitz
24. Martin Rev (Suicide)—Martin Reverby
25. Jak Airport (X-ray Spex)—Jack Stafford
26. Gaye Advert (the Adverts)—Gaye Atlas
27. Johnny Blitz (Dead Boys)—John Madansky
28. Budgie (the Slits, Siouxsie & the Banshees)—Peter Clarke
29. Cheetah Chrome (Dead Boys)—Gene O'Connor
30. Candy Darling (Factory transvestite and performer)—Jimmy Slattery

31. Divine (actor)—Harris Glenn Milstead
32. Billy Idol (Generation X)—William Broad
33. Brian James (the Damned)—Brian Robertson
34. Jordan (SEX shop employee, early scenester and fashion plate, manager for Adam & the Ants, appeared in the seminal punk film *Jubilee*)—Pamela Rooke
35. Nico (Nico, the Velvet Underground; Warhol superstar)— Christa Paffgen
36. Pete Shelley (Buzzcocks)—Pete McNeish
37. Suggs (Madness)—Graham McPherson
38. Johnny Thunders (New York Dolls, the Heartbreakers)— John Anthony Genzale
39. Rob Tyner (MC5)—Robert Derminer
40. Ari Up (the Slits; stepdaughter of John Lydon)—Arriana Foster
41. Dave Vanian (the Damned)—David Letts
42. Cherry Vanilla (singer, actress)—Kathy Dorritie
43. Jimmy Zero (Dead Boys)—William Wilder
44. Jello Biafra (Dead Kennedys)—Eric Reed Boucher
45. GG Allin—Jesus Christ Allin; later changed to Kevin

PATTON OSWALT'S LIST OF PUNK ROCK BAND NAMES TAKEN FROM ONE DAY OF DRUDGE REPORT HEADLINES

1. Peanut Butter Warning
2. Bionic Eye
3. Year of the Pig Will Bring Disaster
4. Hilary Haunted
5. Removed from Forehead
6. Burial Dress
7. Balloons Above the Pentagon

8. Bald Britney Breakdown
9. Touching Ivanka Trump

Comedian Patton Oswalt—a former MADtv *writer,* Seinfeld, King of Queens, Reno 911! *vet, and* Aqua Teen Hunger Force *voice-over guy—has more punk cred than you. At a 2004 stand-up appearance in San Francisco, he was booed off-stage by a mob of angry hippies.*

HOBBIES OF 8 FAMOUS PUNKS

1. Poison Ivy Rorshach
As a kid, Ivy liked to blow up Barbie dolls with firecrackers.

2. Lux Interior
Among Lux's many hobbies is 3-D photography, and his favorite subject is Poison Ivy, who cavorts around the house in fetching fetish wear.

3. Darby Crash
Crash liked to play with his food. He smeared the walls of his living room with spaghetti as if they were canvases; he opened condiment packs and threw them on the audience, smearing himself with salad dressing, peanut butter, or red licorice that would melt over his body.

4. Joe Strummer
In the early days of the Clash the lads went down the pub as often as possible. One day Strummer said, "Right—now we're going to jog." The hungover boys took the bus to the Serpentine River and huffed and puffed away. Over time, all developed into first-class runners. Says a close friend of Strummer, "It changed my life. Now I'm a workout freak." Strummer entered several marathons and successfully ran them while drinking beer.

5. John Lydon

In the years just prior to the formation of the Sex Pistols, Lydon and his teen pals went vampire hunting. In his memoir, Lydon writes that they would break into crypts in Hackney, near their school, "open up the coffins, and have a look. We'd see which bodies hadn't deteriorated . . . it was almost like a social club down there. You'd meet so many people, loonies mostly, running around with wooden stakes, crucifixes, and cloves of garlic." Lydon had money and relative freedom because he worked as a laborer from a young age. He said, "At the time, it was highly unusual for kids to leave their districts and go off into the far reaches of London and dance at nightclubs and vampire hunt." As a 50-year-old, he surfs—"poorly."

6. Joey Ramone

Joey's mom had finally kicked him out of the house at the age of 21, and he and Dee Dee Ramone began sleeping on the floor of Joey's mother's art gallery in New York, the Art Garden. Explained Dee Dee, "Joey was painting then. He would chop up carrots and lettuce and turnips and strawberries and mix it all together and paint with them. His paintings were very good."

7. Johnny Ramone

Johnny collects movie horror posters and autographs and is rumored to have had the world's largest autograph collection.

8. The Replacements

The Replacements were big Scrabble enthusiasts.

BLUE-COLLAR PUNK: 25 PUNKS AND THEIR JOBS BEFORE FAME

1. Henry Rollins (Black Flag, Rollins Band)—worked at a pet store, then as manager of a Häagen-Dazs ice cream parlor in Washington, D.C.

2. Joey Ramone (Ramones)—unlawfully peddled plastic flowers on the streets of New York, and made $50 a week distributing flyers for massage parlors.

3. Ian MacKaye (Minor Threat)—worked in a pet store with Henry Rollins; after seeing the Cramps play, he cut off all his hair with a trimmer meant to be used for grooming dogs.

4. Dave Vanian (the Damned)—was a gravedigger.

5. Bryan Gregory (the Cramps)—allegedly worked in a nuclear weapons plant in California, but, said fellow band member Lux Interior, "they fired him 'cuz he was eating too much of the product."

6. Poison Ivy Rorshach (the Cramps)—hated being a cocktail waitress, and was happy to land a job as a dominatrix. The job, which paid better than the waitress gig, helped finance the Cramps.

7. Maureen Tucker (the Velvet Underground)—worked as a keypunch operator for IBM.

8. Arthur Kane (New York Dolls)—sold snacks in Amsterdam's Vondelpark. Recalled band member Syl Sylvain, "He had a little sign that said, 'Arthur's Cream Cheese Sandwiches.'"

9. Elvis Costello (Elvis Costello & the Attractions)—worked as a data-entry processor for Elizabeth Arden cosmetics. Costello

notes that during the '70s this was a far less skilled job than it is today. Costello had his first studio experience during this period. He sang backup on a lemonade commercial that was so popular in Britain that it played from 1973 to 1984. The lyrics to the jingle: "I'm a, I'm a, I'm a, I'm a secret lemonade drinker."

10. Brody Dalle (the Distillers)—worked at a Betsey Johnson boutique in L.A.'s Beverly Center. Said Dalle, "It was a nightmare. I'd never worked retail in my life. I lasted four months: the mall is a fucking Antichrist."

11 & 12. Gibby Haynes and Paul Leary (Butthole Surfers)— Haynes moved from Texas to Los Angeles in the summer of 1981. He had just dropped out of college one semester short of an MBA. On an athletic scholarship to Trinity University, he studied economics and was named "Accountant of the Year," a bright future in store for him. After graduation, he was given a prestigious post in the accounting firm of Peat, Marwick & Mitchell. Haynes began dropping acid daily and editing a zine called *Strange VD*. When he accidentally left photos of mutilated genitalia in the office copy machine, he was fired. He and Leary had noticed one another's weird appearances at school. Leary said, "We both liked horrible music," and they became fast friends. The future rock stars made a meager living by making Lee Harvey Oswald T-shirts, pillowcases, and bedspreads and selling them on Venice Beach. "Then," said Leary, "we decided that was too much work . . . so we started a band."

13. Jonathan Richman (Jonathan Richman & the Modern Lovers)—was a "rack-puller" in the NY garment district and a busboy at CBGB.

14. Debbie Harry (Blondie)—worked at the Playboy Club and was a waitress at Max's Kansas City. Her first musical job was in a hippie band called the Wind in the Willows.

15. Roberto "Robo" Valverde (the Misfits)—was allegedly a soldier in the notoriously corrupt Colombian army.

16. Paul Westerberg (the Replacements)—worked at a steel mill, then as a janitor in a senator's office. He stole Senator Dave Durenberger's stationery and wrote set lists on his letterhead.

17. Malcolm McLaren (impresario, Sex Pistols manager)—worked as a wine merchant because his mother wanted him to be a sommelier.

18. Paul Cook (Sex Pistols)—was an electrician's helper and occasional petty criminal.

19. Steve Jones (Sex Pistols)—was a thief who had so many convictions he was on his way to a life in the Big House when his career was diverted by rock 'n' roll.

20 & 21. Chrissie Hynde (Pretenders) and John Lydon (Sex Pistols)—penned dirty missives. Said Lydon in *England's Dreaming,* "It was a very pure time then towards sex. People took it as it comes. One of Chrissie Hynde's jobs was to write letters for *Forum*, and I wrote a few with her. Used to sit there making up this utter gunk and then buy it the next month, thinking, 'People are masturbating to this nonsense!'"

22. John Lydon (Sex Pistols)—worked counseling kids, a job he loved, and teaching them woodworking, even though he had no woodworking skills. He also worked as a laborer for his father, bashing and killing rats that attempted to climb up cranes. Lydon recently went on the British reality show *I'm a Celebrity, Get Me Out of Here!,* where in the famous are thrown together in the Australian wilds. Lydon was once again called on to do a bit of rat killing—he hadn't lost his touch.

23 & 24. John Lydon and Sid Vicious (Sex Pistols)—performed public acts of self-mutilation. When the two boys were living together without running water or electricity, they made money by going to pubs and stubbing cigarettes out on their wrists for five pounds. Lydon made a classic cutter's observation: "It relieved some kind of pressure, just to remind myself that I was really alive and all this chaos was really happening."

25. Thurston Moore (Sonic Youth)— was an ice cream man specializing in Chipwiches.

MORE WORK: 13 PUNKS AND THE JOBS THEY HELD DURING (AND AFTER) ROCK 'N' ROLL FAME

1. Jello Biafra (Dead Kennedys)
Biafra ran for mayor of San Francisco in 1979, getting a substantial number of votes, coming in sixth place out of ten, which caused a runoff election. The win eventually went to Diane Feinstein. The singer's campaign slogans included "If he doesn't win, I'll kill myself" and "There's always room for Jell-O."

In 2000, Biafra ran again, this time as a Green Party candidate for president.

2. Clint Conley (Mission of Burma)
The bassist decided to hang on to his day job even after his band had become a success. He worked for the Census Bureau.

3. Johnny Rotten (Sex Pistols)
After appearing on a celebrity reality show in the wilderness (*I'm a Celebrity, Get Me Out of Here!*) to great public acclaim, Rotten made two documentaries about bugs for British television.

4. Walter Lure (the Heartbreakers)

After achieving fame and notoriety in Johnny Thunders' band, Lure became a successful commodities broker on Wall Street. He occasionally took time off from his job for a Heartbreakers reunion gig.

5. Tommy Stinson (the Replacements)

Stinson dropped out of tenth grade to join the Replacements as a bass player. After the band's acrimonious breakup, Stinson worked as a telemarketer. You might have hung up on him. He has since revived his musical career.

6. Alex Chilton (the Box Tops, Big Star)

After gaining teenage fame in the Box Tops, Chilton went on to continued success with Big Star. In the years between the bands' breakups and Chilton's successful solo career, he took a number of odd jobs, among them, working as a tree-trimmer and a dish-washer in Memphis.

7. Dee Dee Ramone (Ramones)

Fed up with sporting a bowl haircut and a leather jacket, and being "a middle-aged man dressing like a juvenile delinquent." Dee Dee changed his last name to "King" and had a brief and unsuccessful career as a rap artist. He went on to do further work with the Ramones.

8. Steve Jones (Sex Pistols)

Following the ugly breakup of the Sex Pistols, Jones continued playing in a number of bands and worked as a producer. Now he hosts a highly popular radio show out of Los Angeles called *Jonesy's Jukebox*. He has a lot of rockin' special guests, including his former band mate John Lydon.

9. Lou Reed (the Velvet Underground)

After the Velvet Underground broke up, Reed scuttled back home to work for his father, an accountant. He has since had a prominent solo career as a musician.

10. Mark Mothersbaugh (Devo)

Post-Devo, Mothersbaugh has created music for McDonald's, Barbie dolls, and 7-Up. He also wrote the *Pee-wee's Playhouse* theme song.

11. Keith Morris (Circle Jerks)

Morris now works as a successful CPA in Los Angeles.

12. Richie Ramone (Ramones)

Unhappy with working for years for a small salary as the Ramones' drummer, Richie quit to take a higher-paying job as a golf caddy.

13. Ross Johnson (Tav Falco's Panther Burns)

Drummer for the infamously deranged Panther Burns, Johnson claims not to have played a gig sober during the band's first four years. He was the only member to hang on to his day job, as a librarian. Said Johnson, "I didn't believe in my 'talent' in the same way that other band members did. I always considered myself the lucky fan or record collector who was just along for the ride."

MICK FARREN'S 10 FOUNDING FATHERS OF PUNK, WITHOUT WHOM . . .

1. Gene Vincent

Coming in the wake of Elvis Presley, with a leg smashed in a motorcycle accident, a serious pill and alcohol problem, and a very bad attitude, Gene Vincent sang "Be-Bop-A-Lula" with pioneer fervor for rock 'n' roll as a high-energy invocation of total anarchic mayhem that was so intense that it would kill him in early thirties. Unarguably the primal punk musician.

2. William S. Burroughs

Novelist, social commentator, poet, junkie, paranoid, homosexual, marksman, Special Agent of Interzone, Burroughs, although generally recognized as one of the towering figures of the Beat Generation, also gave punk its major theoretical underpinning. Burroughs' fragmented and often obscenely brutal narco-visions provided the foundation literature for a punk movement that would mainly aspire to a raucous illiteracy.

3. Arthur Rimbaud

Generally more invoked to impress than actually read, the nineteenth-century anarchic poet was longhaired, unwashed, alcoholic, and stoned on hash. The sexually ambiguous boy genius may briefly have joined the 1871 Paris Commune uprising only to find himself gang-raped by drunken communards. His affair with Symbolist poet Paul Verlaine was so tempestuous it culminated in gunfire. All in all, most punk intelligentsia, from Patti Smith on down, saw Rimbaud as a perfect, and highly crucial, early role model.

4. Jim Morrison

A major invoker of Rambo, Morrison may have been contemporary with the flower power of the 1960s, but he was seeking a much darker place—his "End of the Night," a close cousin to Joseph Conrad's *Heart of Darkness*. In his leather jeans and with a bottle of tequila in his hand, Morrison took the torch of anarchic and culturally dangerous rock 'n' roll, and handed it on to Johnny Rotten, Joe Strummer, Joey Ramone, and especially Iggy Pop and Billy Idol. Of course, he died in the process, but in punk that can only add to one's status.

5. Che Guevara

The professed communist's actions proved him to be a restless and reckless rebel, more non-conforming punk than Marxist ideologue. Handsome and charismatic, Guevara was second only to Fidel Castro as a hero of the Cuban Revolution, but in its wake he found himself unable to cope with the mundane daily business of running of a country. He went in search of other revolutions, winding up in Bolivia, where, in 1967, deserted by his party comrades, he was hunted down and murdered by the CIA. In that final moment, though, he became a posthumous symbol of world revolution, and ultimately exerted more power as an image on a T-shirt than as a living guerrilla fighter.

6. Doc Holliday

The coolest of the all the legends of the Old West, hooked on opium, usually drunk, and coughing up his lungs from tuberculosis, John Henry "Doc" Holliday was an unpredictable gambler, a stone killer with a gun or knife, but also a Latin scholar with the manners of gentleman. In the pantheon of the American frontier, Doc Holliday was plainly the nineteenth-century protopunk.

7. Charles Manson

Charlie Manson was a former pimp and institutionalized petty criminal, with a legendary coven of acid-girl killer slaves, a rap sheet of Hollywood celebrity murders, and links with the darkest psychedelic occult. All this helped make nihilist punk philosophy infinitely more possible by driving a metaphoric semitruck through the utopian flower power of hippie counterculture. Today, Charlie still sits in jail and continues to enjoy his status as a perverse icon.

8. Gavrilo Princip

Gavrilo Princip can only be the most glorious example of a wholly inept political assassin who, by sheer dumb luck, managed to fire the shots that started World War I and was thus responsible for a body count that ran into the tens of millions. A tubercular teenager with little to lose, Princip was a junior member of the Serbian Black Hand. After a bungled bomb attack on the Archduke Franz Ferdinand in Sarajevo in 1914, Princip was able to lose himself in the crowd. He stopped at a café, only to find himself suddenly confronted by the archduke's car. Seeing his chance, Princip shot Franz Ferdinand and his wife . . . and the rest was very definitely history.

9. Charles Starkweather

Well aware that he bore a striking resemblance to James Dean, Charlie Starkweather was the first of the rock 'n' roll generation to unconsciously embrace an inarticulate doctrine of lethal, emotionless nihilism and realize that serial murder might be a shortcut to fame, no talent or guitar necessary. Accordingly, he and his gum-chewing teen girlfriend Caril Ann Fugate went on a murder rampage in rural Nebraska that racked up a total of 11 homicides, and became the basis of at least four movies and a Bruce Springsteen song. Charlie was captured and went to the electric chair on June 25, 1959. Caril Ann was sentenced to life in prison but was paroled in 1976, in time to become a minor punk icon.

10. Elvis Presley

After his death, the *Times* of London noted that Elvis Presley had caused the first cracks that led to the generation gap of the twentieth century. He can't be ignored. As John Lennon—the Beatles' own prototype punk—put it, "Before Elvis there was nothing." Gene Vincent may have been the first visible punk rocker, but it was Elvis who changed the mode of the music and caused the walls of the city to shake. Also, in later life, bejeweled and bloated, he provided an alarming example of what can happen when rock 'n' roll rebellion turns around and makes you King of the World.

Mick Farren is a respected music critic, science fiction author, and journalist based in the U.K. Farren was an early champion of the Pink Fairies and Motörhead and was a bandmate of the original punk rock drummer, Twink. In the 1960s he fronted anarchist psychedelic proto punks the Deviants, who were later signed to Stiff Records.

LAURIE HENZEL OF *BUST* MAGAZINE'S 9 SHOCKING MOMENTS FROM 9 PUNK LADIES

1. In 1967, during a drug raid at Keith Richards' Redlands estate in England, police were shocked that Marianne Faithfull was only wearing a fur blanket and was totally nude underneath it. She later admitted to giving the cops a little flash. Jolly good!
2. In 1970, at the restaurant El Quixote in NYC, Nico overheard a woman complaining about her life, and felt that this person had not suffered enough, so she smashed a beer glass on her head and cut her face open.
(From Nico: *The Life & Lies of an Icon*, by Richard Witts.)
3. In the 1978 documentary *Punking Out*, Lydia gives her used tampon (wrapped in tinfoil) to Stiv Bators of the Dead Boys. He then pledges to eat it onstage.
4. As reported by *Creem* magazine in 1979, at WABX radio in Detroit, Patti Smith punched Ted Nugent in the chest after the Motor City Madman made her wait by taking too much time with his interview—she was scheduled to go on next. Nugent reportedly got even by putting "Double Live Gonzo" stickers all over Patti's limo. *[Patti has a limo?—Ed.]*

5. Perhaps these days no one would bat an eye at something like this, but in the late '70s, Nina Hagen appeared on a German talk show and simulated how to masturbate on live TV (wearing leather pants). The viewers were so outraged they wrote letters and called the station asking for the return of the Führer to rid the county of such terrible punk women!

6. In 1992 at the U.K. Reading Festival, Donita Sparks of L7 got so pissed at the crowd throwing things at her during their performance, she pulled out her tampon and threw it at the audience. Apparently, someone threw it back onstage!

7. In 1996, Björk got off a flight with her son, Sindri, at the Bangkok International Airport, and when a female reporter approached her with a friendly "welcome to Bangkok!" Björk flipped out, grabbed the woman's hair, and bashed her face into the ground!

8. In 1981, during the Pretenders' first U.S. tour, Chrissie Hynde was so angry about being arrested, she kicked out the police car window before being carted off to jail for the night.

9. As reported by *The Daily Mail* in 2006, a drunken Amy Winehouse said, "This girl came up to me and said I was brilliant. Two seconds later, she turned to my boyfriend, pointed at me, and said, 'She fucked up.' So I punched her right in the face—which she wasn't expecting, because girls don't do that." Amy then kneed the girl's boyfriend between the legs and punched him in the face when he tried to calm Amy down.

Laurie Henzel is the publisher and creative director of Bust *magazine, which, under her guidance, along with that of editor Debbie Stoller, has grown from a photocopied, black-and-white zine into an award-winning international, bimonthly glossy with a circulation of 95,000. Laurie resides in New York City with her husband, photographer Michael Lavine, and their two daughters, Olive and Penny.*

NICK TOSCHES' 10 WHO WERE PUNK BEFORE THERE WAS PUNK

1. Christopher Marlowe (1564–1593)
2. Jimmy Durante (1893–1980)
3. Louis Prima (1910–1978)
4. Gorgeous George (1915–1963)
5. Joey Gallo (1929–1972)
6. Sonny Liston (ca. 1932–1970)
7. Little Richard (b. 1932)
8. Jerry Lee Lewis (b. 1935)
9. Stan Stasiak (1937–1997)
10. Charlotte Rampling (b. 1946)

Nick notes that this list has neither rhyme nor reason, but that it is the most important list since the Ten Commandments, and that he only put Louis Prima there because he couldn't think of anybody else. This is the way most of the Ten Commandments got there as well.

Nick Tosches was born in Newark, New Jersey, a long time ago, and he will die in 2021, but he doesn't yet know where. He is the author of many books, including Hellfire, Cut Numbers, Dino, Chaldea, *and* In the Hand of Dante. *It is said that it was he who first used the word "punk" to refer to rock 'n' roll, in a 1970 article called "The Punk Muse." He is presently a life coach who specializes in rich broads, and he likes pork chops.*

KIM FOWLEY'S LIST OF 10 GOLDEN MOMENTS IN PUNK ROCK

1. Kim Fowley producing the Germs live at the Whisky a Go Go.
2. Kim Fowley having sex in the mosh pit with lesbian punk the following week.
3. Kim Fowley judging punk rock talent show in mental hospital six months later.
4. Kim Fowley acting as best man at punk rock wedding a year later.
5. Kim Fowley attending punk rock baptism as godfather of lesbian mother and punk rock dad's deformed child.
6. Kim Fowley doing music for punk rock animal sex movie.
7. Kim Fowley producing Hollywood punk band Venus & the Razorblades and co-writing the punk rock classic "Punk-O-Rama."
8. Kim Fowley doing music for punk rock vomit documentary.
9. Kim Fowley launching U.K. modern punk rock band Trick Baby, June 2007, fronted by Brigitte Bardot look-alike/trailer goddess Charlotte Pain.
10. Kim Fowley attends punk rock funeral, 2007.

Kim Fowley is a punk rock pig boy covered in urine, mud, horror, and innocence; a skeleton giraffe with maniac recoil. Kim Fowley's name as producer or writer/contributor can be found on noisy product by artists such as Kiss, Alice Cooper, Gene Vincent, the Seeds, Blue Cheer, Them, and the Runaways, which prepared him for his cultural contribution to the careers of the Germs and Venus & the Razorblades.

Raising the Bar: 9 Very Tall PUNKS

1. Joey Ramone (Ramones)—6'8"
2. Krist Novoselic (Nirvana)—6'7"
3. Lux Interior (the Cramps)—6'6"
(7' in hot footwear)
4. Angus Andrew (Liars)—6'6"
5. Thurston Moore (Sonic Youth)—6'6"
6. Tesco Vee (the Meatmen)—6'6"
7. Gibby Haynes (Butthole Surfers)—6'5"
8. Peter Garrett (Midnight Oil)—6'4"
9. Sid Vicious (Sex Pistols)—6'4"

STEVE SOTO'S 10 THINGS I LEARNED PLAYING IN THE ADOLESCENTS THAT I NEVER WOULD HAVE LEARNED IN HIGH SCHOOL

1. When you go to record your first album, make sure you remember to bring a bass guitar.
2. Beware of a manager who pays you in pills, especially if his reasoning is that you can sell the pills to your friends and make even more money.
3. If some guy offers you $200 or 30 percent of the door to play Northridge, take the 30 percent—otherwise, you'll feel stupid when, like, 2,000 punks show up.
4. When you meet new girls at Geza's house in Hollywood, make sure they don't have Adam's apples.
5. If you mix pot, Valium, and malt liquor, you might play so horribly that your band will turn your amp off behind your back.
6. If you mix pot, Valium and malt liquor together, you'll be so out of it you won't notice that your band turned your amp off, and you'll still keep playing like it's the best show of your life.
7. If you see a Camaro full of hessians drive up slowly, and "Dancing Days" by Led Zeppelin is blasting on the radio, you might want to start running . . . as fast as you can.
8. Playing a lunch concert at an all-boys Catholic school is always a bad idea. Especially when they forgo eating their lunches and opt to throw them at you instead. Note: An apple a day may keep the doctor away, but not when it's thrown at your head by a baseball jock.
9. Sneaking into clubs as a minor could take a bit of work. It's always good to have a friend who is an artist to fake hand stamps. Sometimes you may have to scale a wall, but be careful going through the roof—you might come crashing through the ceiling and land right in front of the stage next to a security guard. . . .

10. If you sneak out of your house to go to Hollywood, leaving a fake "body" of pillows under your blanket, don't have a heart attack when you come home and your dad has replaced the pillows and is under your blanket waiting to bust you. . . .

Steve Soto (bass) and Tony Cadena (vocals) formed the Adolescents in 1980. While other bands were screaming about Reagan and world politics, the Adolescents focused on what they knew best: teenage alienation in the midst of California's "suburban wonderland." Their self-titled debut (dubbed the Blue Album by fans) helped lay out the blueprint for what would become the California pop-punk sound. Soto also played on the Agent Orange surf/punk classic Bloodstains*, and managed to do all of this before he turned 18. The Adolescents still record and tour to this day*

BLAG DAHLIA OF THE DWARVES' 5 THINGS ASSHOLES ALWAYS SAY WHEN THEY WANT SOMETHING FREE (PLUS 5 THINGS PUNK GUYS SAY TO GIRLS)

1. "Come on, it's punk!"
2. "Rancid's doing it, and they didn't ask for any money."
3. "CBGB is great exposure."
4. "I used to roadie for Murphy's Law back in the day."
5. "You can have three copies of the comp when it comes out."

5 Things Punk Guys Say to Girls

1. "You said you loved me, and you said I could stay here!"
2. "The music industry is doomed, asshole."
3. "She wasn't just your friend—it turned out she was mine, too."

4. "Mom, I only need 50 bucks. Please!"

5. "It's not a sore, it's an abrasion."

Blag Dahlia is a rock legend and the best-looking man in show business.

COULDA, WOULDA, SHOULDA: 5 PUNK ROCK ALMOSTS THAT WOULD HAVE CHANGED THE WORLD

1. We Are Not Pistols, We Are Men

In the words of Mark Mothersbaugh, as told to Marc Spitz and Brendan Mullen in *We Got the Neutron Bomb*: "Richard Branson called me up in Akron in the winter of 1978 and said, 'Hey, you wanna come down to Jamaica?' And I looked out the window and said to myself, 'Well, it's snowing about 30 inches here. Sure, I'll come down to Jamaica.' So he flew Bob Casale and I down there." They all sat around at the Kingston Holiday Inn and smoked enormous joints (impressive to the Devo guys after Akron joints) and discussed the Sex Pistols' last show at Winterland, and Devo's brief meeting with them. "And Branson said, 'I'll tell you why you're here. Johnny Rotten is down here at the hotel. He's in the next room, and there are reporters downstairs from the *New Musical Express*, *Sounds* and *Melody Maker*. . . . Johnny Rotten wants to join your band . . . and I want to announce to them that Johnny Rotten is the new lead singer of Devo.' And I'm going, 'Ohmigod, I'm so high right now.' Regrettably, I didn't just go, 'Yeah, sounds great. Send him to Akron.'"

2. I Coulda Been a Contenda, Part 1

As a boy, Johnny Thunders was a fantastic all-round athlete. He played superbly for New York City neighborhood baseball teams and nearby pickup games. His sports career was rudely ended when it became apparent that the Little League rules called for all the boys' fathers to be present at games. Johnny's father had abandoned the family. This regulation barred Johnny from the Junior League, from which he might have been selected by one of the professional teams that had been scouting him when he was 12. Years later, Thunders would claim that his baseball career was cut short by his refusal to get a haircut.

3. I Coulda Been a Contenda, Part 2

Johnny Ramone's baseball career was cut short by his refusal to get a haircut.

4. Too Intelligent to Be a Movie Star

As told in Dick Porter's *The Cramps*, Lux Interior was offered a role in the gothic superhero movie *The Crow*. "They wanted me to be in the first *Crow* movie. It's funny, because I would have been the guy who shot Brandon Lee, but in the first draft it had me saying all kinds of fart jokes. Just horrible—I could never say that."

5. Prep School Fantasies

Malcolm McLaren had an idea for the British punk group the Damned: he named them Masters of the Backside, and wanted Chrissie Hynde to dress as a boy and whip the band while they performed. The plan never came to fruition. Presumably McLaren was left with his schoolboy fantasies unfilled.

SLAGGIN' OFF: 10 PUNK ROCK JABS, JIBES, AND COMPLIMENTS

1. The members of Black Flag were famous for humorlessness. One fanzine wrote that they possessed "all the humor of a muscular dystrophy telethon."

2. "You get a donkey and you get a baboon and you feed 'em a diet of chili and custard for 30 days and then you get 'em to fuck. Their children would be the Germs."—Kim Fowley

3. "We'd always been quirky," Richard Lloyd said of his band, Television. "Tom [Verlaine] writes lyrics that are like triple entendres, and he didn't have a singer's voice. I think if you slit a goat's throat it would sound like that. Anyway, he never would take singing lessons, so what are you gonna do?"

4. Dee Dee Ramone on the other Ramones: "Wouldn't it be great to be in a band with other junkies instead of guys who collect baseball cards?"

5. Henry Rollins on Black Flag guitarist Greg Ginn: "Greg Ginn practices were like the long march to the sea. Talk about a work ethic—he is like Patton on steroids."

6. Johnny Rotten on the Clash: "[They] looked and sounded like they were yelling at themselves about nothing in particular."

7. The severe hostility between Dinosaur Jr.'s Lou Barlow and J Mascis led Barlow to tell *Cut* zine in 1990, "It makes me sick that I spent six or seven years putting my heart and soul into that band. They're sleazebag snob pigs like no one I have met in my entire life. J's always been an asshole."

8. Robert Quine on Richard Hell: "[Richard] can't make up his mind whether he wants to be a rock star like Elvis Costello or just go die."

9. Shane MacGowan on punk bands: "To early punks, the Clash were just a bunch of bandwagon jumpers, y'know. They were too political. And the Damned didn't take it seriously enough. They were just a comedy band. There were a few other bands that really had the idea, like Subway

Sect and Siouxsie & the Banshees. But there was really only the one group at the end of the day, the one English group, and that was the Pistols. And of course the Ramones, but they were American."

10. John Holmstrom on the Sex Pistols: "It's unbelievable that a rock group that played no more than 100 live performances and existed for only 27 months could become so internationally disliked as the Sex Pistols were."

CHAPTER 2

THE LIVING (AND DYING) SECTION

THEY OD'D: 13 PUNKS WHO ACCIDENTALLY BOUGHT IT

1. Malcolm Owen (the Ruts)

The lead singer for the Ruts—best known for "Babylon's Burning"—died of a heroin overdose in 1980.

2. Lester Bangs (rock critic)

The famous (and infamous) writer (and, for our money, the best rock critic ever) and musician, was an alcoholic who did his heaviest drinking whenever he finished a piece of writing. Bangs went to his first AA meeting in April of 1982. A week later he completed some work and decided not to celebrate in his customary fashion. Instead, Bangs scored pills—Darvon and Valium, which he downed with large quantities of alcohol-based Nyquil, because he had a cold. He OD'd at the age of 44—the combination of alcohol and Valium was probably what killed him.

3. Will Shatter (Negative Trend, Flipper)

Shatter, a pivotal figure in the '80s punk scene, died of an accidental heroin overdose. He often switched to amphetamines to quit heroin, then did the reverse. He died when his system was opiate-free, a classic accident. He was 31.

4. John Dougherty (Flipper)

Dougherty replaced Shatter in Flipper, for a comeback tour, and died of a heroin overdose on Halloween, 1997.

5. Pete Farndon (Pretenders)

The bassist, was kicked out of the Pretenders for using drugs. He died in a bathtub, aged 31, of a heroin overdose.

6. James Honeyman-Scott (Pretenders)

The guitar man died of a cocaine and heroin overdose two days after Farndon was fired.

7. Johnny Thunders (New York Dolls, the Heartbreakers)

Murk and mystery surround Thunders' death. He had played lucrative shows in Hong Kong, had stylish suits made, and still had $10,000 in cash. He flew to England to see his doctor and get a substantial amount of methadone. What followed was a bizarre death. He went to New Orleans planning to get together a group with a number of classic black jazz musicians. He went out to a bar, returned to his hotel, and was found dead the next day in a contorted U-shape. The room showed evidence of a struggle, and all his methadone, clothes, money, and makeup were gone. The New Orleans police were remarkably sloppy—they wrote Thunders off as another OD, even though the coroner found only traces of cocaine and heroin in his system. He also discovered that Johnny was dying of advanced leukemia. The bizarre position of his body led many to believe that Thunders had received a "hot shot," possibly containing LSD and strychnine. The coroner was soon fired, and despite all the efforts of Johnny's family, the New Orleans police have refused to order a murder investigation.

8. Dee Dee Ramone (Ramones)

Dee Dee's death was an accident, another case of taking too much heroin after being clean, thinking one can handle the old dose.

9. Jonathan Melvoin (Smashing Pumpkins)

The keyboardist OD'd while on tour.

10. Sid Vicious (Sex Pistols)

Vicious, a chronic OD'er, cleaned up in Rikers after being charged with the murder of his girlfriend, Nancy Spungen. When he was released on bail, his mother threw a party to celebrate his homecoming. She bought him heroin, which she attempted to keep on her person and dole out. When she fell asleep, Sid went through her purse, found the China White, and overdosed. He was 21. His mother said, "He would *never* go through my things!" Sid's mother dropped the urn of his ashes at Heathrow Airport, so he will forever be going through the ventilation system. Said John Lydon, "At least he won't be bored."

11. Stiv Bators (Dead Boys, Lords of the New Church)

The official story is that the front man died of internal injuries after being hit by a car crossing the street in Paris. He spent the night with his girlfriend, rather than going to the emergency room. Those in the know, who prefer not to be named, concur that "it was a straight-up OD."

12. Roger Rogerson (Circle Jerks)

The bass player died of a heroin overdose.

13. GG Allin

For many years, the legendary punk singer threatened to commit suicide onstage on Halloween. However, each Halloween found him in jail. Allin's last show was at the Gas Station, a small New York City club (the event is captured on video). GG did a few songs before the power went out; then he trashed the venue, fled the police, and walked the city streets covered in feces and blood, surrounded by adoring fans, whom he embraced. Allin went to a friend's apartment, where he snorted three bags of heroin and discussed plans for an upcoming recording before nodding out. Several party guests posed for photos with the unconscious singer, unaware that he was already dead. Allin's girlfriend—who as a 13-year-old had written to him in prison—was on the roof chatting with a friend about her and GG's plans to marry. Not until the morning did friends realize he was dead.

THEY DIDN'T OD: 21 PUNK DEATHS

1. Joe Strummer (the Clash)

Strummer succumbed to a heart attack at age 50.

2. Joey Ramone (Ramones)

The front man died of lymphoma, a virulent form of cancer.

3. Jerry Nolan (New York Dolls, the Heartbreakers)

The drummer died of a stroke.

4. Johnny Ramone (Ramones)

Prostate cancer claimed the guitarist.

5. D. Boon (Minutemen)

Boon died in a car accident after his girlfriend fell asleep at the wheel while driving their van.

6. Bryan Gregory (the Cramps)

The freakish fuzz guitar man, who appeared on the Cramps' first (and best) recordings, suffered a lengthy illness and died of a heart attack at California's Anaheim Memorial Hospital. He was 46.

7. Nico (the Velvet Underground)

The chanteuse, who lived in the Balearic Islands, took her bike out on an exceptionally hot day. Self-conscious about her weight, she swathed herself in heavy clothes and scarves, and died of a brain aneurysm.

8. Lance Loud (Mumps)

Television's first reality star died of AIDS.

9. Kirsty MacColl

A tragic boating accident took the singer's life.

10. Lee Brilleaux (Dr. Feelgood)

The protopunk pub rocker died of cancer.

11. Ian Dury (Ian Dury and the Blockheads)

The gravel-voiced singer succumbed to cancer.

12. Sterling Morrison (the Velvet Underground)

A founding member of the influential group, Morrison was just 53 when he died of non-Hodgkin's lymphoma.

13. Billy Murcia (New York Dolls)

Commonly believed to have overdosed, the drummer actually died of drowning and choking in a bathtub. On his first trip to London, he was invited to a party and introduced to Mandrax (a British quaalude), which he mixed with alcohol, whereupon he passed out. Most of the terrified party guests fled, but a few decided that the best way to revive him was to immerse him in an ice-cold bath. When the doctor arrived, it was revealed that he had drowned and/or choked on his own vomit, and would have been fine if he'd been left to sleep off the cocktail's effects.

14. Arthur "Killer" Kane (New York Dolls)

Kane died of leukemia, immediately after a stunning comeback with the Dolls.

15. Mia Zapata (the Gits)

The singer was raped and murdered in Seattle; her killer was found and convicted more than ten years later.

16. Greg Shaw (Bomp! Records founder)

Shaw died of heart failure.

17. Peter Laughner (Rocket from the Tombs, Pere Ubu)

Although it was said of heavy drug user Laughner that "he would inject a cough drop," the autopsy report on his death gave the mysterious cause as "systemic failure."

18. Sandy West (the Runaways)

The drummer died following a long battle with lung cancer.

19. Bob Stinson (the Replacements)

It is widely believed that Stinson overdosed after getting clean and getting kicked out of the Replacements. However, his body was found with an unused insulin syringe beside it, and the doctors turned in a strange verdict: that he had worn his body out from excess. No precise cause of death was given.

20. Kurt Cobain (Nirvana)

Suicide . . . or murder? For many, Cobain's suicide note speaks for itself, but it has been inspected by handwriting analysts, who claim that the bulk of the letter can be read as his plan to divorce his wife and leave rock 'n' roll. The final sentences appear to be in a different handwriting.

21. El Duce (Mentors)

The lead "singer" was allegedly contacted by Courtney Love, Kurt Cobain's wife, and asked to kill her husband for the measly sum of $50,000. He died by stepping in front of a train while supposedly drunk, further adding to the possibility that he was involved with Cobain's murder—and leading many to speculate that he was murdered himself as part of a cover-up.

JOHNNY THUNDERS' GREAT BIG KISS OF DEATH

Johnny Thunders, who died in New Orleans in 1991 under questionable circumstances, left a string of dead playmates behind him.

1. Billy Murcia (New York Dolls)

The original New York Dolls drummer was the band's first drug-related casualty. On the Dolls' first trip to England, Murcia ingested a lethal cocktail of pills and booze. Throughout the night, Murcia's girlfriend, aided by partygoers, tried to keep him from nodding out by pouring coffee in his mouth and throwing him in a cold bathtub. The coroner's report lists drowning as the official cause of death, no doubt a result of a hard night of partying.

2. Jerry Nolan (New York Dolls, the Heartbreakers)

Billy Murcia's replacement went on to play on the Dolls' two studio albums and left with Johnny Thunders to form the Heartbreakers. Hard drug use ran rampant throughout the Dolls' and Heartbreakers' careers, but in the end, Nolan died in a coma resulting from a stroke while undergoing treatment for pneumonia and meningitis.

3. Arthur "Killer" Kane (New York Dolls)

One of the few Thunders acquaintances not to die in a drug-induced stupor, Arthur Kane fell victim to leukemia shortly after the New York Dolls reunited in 2004. Besides playing with Thunders in the Dolls, Kane backed him on several tours in the 1980s before finding religion and relocating to Los Angeles.

4. Phil Lynott (Thin Lizzy)

The bassist and vocalist made a notable guest appearance on Thunders' 1978 solo record *So Alone*. Lynott sang a verse of the blues standard "Daddy Rolling Stone" and was also known to back Thunders up live on occasion. A notorious substance abuser in his own right, Lynott ultimately succumbed to heart failure brought on from years of hard living.

5. Steve Marriott (Small Faces, Humble Pie)

The British rock 'n' roll legend and founding Small Faces and Humble Pie guitarist also sang a verse on "Daddy Rolling Stone." In 1991, at the age of 44, Marriott met his fiery end when he fell asleep while intoxicated. A lit cigarette left burning set his house ablaze.

6. Sid Vicious (Sex Pistols)

Vicious and Thunders played together around the time of the Sid and Nancy Chelsea Hotel fiasco. Though no official recordings exist, they were occasionally known to turn up together at Max's Kansas City and CBGB. Vicious went on to become perhaps the most notorious death in punk.

List compiled and annotated by Mike Edison and Aaron Lefkove.

5 PUNKS WHO TOPPED THEMSELVES

1. Ian Curtis (Joy Division)

The singer hung himself just when he appeared to have "everything to live for": a hugely successful career, his biggest single yet ("Love Will Tear Us Apart"), a wife, and a child. Curtis had always been a depressive fellow, and the key to his departure may be in the in the lyrics to the aforementioned song, which refers to an increasingly estranged marriage. He was 23.

2. Jason Thirsk (Pennywise)

The bassist shot himself in the head in 1996 after a long spell of alcoholism. He was 28.

3. Darby Crash (the Germs)

Crash has been promising to commit suicide for so long that his friends thought it was a case of crying wolf. However, after the Germs' successful reunion concert, he and his close friend Casey Cola decided to die together using uncut heroin. Casey survived and was ostracized for years; Crash succeeded, dying at the age of 22. He left a brief suicide note and his leather jacket to a friend, Bosco.

4. Robert Quine (Richard Hell & the Voidoids)

Quine, legendary guitarist for the Voidoids, among many other greats, was found dead in his New York apartment. Richard Hell, in his beautiful obituary for Quine, noted that "he never injected drugs," so the presence of empty bags of heroin and a syringe indicated that his death was not an accident. His wife, Alice, whom he'd been with since the mid-'70s, had died of sudden heart failure the previous August. Quine did not care to go on living without her, and he had already attempted suicide since her death. Wrote Hell, "In fact, if you're not crying, it's hard to think of him without smiling. Or perhaps you could do both at once."

5. Wendy O. Williams (Plasmatics)

The singer succeeded on her third suicide attempt, shooting herself in the head. She left a note for her partner, with love letters, gifts, and a map to the location of her body, a rustic spot where she loved to feed squirrels. She left her money to an animal sanctuary.

MUSIC 5 PUNKS LISTENED TO AS THEY LAY DYING (OR, IN ONE CASE, AFTER HE WAS ALREADY DEAD)

1. Joey Ramone (Ramones)

As he was dying in the hospital, he put on the U2 song "In A Little While."

2. Kurt Cobain (Nirvana)

He put in *Automatic for the People* by R.E.M. on CD before he pulled the trigger or was murdered.

3. Ian Curtis (Joy Division)

Not to be outdone by mere music-listeners, Curtis watched Werner Herzog's depressing *Stroszek* the night before he hung himself in his wife's kitchen. Before doing the deed, he put Iggy Pop's *The Idiot* on the turntable.

4. Lester Bangs (rock critic)

Bangs died of an accidental overdose at 44 from combination of Darvon, Valium, and Nyquil. He was listening to the Human League's album *Dare* at the time.

5. GG Allin

Per Allin's instructions, his brother Merle put on GG's band's *Suicide Tapes* while he lay in his coffin.

13 PUNK SELF-MUTILATORS

1. Henry Rollins (Black Flag)

Along with the usual rolling in broken glass, the Black Flag singer pulled another punk cliché in Northern California, tearing up his chest with broken glass.

He wrote in his diary, "Blood started flying all over the place. It felt good to feel pure pain. Helped me get perspective." He broke his wrist twice against audience members' heads—the first time by accident, the second when attacking a fan.

2. Greg Ginn (Black Flag)

The guitarist played so ferociously that blood and sweat would leak into his guitar and short-circuit it. He resolved the problem by tuning the volume knob up to ten, soldering it in place, and installing a waterproof switch.

3 & 4. Shane MacGowan (the Pogues) and Jane (the Mo-dettes)

Mr. MacGowan took part in a much-publicized biting frenzy while pogoing at a punk club. In *A Drink With Shane MacGowan* by MacGowan and his wife, Victoria Mary Clarke, he describes the incident: "What we [Jane and Shane] were doing was having a kind of sado-masochistic love ritual in front of the stage with broken bottles. It felt like a good idea at the time. I got off on the pain, both inflicting pain and being on the receiving end. . . . She wasn't my girlfriend . . . she was just a bird who grabbed me in the crowd . . . and carved me up with a broken bottle." According to Shane, they were biting each other very hard, "on the arms and shoulders and necks," but the press zeroed in on Jane biting a piece out of Shane's ear. He explained, "Ears bleed a lot, so there was loads of blood pumping. . . ." Then Jane excitedly slashed her wrists with a bottle and was taken away by security.

5. Iggy Pop (the Stooges)

An early self-mutilator, Pop is well known for putting cigarettes out on himself, hacking at himself with broken beer bottles, and especially rolling in glass, usually after covering himself in peanut butter.

Pop self-mutilation stories are legion. One night, before an L.A. gig, he announced that he was going to kill himself at the end of the act. At the finale he got out a butcher knife and carved up his chest, and had to be carried off by security guards.

On another occasion he asked Ron Asheton to wear a Nazi uniform and whip him during the show. Asheton used a fake whip, which dissatisfied Iggy.

Iggy begged his friend to "thrash me—really do it." Two of Asheton's buddies arrived with homemade blackjacks, with which they proceeded to flail Iggy. This excited Mr. Pop so much that he took out a rusty pocketknife and began to hack at his body. Finally he asked to be put in a gunnysack and dragged through the club into the gutters of Sunset Boulevard. The guys dragged him out, kicking him in the bag, and dumped him on the street.

Iggy named this "piece" "Murder of a Virgin."

6. Darby Crash (the Germs), part 1

The Germs played at San Francisco's Mabuhay Gardens the same week that the Sex Pistols broke up after their last concert at Winterland. Germs singer Darby Crash knew that Sid Vicious was in the audience at the Mab and wanted to impress him.

As Nicky Beat reported in Marc Spitz and Brendan Mullen's *We Got the Neutron Bomb*, "Darby ran onstage, put his hands on my shoulder, jumped right onto me, grabbed a glass full of booze, downed the whole thing, carved a circle in his chest, grabbed the mic, and started singing the first part of the first verse in perfect time. . . . From then on it was pandemonium."

7. Darby Crash (the Germs), part 2

In *We Got the Neutron Bomb*, interviewees explain the "Germs burn." Said Hal Negro, "Germs burns were inflicted with a lit cigarette. You were supposed to get one from somebody who had one. It was like pledging allegiance to Darby Crash." Darby administered many burn circles, which gave the wearer the right to pass it on to others. As band member Pat Smear said, "It was his idea of something permanent, so that in ten years you'd be at the supermarket, and some lady would give you change, and you'd see the burn and make a connection."

8. Sid Vicious (Sex Pistols), part 1

One of the most enduring images in punk is of Sid's skinny, 90-pound weakling chest sliced every which way with a broken bottle, blood coursing down it. Equally memorable are the pictures of his chest with "Give Me a Fix" carved on it. This optimistic piece of performance art was created on the Sex Pistols' tour across the American South, during which Sid rode on a bus with Johnny Rotten and some bikers whose job it was to keep Sid off dope. (The rest of the band flew from gig to gig.) Sid was experiencing terrible heroin withdrawal during the journey. In desperation, Vicious slashed his plea across his already mutilated chest in hopes of meeting a sympathetic fan. It wasn't until reaching San Francisco that he managed to give his minders the slip and OD.

9. Sid Vicious (Sex Pistols), part 2

Everyone's favorite Sid self-mutilation story was told by photographer Bob Gruen, who traveled across America on the Pistols' bus. One night, Sid and Bob stopped at a roadside truck stop to have a bite. Sid ordered steak and eggs, and was just tucking in when a big redneck left his family at a nearby table and approached the punk star.

"You're Vicious, huh? You're so tough, let's see you do this!" And the guy burned his hand with a cigarette.

Sid replied, "Can I hurt myself? Yeah."

He took his steak knife, made a deep cut in his hand, from which blood steadily dripped onto his eggs, and kept on eating without missing a beat.

The tough guy watched in horror as Sid shoveled down bloody eggs—then he grabbed his family and escaped in terror.

10. GG Allin

Allin's self-loathing exploits are renowned—he mutilated himself at almost every show, usually cutting his face and body with broken glass. Captured on film is a sequence of Allin sodomizing himself with a chair leg, something he did periodically.

Depending on your viewpoint, this could be called an act of self-mutilation or a romantic interlude.

11. Alan Vega (Suicide)

While Vega is also known for attacking and threatening the audience (wielding chains, etc.), he is more renowned for his self-mutilating. Joe Strummer recounts a memorable incident he witnessed at the Music Machine in Camden Town, London. Strummer saw "a bottle miss [Vega's] head, and he bent down to pick it up and threw it at his *own* head." Vega often beat himself senseless with bottles.

12 & 13. Shane MacGowan (the Pogues) and Shanne Bradley

This merry incident has often been misreported as "MacGowan getting his ear bitten off" and thus has become confused with the "Shane and Jane from the Mo-dettes" incident. In fact, Shane and his girlfriend Shanne were dancing furiously to the Clash when, as MacGowan explained in his memoir, *A Drink with Shane MacGowan*, they started "biting each other's arms till they bled—it was a kinda tribal, primeval, love-hate, violence-affection ceremony. It was a hypnotic trance kinda thing. . . . Then she broke a bottle and slashed my earhole, causing loads of blood to splatter all over the place."

14 & 15. The Kipper Kids

The Sex Pistols once played in Reading, supported by he Kipper Kids (both named Harry), who performed a piece called "The Boxing Match." Explained Genesis P-Orridge, in *England's Dreaming*, "The basic gist was that there was one boxer and one referee. The idea was that whichever Harry was the boxer had boxing gloves on and boxed himself. So he would be punching himself in the face, as hard as possible. Because the performance did not end until Harry Kipper the boxer had knocked himself out, it was a very bloody sight."

16. Adam Ant (Adam & the Ants)

In 1977, filmmaker Derek Jarman decided to follow SEX employee and scenester Jordan around with a Super-8 camera. These experiments evolved into what Jarman called a "prophetic" punk film, *Jubilee*, starring Adam Ant. Said Jarman, "Jordan brought Adam [Ant] along. I'd seen him on the street with 'Fuck' written on his back in what I thought was eyeliner, but Jordan told me he'd had it carved in with a razor blade." Perhaps, like Sid Vicious' "Gimme a Fix," it was a request.

17. John Lydon (Sex Pistols, PiL)

Lydon wrote in his autobiography, "Sid and I used to mess around with cigarette burns. It was mostly me. I don't know what prompted it. Insecurity. I got it from a Michael Caine movie—they were torturing him with cigarettes. I thought, That doesn't look too painful. I can handle that . . . there's scars all up and down my arms by my shoulder. Forget it, there's a lot of muscle tissue around there. I think it was a badge of self-pity more than anything."

18. Henry Rollins (Black Flag), redux

Rollins kept a tour diary, writing about a German show: "Bit a skinhead on the mouth and he started to bleed real bad. His blood was all over my face." Rollins was so aggressive with the audience that he became a masochistic violence magnet. Fans bashed the singer in the mouth with the mic, burned his legs with cigars, and put cigarettes out all over his body. They also doused him with cups of urine, stabbed him with pins, scratched him brutally, and hit him in the groin with water balloons. Rollins loved all this, writing in his diary about the ecstasy of his suffering: "I hope I get bashed up soon. I need the pain to play." He eagerly attacked audience members, slithering through the crowd on broken glass, biting kids' ankles. In a typical scenario, he grabbed a guy by his Mohawk and beat his face into the floor (must have been all that coffee). He often invited fans to fight him, then became outraged if they refused.

6 GREAT MOMENTS IN PUKING

1. Lux Interior (the Cramps)
A young Ian MacKaye saw a life-changing Cramps show during which Lux vomited onstage. Inspired by this event, and by the black punk group Bad Brains, MacKaye formed his first band. In September of 1981, the Cramps played a festival in Leeds, England. Lux threw up during the encore and later remarked, "That's when I knew I was a success—I got paid $15,000 to throw up."

2. Johnny Thunders (New York Dolls, the Heartbreakers)
Johnny did a good deal of hurling, either due to a stiff dose of heroin or junk-sick withdrawals. Heartbreakers manager Leee Black Childers often stood by the stage with a bucket to catch Johnny's heaves. Of Thunders' many recorded pukes, he is most renowned for the upchuck of November 28, 1973. After the Dolls' London debut, the group flew to France to continue their tour of the Continent. Landing at Orly Airport, Thunders lurched off the plane and projectile-vomited all over the crème de la crème of the European press, who had been invited by the record company. Wrote journalist Nick Kent, "The members of the band look stone-faced and wasted, wondering if maybe he's going to fall into his own vomit." The band soon played the Olympia Theatre in Paris, where Johnny spent five minutes throwing up behind an amp.

3. Stiv Bators (Dead Boys)
In a movie of Dead Boys' concert footage, singer Bators can be seen stroking his throat and forcing out vomit. It looks stupid because he's trying so hard.

4. Fletcher Dragge (Pennywise)
Guitarist Dragge is known as "the Sid Vicious of Orange County." He is the most badly behaved of this crew of surfer/skate punks, and is known for vomiting on audiences.

He also has a tendency to puke on celebrities—radio/TV personality Riki Rachtman got covered with a massive amount of upchuck while Pennywise was performing at a KROQ-sponsored concert.

5. Iggy Pop (the Stooges)

Of course, Mr. Pop was a frequent puker, due to substance excess or hangover. In Please Kill Me, Alan Vega is quoted: "Iggy came out and he's wearing dungarees with holes, with this red bikini underwear with his balls hanging out. He went to sing and he just pukes all over, man. He's running through the audience and he jumped Johnny Winter, who was sitting beside Miles Davis. Johnny Winter hated them, but Miles Davis loved it. It was one of the greatest shows I've ever seen in my life."

6. Sex Pistols

The Pistols alleged heavy vomiting is something of an urban legend. It is the case that Johnny Rotten spat and blew his nose a lot onstage due to a serious sinus condition (it's rumored that fans imitated him and started the gobbing craze)—but there is little evidence that he was a frequent vomiter. Certainly, the Pistols weren't in a league with Johnny Thunders. Rumor has it that Steve Jones threw up on an old lady in an airport departure lounge. Apparently he was drunk and did vomit at the airport, but not on anyone. Johnny Rotten is said to have puked a lot, but again, there is no evidence to support this: in his autobiography he recalls "being sick in a rubber plant" at a record executives' party. Sid Vicious came closest to the stereotype, and being a serious junkie, it was probably more likely for him to vomit than for the other guys. Wrote Legs McNeil, "After a wild signing at the A&M offices, Sid trashed the managing director's office and vomited on his desk—the Pistols were dropped the following week from A&M Records."

GOBBING'S GREATEST HITS

1. Johnny Ramone Cries

On their first trip to England in 1976, the Ramones opened for the Flamin' Groovies at the Roundhouse. Groovie Chris Wilson reported, "When they came off, Johnny Ramone was in floods of tears because the punks had been spitting on the band. That was a purely London thing—nobody did that in New York. I remember him saying, 'They got it on my guitar . . . they got it on my pick!' And Joey still didn't know if they'd gone down well or not. 'Did they like us? Did they hate us?' He couldn't tell." The Ramones were a massive hit in Britain.

2. Lita Loves Loogies

Lita Ford, solo performer and former lead guitarist of the Runaways, had an appreciation for spittle. She remarked, "[In England], the more spit you got, the better you were. Oh, fuck, yeah. We had loogies hanging over us by the end of each set. It was great. Now I'd run for some antibacterial wipes, but then it was awesome. 'Man, look at that loogie on your neck, that's cool!' We just got spat on left and right."

3. Mudhoney Plays a Prank

In the book *Our Band Could Be Your Life*, author Michael Azerrad wrote of the Mudhoney/Sonic Youth tour of the U.K., "In Manchester some of the audience started spitting on Mudhoney, apparently thinking the old punk custom still prevailed in the States. [Vocalist Mark] Arm deadpanned into the mike that although gobbing was not a Seattle thing, it was very much appreciated in Sonic Youth's hometown of New York. The hail of saliva stopped, then resumed tenfold when Sonic Youth hit the stage. By one report, Thurston Moore's hair was matted with spit and he would periodically have to flick spew off his hands."

4. Johnny Rotten's Sinuses

It's probable that the gobbing craze began because Johnny Rotten suffers from nasal and throat congestion. He often blows his nose into a hanky and spits onstage, or into the hanky. In the Sex Pistols' early days, young punks attempting to emulate their hero began to hock up loogies. The Pistols were the first band to be associated with spitting and vomiting.

5. Gobbing in Belfast

TV Smith of the Adverts describes a night in Belfast, 1978, in the history of Irish punk, *It Makes You Want to Spit*: "We hit the stage to the most concerted barrage of gobbing I'd ever seen. The Belfast audience had heard about the spitting craze . . . in the English punk rock scene . . . and were out to show that they were as punk as anyone. For us, though, playing under a storm of spittle and having our clothes crusty and reeking for the rest of the tour was something we'd long ago grown to hate. . . . The gig descended into chaos as our manager came on and begged the crowd to stop spitting. . . . He was met with the inevitable hail of gob. . . . That was the Adverts in Belfast. We never went back."

6. A Snappy Comeback

Peter Perrett, of the Only Ones, was spat on in a Birmingham club. He kicked the offender in the head, telling him, "Look, if you really want to do something, I'd rather you pissed on me, because I'm into water sports."

7. Mythic Spittle Imagery

Filmmaker Julien Temple, who made the much-lauded Sex Pistols documentary *The Filth and the Fury*, reported on an early show: "When the Pistols finally played at Leeds, all the kids in the audience felt that they had to wear safety pins, tear their clothes, and spit at the stand. I still remember that amazing image. When Rotten finally came out onstage, it was like Agincourt. There were these massed volleys of gob flying through the air that just hung on John like a Medusa. It was like green hair, or snakes."

8. Projectile Injuries

Siouxsie of Siouxsie & the Banshees caught a gob in her eye and got an infection. Adam Ant got conjunctivitis from getting spat on in the eye at a Sex Pistols gig. Wrote Lydon, "That's why he had to wear his eye patch. Everybody thought it was part of his pirate scene, his big look."

9. Handsome Dick Manitoba Fights Back

Exclusive to this book, Manitoba says, "I remember going to England to open up a Stranglers tour in '77. I was famous in those days for a thing called 'the spit trick.'"

The spit trick occurred when Mr. Manitoba would drink either orange juice or ginger ale. A glandular miracle would take place soon afterward—Manitoba would be able to release from his mouth a huge gob of saliva that would slowly wend its way down from his mouth toward the floor. Two, three, even four feet of gob stretching from Mr. Manitoba's mouth toward the floor was a common occurrence. The gob was quickly, in a snakelike manner, 'sucked' back up into Mr. Manitoba's mouth before hitting the ground. Then, in rapid-fire succession, he would let the spit go up and down, in and out of his mouth. People would go crazy. Screams of "Spit trick!" followed on stages all over the world, once fans caught a glimpse of this modern miracle. Having mastered his art, Manitoba was in no fear of the British. "It was nothing to me," he reports. "I can handle this shit! I fuck-you'd the English crowd with a giant 20-foot spit missile, to which they responded with a nauseating cascade of gobs that covered everything on the stage. They won, and Mark 'the Animal' Mendoza, our bass player, almost left the tour then and there. But he was man enough to stay."

HEALTHY LIVING: 21 DIETARY HABITS OF PUNKS

1. Bubble Gum Rock

Minor Threat was crossing into Canada and was stopped by the border patrol. The guards obsessively searched the band's van in hopes of finding drugs. When they found a secret door into a space that held equipment, a guard said, "And what's in here?" Inside were 800 pieces of bubble gum.

2. Meat Deprivation

When the New York Dolls first came to L.A., singer David Johansen was irritated when he couldn't find hand-cut pastrami. According to writer Harvey Kubernik, in *We Got the Neutron Bomb*, "He was like, 'Where's Nathan's?' I said, 'There's one in the Valley.' We had to do a hot dog run to Nathan's with him. I'd never seen anybody put sauerkraut on a hot dog. I was like, 'Wait a minute, you eat this at ten in the morning?' He said, 'Oh yeah. Anytime.' He was always going, 'Where's the vendor carts?' I never knew you could get a hot dog on the street."

3. Doggie Bag

The Poverty Diet took many forms among punk bands. Any number of punks claim to have eaten dog food, but many say Mugger, a Black Flag roadie, actually does it. Pragmatic about his nutritional needs, he wrapped dog food up in a ball of Wonder Bread and chucked it down his gullet fast.

4. Only in Florida

Rat Cafeteria, a Tampa, Florida, band, lived up to its name. Band members ate one another's "snot and spit," and one member, Jimmy Barf, specialized in cockroaches and cigarette butts.

5. The Go-Go's Diet

The Go-Go's Diet, as the girls in the band called it, was caused by a combination of poverty and borderline anorexia, the latter induced by their manager, Kim Fowley, who viciously humiliated them if they were "fat." Says original bassist Margot Olaverra. "We were on a stipend of $40 a week, which nobody can live on, and we would get a bonus if we lost ten pounds . . . Jane got really pimply 'cause she was doing crystal meth to lose weight. I would throw steamed vegetables in a blender and call it soup. . . . The 25-cent box of macaroni and cheese was affordable but too fattening. . . . I was living on celery soup and then we'd go to a club and have an open tab because now we [had a record in the charts]. Basically, I fucked up my liver. . . . [One of the reasons] they fired me, they said, was that I got hepatitis."

6. Fine Dining

Elvis Costello toured with a *Good Food* guidebook. In the Costello biography *Complicated Shadows*, Bruce Thomas reminisced, "It would be Japanese meals all the time; we'd take a cab 60 miles to go to lunch together. And we polished off some good wine. I remember having a waiter literally weeping on the table because Elvis and I ordered the last bottle of '61 Haut Brion whilst having very erudite conversations about social reform, Jeremy Bentham and William Blake. We weren't idiots." Costello also had food quirks: he'd go into the kitchen and emerge, said a friend, with "a peanut-butter sandwich with blackberry jam with tomatoes on it. Really weird stuff." Around 1983, Costello saw a documentary about animal abuse and became a vegetarian.

7. The Poverty Diet

When Bruce Pavitt of Mudhoney first moved to Seattle, in 1983, he was so poor he sold his blood twice a week and subsisted on a case of sardines a friend had stolen from her father's fishing boat. This was probably a healthier diet than that of San Francisco's Flipper, whose members lived on methamphetamine and potatoes.

8. Sucking on Inanimate Objects

In the legendary feud between Dinosaur Jr.'s Lou Barlow and J Mascis, what they did with their mouths played a major part. Barlow said of Mascis, "The guy chewed like a cow. Loudly." Barlow himself upset Mascis by putting things in his mouth. "Just random things," he explained, "and [he'd] chew on them." Complained Mascis, "I bought this Cookie Monster doll on the tour, and I looked in the van once, and Lou was there sucking on its eyeball. Something about that disturbed me to the core. I couldn't handle it. I had to throw the thing out."

As the guys' relationship degenerated, Barlow said he "took this martyr role. . . . I made sure I didn't put things in my mouth."

9. According to Joey Ramone . . .

Joey told Offspring singer Dexter Holland, "Our drummer [Marky] eats bugs for money." On Yoo-hoo: the Ramones' rider included ten cases of the gooey chocolate soda. Said Joey, "It's rough singing [after] drinking Yoo-hoo, because of all the mucus. I had to give up drinking Yoo-hoo. It's a sticky situation." Johnny Ramone reportedly kept drinking it. Joey's No.1 favorite food was popcorn. When possible, he ate it every night before dinner. Another favorite food was sushi.

According to all the Ramones and their entourage, they had one important food ritual: before every gig, they ate a plain cheese pizza. The pizza was in the rider, and the guys got extremely upset if it wasn't provided.

10. Mr. Natural

In *Please Kill Me*, Scott Asheton reminisces about Iggy Pop's way with the ladies: "It used to just blow my mind the way Iggy could get the girls to just flock around him. You know, they'd sit around and watch him eat boogers. Once I saw him pick up his usual four or five girls . . . he's got all these young girls just grouped around him—'Oh, Iggy, oh, Iggy . . .'

"They were all around him in a semicircle, just staring and gawking at him. All of a sudden, he blew his nose into his hand, and then just guided it right down into his mouth.

"And I swear, they were still gazing at him like they didn't even notice."

11. The World War II Diet

Geza X, musician and producer for the Germs, told the authors of *Lexicon Devil* about dining at L.A.'s underground club, the Masque:

"I lived in the Masque when it first opened up. It was so cheap a bunch of unsigned local bands moved in. It was like a bomb shelter. There was a giant storage room with food rations from WWII. They were stored in these tins. We were all starving so we stared opening them up and they were full of crackers and dried food. We'd go back there, drunk out of our minds, and eat these food rations."

12. Noshing Onstage

The Germs performed a cover of the Archies' "Sugar Sugar," during which they emptied two-pound bags of sugar over the stage and the audience. At the same show, they told everyone they knew to bring food, which they mixed in tubs to pour on themselves and on the crowd: a combination of whipped cream, salad dressing, rotten beans, mayonnaise, bread, Campbell's soup, sour milk, and peanut butter.

13. A Wee Prank #1

In Johnny Rotten's autobiography, he shares a culinary secret: "It was laughable when Glen [Matlock] was in the band. When Steve Jones would masturbate, he'd pour hot water down a hollowed French loaf, chuck some raw liver down it, and then fuck it. The hot water would cook the liver, and I suppose his dick cooked it, too. Then he'd come in and set it aside.

I would turn up and Steve would say, 'I'm sorry, I've done it again. Should we make Glen Matlock a sandwich?' I particularly remember how he used to love how soft the bread was."

14. A Wee Prank #2

Johnny Rotten gives away another secret recipe in his book. "Nora" is Rotten's wife, his girlfriend at the time of this tale: "It was at Nora's house. I arrived there and she said, 'Of course I'm faithful,' and there was Vic Goddard of Subway Sect hiding under the table. That was it. That was your starter for ten. There were all these horrible Hells Angels chaps there, and everyone decided an hour later that they were hungry. I was with a couple of mates, and Nora was foolish enough to let us cook the food. Now Nora would never eat anything we cooked in the kitchen, so we served it to Nora's friends. It was literally a shit in the frying pan cooked in olive oil. Then we all wanked into the fucking omelet—one egg and at least four good doses. They all thought it was the best food they ever ate. The shit sandwich was the killer. It was deep fried and put between two toasted slices of bread. They ate it and thought it was corned beef."

15. Junk Food Pride

Jeff Pezzati, the singer for Naked Raygun and the bass player for Big Black, is a health-conscious guy. Not so former Big Black bandmate Steve Albini. "I'll say one thing for him—he had a terrible diet, man," said Pezzati. Albini was addicted to Slim Jims, and his favorites were the ones with the gold wrapper because the ink from the label stuck to the mystery meat. Recalls Pezzati, "He would always show it to me, every time, and say, 'Look!' And then he would eat it."

16. Breakfast for a Champion

This is the daily breakfast of J Mascis, of Dinosaur Jr.: Jell-O and whipped cream, cut up and stirred until it makes a gummy paste.

17. Colon Cleanse

The Minutemen's D. Boon ate a lot of spirulina—a healthy "green food," and the band had to make regular stops in the van to accommodate his bowel needs.

18. Brit Punk Food

As pizzas and burgers are American punk food, heavily fried things and scary sandwiches are British punk food. In *John Lydon: Stories of Johnny*, American Judy Nylon of the band Snatch recalls English punk fare: "Punk cuisine was limited to bags of crisps, fish and chips, canned beans on toast, and that foul concoction know as a chip buttie. For those who have never run into one, the ingredients are chips (fried potatoes, for my fellow Yanks) between two slices of 'mother's pride,' (cheap nasty white bread) slathered with salad cream (a vinegary, low-grade mayonnaise). The first time I was offered this delicacy was at the Slits' hangout. . . . I wanted so much to feel included that I closed my eyes and swallowed the whole thing in about five quick bites. The attempt to find a new 'comfort food' wasn't very successful, but the reverb I associate with this period is still deeply imprinted."

19. Going Veg with John Lydon

A number of punks, from Chrissie Hynde to modern-day hardcore kids, are either vegetarian or vegan. In a 1986 interview with Kris Needs, John Lydon describes giving up meat: "I found it made me sick a lot. I think I'm actually allergic to it. Red meat, anyway. It works against you. I haven't looked back to a toilet since. I remember those meaty shits! Oh ho ho! No thanks! Bye-bye! Who needs the past?"

20 & 21. Iggy and Nico Go Macro

It's hard to know how it all got started, but David Bowie's ex-wife, Angela, supposedly hired a macrobiotic cook for her husband's band and for the Stooges. The Stooges were appalled and demanded to know where the hell the meat was. Iggy went along gamely for a while, telling friends, "My shit don't stink now! Really! It don't stink!" Nico and Iggy were having a torrid affair about this time, and one famous tale of Health Food Hell occurred under Nico's reign. She would make a pot of brown rice and then pour a bottle of Tabasco sauce into it, in the belief that the chili sauce would cure her ear pains. The macrobiotic period did not last long.

MYKEL BOARD'S 9 WAYS THAT VEGETARIANS ARE DESTROYING THE EARTH

Vegetarianism is a strange and alienating brand of fanaticism that masquerades as a dietary philosophy. Its tenets are as toxic as the poison ivy its proponents prefer to a T-bone steak. The cult is conceived in the egg of intolerance, weaned on the milk of totalitarianism, raised on the bread of narrow-mindedness, and spread through the germs of fanaticism.

If it were private, a lone stupidity that affected no one but the practitioner, vegetarianism would be laughably harmless. But it is far from private. The rise of vegetarianism has the potential to destroy the entire Earth. Here are nine ways it can do it:

1. Creating Cultural Hostility

What would Italian culture be without spaghetti and meatballs? What would pass for Brazilian if not churrasco steak on a spit? Texas wouldn't be the same without cowboys and cattle roundups. Culture is food. And for many cultures, that food is meat.

2. Destroying the Air Quality with Methane

Grazing cattle gobble up thousands of acres of the Earth's surface. Every day, those cattle expel enough methane to burn an area the size of Oklahoma. It's easy to laugh at cow gas, but those cow farts create more air pollution than all the factories in Cleveland. The only check we have is the insurance that those cows will be killed. Dead cows don't fart.

3. Destroying the Rain Forests with Clear-cutting

Methane isn't the only problem with feeding all these extra animals.

In Brazil, 70 percent of land that was once rain forest is now being used as pasture—to grow animal feed. Vegetarians want the world's cows to live a long and consuming life. But they are living those lives on what was once a thriving ecosystem. Can you imagine how many more trees would have to be cut for every extra year those cows live to chew more cud?

4. Creating a Master-Race Mentality

Even among vegetarians, there's a split on what constitutes a plant. Vegans say anything that comes from an animal is taboo—even honey. More liberal vegetarians will eat anything that doesn't move when it's alive. For most, that's the defining factor. If it moves, it has value. If it doesn't, it's okay to kill and eat it.

What does this mean in human-to-human interaction? What does this mean for the thousands of people confined to hospital beds or suffering in comas? It means they're vegetables. Kill 'em! They don't move, so it's okay to destroy them. Pull 'em up by the roots. Cut 'em down like so many celery stalks.

And if movement is life, more movement is more life. After we go after the still, we can start on the slow. Old people—hah, they're almost vegetables. Why not kill 'em too? In motorized wheelchairs? That's not real movement. It's like broccoli on a shopping cart. Off with their heads. Into the ovens with 'em.

Scratch a vegetarian and a fascist will yell, "Ouch!"

5. Causing Unemployment, Starvation, and Death

It's difficult to guess how many people are employed in the meat industry. There's the entire meat chain, from the feed growers, to the veterinarians, to the cattlemen, the abattoir operators. Then there are the meat cutters and packers. (Somehow "Green Bay

Potato Skinners" just doesn't have the same ring to it.) And the host of suppliers from chicken coop makers to hamburger flippers all rely on meat for their livelihood.

6. Destroying the Balance of the Ecosystem

Everyone who's been to junior high school knows about the food chain. Tiny single-cell animals gobble up even tinier bits of something. Then something bigger eats *them*. Then a plant sucks them up and something eats the plant. Something eats that something, until the top of the food chain eats that and shits it out. The shit fertilizes the next level of plants, and the whole thing starts again.

That's how the ecosystem has been working for the last several million years. The sponge was the world's first animal. (Do vegetarians use sponges?) Animals have developed from there on the basis of eat, be eaten, shit, be shat upon. Who knows what damage we'll do by cutting out an entire link in the chain of evolutionary history?

7. Encouraging a Defiance of Nature

Nature works through the harmonious interaction of species. Just as the U.S. Constitution lays out a system of checks and balances meant to keep our government running smoothly, nature uses plants and animals to protect and control each other. Gazelles don't overrun the plains, because lions eat enough of them to maintain equilibrium. Carrots don't take over fields, because rabbits eat enough to prevent that from happening. The greatness of nature is its ability to arrange things in a balance.

8. Causing Animal Starvation

Right now, animals don't need to starve. Humans cull their population naturally. We don't eat them out of house and home, because we eat them, period. Those that remain have enough food to live and prosper.

Imagine a powerful alien invader. Not understanding Earth's culture, this alien decides to protect humans by only eating their food and not hurting them. Imagine every cupboard raided, every box of Rice-A-Roni torn open and swallowed whole by some green creature, every TV dinner downed by a three legged Venusian that wants to protect us. With no food, humans would be at each other's throats. We'd be murdering our neighbors and feasting on their flesh. That's what would happen to animals if we decided not to eat them but eat their food instead.

9. Destroying Vegetation That Would Provide Oxygen

Oxygen is the substance that allows all animals to live. It's generated only by plant matter. Animals breathe out carbon dioxide. Plants breathe it in. Plants breathe out oxygen. Animals breathe it in. If we don't eat animals that create carbon dioxide, then we have to eat plants, which create oxygen.

Scientists already say that the Earth is oxygen-depleted. The cutting of rain forests to grow crops is one of the major reasons. If the vegetarians got their way, *more* plants would be destroyed to feed humans. We'd need even more than that to feed the animals we don't kill and eat.

All those eaten plants are plants that won't produce oxygen. Eventually, plant life itself could vanish. With no plants—and a lot more animals—life as we know it will end.

Mykel Board is detested by thinking people everywhere. During the '80s, he lived as an anonymous writer of porno novels. Later he was the "singer" for several "bands," including Artless, and has issued some of the world's worst records on his own label, The Only Label in the World, including "artists" such as GG Allin and Swanic Youth. He's been writing a column for Maximumrocknroll *for 20 years. In 2005, he wrote two books that were published with his name on the front.* I, A Me-ist *is an anthology of his writings.* Even a Daughter Is Better Than Nothing *is the true story of his year in Outer Mongolia.*

VIKING THRUST'S 5 DISGUSTING BURGERS YOUR BAND CAN HAVE NEXT TIME YOU TOUR AMERICA

1. WHAT IT IS: The Gandy Dancer—More than two pounds of meat plus all the trimmings you can think of and probably some you don't want to, the Gandy Dancer is a staple with the local logging community. From personal experience, I know it once took two grown men four days to finish one. For anyone passing through the lower Northwest on a budget, the Gandy Dancer can't be beat for both price and quantity. A full band on a skimpy budget can all gorge themselves like true gluttons and still have enough gas money to get to the next town.

WHERE YOU CAN FIND IT: Somewhere just east of The Dalles, Oregon. Look for the signs.

2. WHAT IT IS: Pastrami King's Pastrami Burger—The Pastrami King claims to be central California's No. 1 provider of pastrami, and one is hard-pressed to argue. The burger itself is a thick patty grilled medium rare, then topped with cheese and a half-inch layer of deep-fried pastrami. Bacon is also an option, although those without a capable cardiologist should just stick to the standard issue. Critics will argue that Fatburger, Astro Burger, or In-N-Out are superior California outposts, but for sheer originality, the Pastrami King wins hands down.

WHERE YOU CAN FIND IT: Just past the last In-N-Out on I-5, about an hour and a half north of L.A.

3. WHAT IT IS: Culver's Butter Burger Deluxe—As far as cheeseburgers go, regional fast food chains are a pretty safe bet. The menu options are much less pedestrian than your standard McDonald's or Burger King fare and tend to offer amazing side orders not found elsewhere in the country, like Wisconsin Dairyland cheese curds. Of all the regional fast food chains,

Culver's and their Butter Burgers lead the pack in both the taste and cholesterol categories. The double patty on the Deluxe is topped with cheese and bacon, then along with the bun slathered in butter and fried to perfection. It's a meal your heart and waistline won't soon forget.

WHERE YOU CAN FIND IT: Found throughout the Midwest.

4. WHAT IT IS: The Varsity Double Chili Cheeseburger—A venerable local favorite and a southern tradition, the Varsity's burgers are paralleled only by their hot dogs. The patties aren't huge by any stretch of the word, but what they lack in mass they make up for in taste. The thick chili topping is rich in ground beef and doubles the overall meat quotient. No trip to Atlanta (or the Varsity, for that matter) is complete without onion rings, and luckily, they have you covered on that front. The flagship location on North Avenue is conveniently located near all the city's scummy punk rock dives, so you should have no problem navigating your way there either before or after a rough night out.

WHERE YOU CAN FIND IT: Atlanta and Athens, Georgia.

5. WHAT IT IS: Wild Willy's Wicked Good Burger—With its covered-wagon-chic décor and 15-strong list of burgers, Wild Willy's tops the charts when touring through New Hampshire, Maine, and Massachusetts. The perennial New England favorite Wicked Good Burger elevates Willy's from a small regional chain to a real contender. Piled onto the all-Angus-beef patty are sautéed mushrooms and onions, in addition to both cheddar and Swiss cheese—that's right, not one but two cheeses! If you want to avoid the blasé chowder that seems to abound throughout New England, check out Willy's for something that will really stick to your ribs.

WHERE YOU CAN FIND IT: Watertown, Massachusetts, with three
other locations throughout New England.

*Viking Thrust claims to be an accomplished musician and has quit
more bands than you'll ever be in. The next band he plans to quit is
LiveFastDie.*

THE MAGNIFICENT 7: PIZZAS OF THE WORLD, ACCORDING TO MARIO BATALI

*Author's Note: Pizza is the most punk rock of all foods, but there
are far too many ordinary slices in New York. And outside of New
York? Fuhgeddaboudit. So I asked my friend Mario Batali to
educate you ham 'n' eggers on the real deal. Herewith, Pizza 101,
special for* The Official Punk Rock Book of Lists. *—HDM*

1. Napolitana—thin blistered yet soft and pliant crust, cooked
in a wood-fired oven, very lightly dressed, with as little as
just tomato sauce and oregano (marinara) to *cuattro stagioni*
(anything four things the *pizzaiolo* wants).

2. Romana—is similar to the Napolitana. It is slightly more crisp
and less pliant. Cooked in a wood-fired oven, it generally features
the same suspects in the topping dept.

3. Stazione—takes its name from "train station" in Italian.
Cooked on sheet pans in electric ovens, the Stazione boasts a soft,
thicker crust, with more sauce, and toppings as varied as canned
tuna and olives, or even sliced hot dogs.

4. Providence—is generally considered to have been perfected
by the Al Forno restaurant in (where else?) Providence, Rhode
Island. This is very thin, grilled over hot coals, and dressed

lightly with both very traditional Neapolitan ingredients and creative ones.

5. New York—has a thin, flexible crust, great for rolling up tube style. Cooked in an electric deck oven, the New York is generally dressed with a thin amount of sauce, too much cheese, and many other things (e.g., "the works").

6. Chicago-style deep-dish pizza—has a thick, pastrylike crust, is cooked in a deck oven, and is constructed in reverse and opposite of the Napolitana: i.e., crust first, then cheese, then lots of topping (lots), then sauce, and then sometimes even another crust. (This is also known as "stuffed" pizza.)

7. West Coast—exhibits almost no consistent characteristics, can have whole wheat or sourdough crust, can be grilled or baked, and can feature barbecue sauce or salsa. There is no limit on the imagination (for better or worse) in the topping department, up to and including the Hawaiian, with Canadian bacon and pineapple.

Mario Batali believes that olive oil is as precious as gold and that shorts are acceptable attire for every season. Mario hosts two Food Network programs, Molto Mario *and* Ciao America. *He also engages in fierce culinary battle in the Food Network series* Iron Chef America *and is the author of many fine books. His restaurant Babbo is widely regarded as the best in New York City.*

HANDSOME DICK MANITOBA'S 5 FAVORITE PIZZA TOPPINGS

1. Sausage—NOT pepperoni. I HATE PEPPERONI. There's lots of shitty sausage in the world. It's gotta be great-quality sausage.

It's like a great tomato. Most are mediocre, but when you get a good one, it's one of the world's great foods. Same with sausage—high-quality, flavorful, thinly sliced, well done, CRISP. The perfect accompaniment

2. Soppresotta—Here's a MANITOBAN food idea: Instead of sheepishly saying, "Okay, I'll pick from the list," when you enter your pizzeria and see the list of extras, why not bring in some thin slices of spicy soppresotta from your local deli? Chop 'em up, ask the pizza maker to "throw this on top of my slice, please." Make the slice hot, so the meat gets chewy, crispy, slightly oily from the fat. THIS HAS TEXTURE! Texture, baby, texture—the true sensuality of food. Flavor is obvious, but texture is sexy! Sprinkle grated cheese on top, and you have the second-best slice goin'! By the way, if your pizza maker doesn't do this "extra stuff that you bring in yourself" thing for free, then find yourself a new pizzeria!

3. Anchovies—I adore anchovies. I like the way, when heated, they release their fishy oils all over the slice. Get napkins!! Grated cheese and hot red pepper flakes are a must on top of the little fishies. If you don't like anchovies, then you're too squeamish! I hope for your sake this doesn't spill over into other categories in life!

4. Black olives, fresh garlic, grated cheese, hot red pepper flakes—These make for a great, chewy, overstimulating concoction. (I've been told I'm a stimulation freak—that's why I like hot pepper so much.) As you can see, grated cheese and hot pepper flakes are a must in the Pizza World of Handsome Dick Manitoba.

5. Sliced meatballs, thinly sliced boiled ham, fresh littleneck clams—This is the "whatever floats your boat" category. There's a legendary pizza joint in New Haven, Connecticut, that does an amazing clam/garlic pizza. Contrary to what my pal, world famous chef Mario Batali, sez, I love grated cheese on top of my clam pizza, or for that matter, linguine with white clam sauce. (Mario don't like the cheese on da' fish!) All this stuff in this category works well with pizza. Just don't get too California. NO PINEAPPLE, CHICKEN, OR GOOFY VEGETABLES! It might be food, but it won't retain its pizza status. California fucked up the great American hamburger (lettuce, tomato, onions, ketchup, and mustard)—don't let 'em fuck up the greatest punk rock food of all—PIZZA!

Handsome Dick Manitoba promises to wax effusive about his other favorite food, White Castle hamburgers, in a future edition of The Official Punk Rock Book of Lists.

It's hard to put a number to their girth, but these guys played in a league of their own.
1. Gary Floyd—the Dicks
2. D. Boon—Minutemen
3. Pig Champion—Poison Idea
4. Dave Thomas—Pere Ubu
5. Kike Turmix—the Pleasure Fuckers
6. Ron Reckless—Mighty Sphincter
7. Randy "Biscuit" Turner—the Big Boys
8. Marco Pirroni—Siouxsie & the Banshees, Adam & the Ants
9. El Duce—the Mentors

JON SPENCER'S 14 FOODS TO AVOID ON TOUR, PLUS ONE BIT OF ADVICE FOR WHEN YOU ARE IN JAPAN

1. **Fast food (McDonald's, Burger King, etc.)**—Avoid at all costs. Sometimes this is hard to do: there just aren't many options in some places. This food will come back to haunt you and definitely make you feel crummy. Conversely/perversely, White Castle, which definitely always makes ya shit, should still be consumed at any and all opportunities.

2. **Food made by punk rockers at their homes**—Late-night grill, strange breakfast, weird loaves . . . nice gesture, but beware! These people can barely take care of themselves. Look at the filthy house/apartment. Of course, there is always an exception, and sometimes you do end up with a great meal . . . *but you never know.*

3. **Indian food**—Never eat this before a show.

4. **Freshly killed snake in Taiwanese outdoor market**—Avoid.

5. **Local liqueurs and house drink specials**—Always approach these with caution, especially if they are being pushed on you by a stranger and/or you did not see the drink poured. But if someone offers you a swig of homemade car battery 'shine from a bottle fashioned out of a child's doll? Go for it. You have to be polite.

6. **Foods that don't match the locale**—Don't order paella in Moscow. Or eat sushi in Denver. *Eat local.*

7. **Cow balls**—do not eat cow balls at interstate truck stops in Middle America. In fact, don't eat any kinds of balls, anywhere.

8. Roadside chain restaurants—Avoid Cracker Barrels, although Waffle Houses are acceptable, as long as you play at least three of the Waffle House songs on the jukebox. Or just the same song three times in a row. "Waffle House Thank You" by Mary Welch Rogers is good. So is "Special Lady" by Billy Dee Cox.

9. Starbucks—Never patronize a Starbucks that is not freestanding, like one that is inside a bookstore. (This rule comes courtesy of Mike Belitsky of the Sadies.)

10. Autogrill rest stops in Italy—Freshly squeezed orange juice done by machine is very tasty but usually contains at least two flies. They seem to live and nest in the squeezing machines. Who can blame them?

11. Turkish pizza—Found mostly in Germany, this is not really pizza; it's closer to a gyro. Always seems like a good idea late at night. Never is.

12. Dunkin' Donuts—Stay away! Not even good donuts, and even worse coffee. Plus, they assault your eyes with their sickening color scheme, poorly designed logo, and insipid Rachel Ray endorsement. Canada's Tim Hortons, however, is more than okay. Try the sour cream glazed.

13. U.K. gas station prepackaged sandwiches made from shellfish—Steer clear of these. Really. Go to a café and get a proper full breakfast, cooked hot. But don't order coffee—it will likely be instant.

14. Never eat chicken at a rock festival.

15. Eat anything in Japan—It's Japanese!

After the demise of his groovy hate-fuck band Pussy Galore, Jon Spencer formed the Jon Spencer Blues Explosion and has continually proven himself the most exciting and innovative performer in rock 'n' roll. On stage and in the studio he has destroyed and rebuilt American roots music with such abandon it is hard to believe that there is anything left. While the Blues Explosion is on a much-deserved hiatus, Jon has found time cook up adult-size doses of psychotic rootsabilly rhythm 'n' noise with his pal Matt Verta-Ray and their stomping roll 'n' rock combo, Heavy Trash.

EAST VS. WEST: MIRIAM LINNA'S PUNK ROCK DELICACIES FROM THE MAX'S KANSAS CITY AND WHISKY A GO GO MENUS, CIRCA 1977

These menus were found at the bottom of my "That Seventies Box," which includes letters, diaries, photos, and a pair of red sneakers signed by the Ramones in '76.

The bar at Max's named the complex and very alcoholic beverages after bands.

1. The Ramone

Your favorite beer, molested by a straight shot of whiskey.

2. Suicide

Green Chartreuse and 151-proof rum . . . on fire. Only attempt it at the bar.

3. Blondie

A silky-smooth bombshell, with Galliano, crème de cacao, and a good head.

4. The Doll

Don't ask. Just drink it!

5. The Heartbreaker

A bittersweet affair between icy vodka, sloe gin, and juicy cranberries.

6. Cherry Vanilla

A hot-pink cherry-tasting cream dream.

7. Wayne County Punch

A nice fruit punch with a heavy dose of Southern Comfort.

8. Milk 'n' Cookies

An old-fashioned brandy-milk punch, tall, with a cookie.

9. Mink DeVille

A high-powered blast of orange-rum-flavored Coke.

10. The Fast

Tequila gone bananas. Drink it FAST!

11. Tuff Dart

A tall, cool, vodka-licorice combination that will have you seeing double . . . in black and white!

12. The Brat

A bit of the spoils.

13. John Collins

What else?

14. Joe Cool

Iced coffee, of course, with mint and mocha brandy.

15. Just Water

A serious amount of gin, Cointreau, and 7-Up.

16. The Planet

Out of sight.

The Whisky seemed a tad more responsible (and less imaginative), skipping the booze and naming their chow after rock acts.

1. Sex Pistol

Cheeseburger and french fries.

2. Blondie

Cheeseburger with bacon and french fries.

3. Kim Fowley

Bacon, lettuce, and tomato.

4. Johnny Rotten

Grilled cheese.

5. Ramone

Hot dog and french fries.

6. Iggy Pop

Fresh fruit salad.

7. Runaways

Large green salad with lettuce, tomato, and choice of dressing.

8. Phast Phreddie

French fries.

9. Rodney Bingenheimer

Hamburger and french fries.

10. Elvis Costello

Fish and chips.

11. Van Halen
10-ounce grilled Delmonico steak, salad, and french fries.

Miriam Linna left Ohio for NYC in July of 1976. She was the first drummer for the Cramps, Nervous Rex, and the Zantees; worked publicity for Marty Thau's Red Star Records; and wrote for the New York Rocker *and* Young, Fast & Scientific, *among other fanzines. She founded* Kicks *in 1979 with husband Billy Miller, and the pair subsequently branched out with* Bad Seed *and* Smut Peddler. *Nowadays, Miriam and Billy blast forth with their label, Norton Records, and make a racket with the A-Bones. She admits to having had one drum lesson ever—from Tommy Ramone.*

17 PUNKS' FAVORITE TIPPLES

1. Johnny Thunders (New York Dolls, the Heartbreakers)
When Thunders was off heroin, or on a low dose, he drank vodka. At one show his dope connection didn't arrive, so he knocked back eight double vodkas before going onstage.

2. Ian MacKaye (Minor Threat)
When MacKaye was in the Teen Idles, he drank milk or Coca-Cola with a side of Twinkies. One of their tracks is titled "I Drink Milk."

3. Henry Rollins (Black Flag)
Rollins is a hardcore coffee addict. While the other guys in Black Flag smoked pot, Rollins caffed up, drinking pot after pot of java, which led to excruciating headaches. Known as "caffeine-withdrawal headaches," these plague addicts when they have gone for a span of hours without their drug.

4. Sid Vicious (Sex Pistols)

Vicious preferred peppermint schnapps, straight. Or, when he could get it, peppermint schnapps mixed with Southern Comfort and a beer back. Really.

5. Iggy Pop (the Stooges)

Pop went for variants on White and Black Russians: sometimes the traditional vodka, Kahlúa, and milk; sometimes just Kahlúa and milk. On one occasion he drank 16 Kahlúa and milks in a row. (Dylan Thomas drank 18 straight whiskeys in a row, said, "I believe that's a record," and died.) Lamented Pop, "I only like pussy drinks."

6. Elvis Costello (Elvis Costello & the Attractions)

Once he could afford them, Costello tended to choose very fine wines, to accompany his epicurean tastes. However, he never handled his drink very well (see the "Oops" list.) According to *Complicated Shadows*, when he enjoyed his favorite spirit, Jameson Irish whiskey, "he needed watching."

7. Steve Nieve (Elvis Costello & the Attractions)

When 19-year-old classically trained pianist Steve Nason auditioned for Elvis Costello, he knew nothing about rock and thought he was trying out for an Elvis Presley tribute band. At the audition Nason (who would later change his name to Nieve) drank a bottle of sherry—his favorite poison—and fell asleep on the floor, thus winning the job.

8–10. The Beastie Boys

Back when the Beastie Boys were punks, they requested the following on their rider:

   a. Six cases of Budweiser—not for drinking, but for throwing around onstage
   b. A couple of cases of quality beer for consumption

    c. One bottle of 151

    d. One bottle of Jack Daniel's

    e. One bottle of Cuervo Gold

    f. One bottle of Stolichnaya

    g. A rainbow assortment of condoms (they were studying the habits of Great Rock Stars Before Them)

The Beasties got quite upset when anything on the rider didn't appear.

11–14. The Clash

These boys were hearty beer-drinking lads, except for a Pernod phase that they went through, thinking they were actually drinking absinthe.

15. Marky Ramone (Ramones)

The Ramones' manager, Monte Melnick, said, "I once saw Marky drink 16 double martinis in Cleveland. The next morning during interviews, he threw up every ten minutes.

16. Handsome Dick Manitoba (Dictators)

Back in the day, Manitoba preferred "Rémy in the winter, vodka in the summer, scotch from Mommy and Daddy's home bar or wherever I could get it."

17. John Lydon (Sex Pistols)

Generally known to be a beer man, Lydon recalls his first hangover in his autobiography, *Rotten: No Irish, No Blacks, No Dogs*: "I got my first nasty hangover after Sid and I mixed up a punch bowl of Southern Comfort, Cinzano Bianco, and Martini & Rossi and drank it in a rush. I've never touched any of those drinks since."

PRETENTIOUS? MOI? ANDY SHERNOFF'S 10 RULES FOR THE PUNK ROCK SOMMELIER

1. Swallow, don't spit.
2. Screwtops are cool. Save the cork tree.
3. Use paper cups.
4. After being handed the wine list by the square sommelier, point and laugh.
5. In French restaurants, order in Esperanto.
6. Pair red wine with bagels and lox.
7. Pair white wine with pizza.
8. Pair rosé with White Castle.
9. Drink Burgundy when someone else is paying
10. Pinot Noir, Northern Rhone, and Spanish wines rule. Vintage Bordeaux sucks!!

Andy Shernoff, a.k.a. the Christopher Columbus of Punk Rock and the Punk Rock Sommelier, is the songwriter/bass player for the Dictators, as well as a world-renowned record producer, social critic, and bon vivant.

SUPERSTAR SOMMELIER JEAN-LUC LE DÛ'S PUNK ROCK WINE LIST

1. The Clash, The Clash (U.K. Pressing)—Barolo (Piedmont; Italy) There's nothing like a blitz of razor-sharp guitars and incendiary political wit from the Strummer/Jones team to echo this classic, sharp-as-a-knife gem from Northern Italy, where they still display posters from the Communist era in three-star hotels.

2. New York Dolls, New York Dolls—Gevrey-Chambertin (Burgundy; France)

What can I say? These are both are flashy, smelly, sometimes sloppy, and often magnificent.

3. Sonics, Here Are the Sonics—Châteauneuf-du-Pape (Southern Rhone; France)

If you could take a chunk of meat, let it ferment, and make wine from it, Châteauneuf-du-Pape is probably what you'd get. Well, Gerry Roslie and his gang from Seattle used that same technique in the same manner, but laid some of the foundations of punk rock instead.

4. Eddie Cochran, 12 of His Biggest Hits—Rioja (Spain)

Total classics one can't go without. Emulated and imitated worldwide, but nothing matches the original. Hey, they probably lost the plans somewhere along the way, and that's not a bad thing.

5. The Ramones, It's Alive—Beaujolais (France)

Simple, direct, classic. No bullshit.

For almost ten years Jean-Luc Le Dû was the head sommelier for New York City's famed Restaurant Daniel. While at Daniel, Jean-Luc won the title of Best Sommelier Northeast America in the 1997 Sopexa Competition. In August 2002, Jean-Luc's wine list merited Wine Spectator magazine's Grand Award, as one of the best in the world. Shortly afterwards, having been already nominated in 2000, Jean-Luc was honored with the James Beard Foundation 2003 Award for Outstanding Wine Service. More recently, he has left the restaurant business to follow his dreams. He has opened a temperature-controlled wine store in New York's West Village called Le Dû's Wines, and has finally made the perfect pairing of punk rock and vin rouge.

29 PUNK ROCK BOOZE SONGS

1. "House of Gods"—the Pogues
2. "Six Pack"—Black Flag
3. "Drinking & Driving"—Black Flag
4. "Red, Red Wine"—the Replacements
5. "Knockin' 'Em Back"—Paul Westerberg
6. "Punch Drunk"—Hüsker Dü
7. "Bottle Now!"—the Raunch Hands
8. "Dames, Booze, Chains and Boots"—the Cramps
9. "Pizza-n-Beer"—Adrenalin O.D.
10. "Drink, Fight & Fuck"—GG Allin
11. "Drunk & Disorderly"—Black Market Baby
12. "Too Drunk Last Night"—Civil Disobedience
13. "Alcohol"—Gang Green
14. "American Wino"—the Lewd
15. "Jesus and Tequila"—Minutemen
16. "Beer"—Murphy's Law
17. "A House Full of Drunks"—Necros
18. "Drunk & Stupid"—Section 8
19. "I Was Drunk"—Willful Neglect
20. "Michelob"—the F.U.'s
21. "Milk and Alcohol"—written by Nick Lowe, performed by Dr. Feelgood
22. "Ripped to the Tits"—the Pleasure Fuckers
23. "Alcohollywood"—the Raunch Hands
24. "The Bottle"—Rancid
25. "Hair of the Dog"—the Ramones
26. "The Alcohol of Fame"—Peter Laughner
27. "Kaos"—Alcoholiday
28. "The Lewd"—American Wino
29. "I Drink Milk"—Teen Idles

30 PUNK ROCK PILL SONGS

1. "Bop Pills"—the Cramps
2. "Downs"—Alex Chilton
3. "Pills"—Bo Diddley (The song was covered by the New York Dolls. When the Dolls asked Bo to sing it with them, he couldn't remember the song, and thought they were asking him for drugs.)
4. "Pills and Soap"—the Imposter (a.k.a. Elvis Costello)
5. "The Bitterest Pill"—the Jam
6. "Lithium"—Nirvana
7. "Valentine"—the Replacements
8. "I'm Just Like You"—the Tards
9. "Yellow Pills "—20/20
10. "Rouche Rumble"—the Fall (Rouche is a drug manufacturer.)
11. "Mr. Pharmacist"—the Other Half
12. "Mr. Pharmacist'"—the Fall (covering the Other Half)
13. "New Kind of Kick"—the Cramps
14. "Amphetamine Blues"—Fallen Angels
15. "My Baby Takes Valium"—Family Fodder
16. "Gimme Sopor"—the Angry Samoans (Sopor was a brand name for quaaludes, R.I.P.)
17. "Sleeping Pill Suicide"—Chin Ho
18. "She Took a Lot of Pills and Died"—Robbie Fulks
19. "Valley of the Dolls"—Generation X
20. "714"—the Godz (714 was the number printed on Quaaludes.)
21. "Pills"—Green Apple Quick Step
22. "DF118"—Charlie Harper (DF118 is more or less Britain's Vicodin.)
23. "Ms. 714"—the Joneses (Another Quaalude song, God love them.)
24. "Diet Pill"—L7

25. "Give Me Dr. Rock"—Roger Ruskin
26. "Little Blue Pill"—Mac McNally
27. "Miss Teen USA"—Streetwalkin' Cheetahs
28. "Lie Still Little Bottle"—They Might Be Giants
29. "Thorazine"—Angry Samoans
30. "Weekend"—Handsome Dick Manitoba's Wild Kingdom

13 PUNK BANDS WITH DRUGGY NAMES

1. China White
2. Pharmacy
3. Diazepam Nights
4. Night Nurse (Night Nurse is the U.K.'s answer to NyQuil.)
5. Little White Pills
6. Dr. Feelgood
7. The Junkies (Johnny Thunders & the Heartbreakers released one recording as the Junkies)
8. Morphine
9. Halcion
10. Xanax-25
11. The Queer Pills (The Angry Samoans used this name when releasing a 7".)
12. Thorazine (This Philadelphia band was threatened with a lawsuit by the pharmaceutical company SmithKline Beecham. The band argued that they'd already spent nearly $1,000 on T-shirts and stickers to promote their debut record, Coffee, Tea or Thorazine, so they couldn't possibly change their name. The incident was excellent promotion for the band.)
13. LSD (This was a pseudonym for the band Chelsea, with Billy Idol, used on an occasion when "something really naff" was needed.)

11 ODES TO THE HUMBLE POPPY

1. "Chinese Rocks"—written by Dee Dee Ramone, the song was made famous by Johnny Thunder & the Heartbreakers
2. "Heroin"—the Velvet Underground
3. "(I'm) Waiting for the Man"—the Velvet Underground
4. "Too Much Junkie Business"—Johnny Thunders, again
5. "Junky Dare"—Fang
6. "Mainliner"—Social Distortion
7. "We Were on Heroin"—Wasted Youth
8. "Pretty Green Eyes"—the Pogues
9. "Junkie Man"—Rancid
10. "Love in Vein"—the Ruts
11. "H-Eyes"—the Ruts

I WANNA BE SEDATED: 36 JUST PLAIN DRUG SONGS

1. "Drug Train"—the Cramps
2. "Let's Get Fucked Up"—the Cramps
3. "Dopefiend Boogie"—the Cramps
4. "Strychnine"—the Sonics
5. "Strychnine"—the Cramps (covering the Sonics)
6. "Dr. Fucker MD"—the Cramps
7. "I Wanna Be Sedated"—the Ramones
8. "Carbona Not Glue"—the Ramones
9. "Drug Me"—Dead Kennedys
10. "Lust for Life"—Iggy Pop
11. "Fun with Acid"—Fang
12. "Dope Fiend"—Hose
13. "Up the Dose"—Mentors
14. "A Pack of Kools"—Necros

15. "YHWH on Acid"—Saccharine Trust
16. "Speed Rules"—Sick Pleasure
17. "Glue"—Society System Decontrol, a.k.a. SSD
18. "Skinheads Smoke Dope"—Fang
19. "Housewife on Valium"—Vatican Demands
20. "Amphetamine Addiction"—Zero Boys
21. "She Fucks for Drugs"—B-Day Vacation
22. "Drug-Induced State"—the Ralphs
23. "Tony Gets Wasted in Pedro"—Minutemen
24. "Drugs and Sex"—N.O.T.A.
25. "Drug-Related Death"—Blood Mobile
26. "Now I Wanna Sniff Some Glue"—the Ramones
27. "Speedball"—Handsome Dick Manitoba's Wild Kingdom
28. "I'm So Fucked Up"—Peter Laughner
29. "Amphetamine"—Craig Bell
30. "She's Like Heroin to Me"—Jeffrey Lee Pierce
31. "Love in Vein"—the Ruts
32. "Syringe"—Butthole Surfers
33. "Cocaine Werewolf"—the Pleasure Fuckers
34. "Black Coffee"—Black Flag
35. "Down at the Doctor's"—Dr. Feelgood
36. "Skin Poppin' Slut"—Dwarves

MIKE EDISON'S 5 BEST DRUGS FOR PLAYING PUNK ROCK, ONE HONORABLE MENTION, AND 6 REASONS WHY MARIJUANA IS THE WRONG DRUG FOR PUNK ROCK

1. Speed—This is how we win wars, how *The Who Sing My Generation* came to be, and the key ingredient in the Motörhead formula.

2. Booze—Macbeth used to argue that it "provokes the desire, but it takes away the performance," but I doubt the Replacements had much truck for him, anyway.

3. Cocaine—Coke is no longer the plaything of rich toffs and assholes like the Eagles, thanks to the War on Drugs, which brought us expensive weed and fifty-bucks-a-gram blow. Not as edgy as real amphetamines, which means you can snort a whole lot of it before your brain explodes. Buy in bulk.

4. Coffee, Coca-Cola, etc.—Here, we're just working our way down the family of friendly uppers. See also: Snickers bars.

5. Smack—Not for me, but others have had great success with it. You could ask them yourself, but mostly they're dead.

One Honorable Mention . . .

Ibuprofen—This drug is absolutely necessary to quell your hangover so you can get through sound check without dying. One time I took 12 and felt my heart slowing down, so ten is probably the limit. Alka-Seltzer is a fine drug, too, if a bit old-fashioned. The only real drawback is that incessant fizzing.

. . . And 6 Reasons Why Marijuana Is the Wrong Drug for Punk Rock

1. Side one of *Sandinista!*
2. Side two of *Sandinista!*
3. Side three of *Sandinista!*
4. Side four of *Sandinista!*
5. Side five of *Sandinista!*
6. Etc., etc., etc.

Mike Edison is the former publisher of High Times, *a former* Hustler *and* Penthouse *scribe, a* Punk *magazine contributor, the former editor in chief of* Screw *magazine, and a professional wrestler of no small repute. He is the drummer for amped-up garage superheroes the Raunch Hands, and performed and recorded frequently with GG Allin. Currently, he can be found doing damage with his band Edison Rocket Train. His memoir,* I Have Fun Everywhere I Go: Savage Tales of Pot, Porn, Punk Rock, Pro Wrestling, Talking Apes, Evil Bosses, Dirty Blues, American Heroes, and the World's Most Notorious Magazines, *will be published in May 2008. He is also the editor of* The Official Punk Rock Book of Lists.

Tony Cocaine's 5 Tips for PUNK Parenting

1. Every time a Republican comes on TV, hit the kid with a stun gun so he learns: Republicans, bad.

2. Encourage your child to cut his own hair.

3. The only baby talk allowed: "Gabba gabba hey."

4. Hide all of your Sex Pistols, Ramones, Stooges, etc., records, but in a place they can be easily found, so when your child comes across them, he thinks it is contraband and really gets into it.

5. Wear tie-dye when you yell at them so they learn to hate hippies.

"Tony Cocaine" is the pseudonym of a famous punk rock parent who would like to avoid any more trouble with the law.

50 PUNK FASHION MUST-DOS!

1. Torn anything (peg-leg jeans, your T-shirt)
2. Safety-pinned torn stuff (safety pins in general, especially through parts of your face)
3. Spiked hair
4. Pointy boots
5. Giant tricolor Mohawk
6. Doc Martens
7. Bondage pants and bondage suits
8. Bandanas and chains around your boots
9. Jackson Pollock look (like the early Clash)
10. Suspenders (over your ripped T-shirt or your pallid bare chest)
11. Old men's suits and hats/looking like a bum
12. Underwear worn over your clothes
13. Tartan/check/plaid miniskirts, kilts, trousers
14. Fuzzy, torn mohair sweaters

15. Dog collars, especially spiked
16. Spiked anything
17. Razor-blade earrings (first worn by Ian Dury)
18. Fetish/bondage wear
19. Rubber clothes
20. Ripped fishnets
21. Converse All-Stars or Keds (High-tops are good.)
22. Dockers and Vans (preferably checked)
23. Winkle pickers
24. Pork pie hats
25. Lots of pins/badges
26. Slogans all over your clothes and body
27. Trash bags, a.k.a. bin liners (These make great dresses, but any form of bin bag attire is okay.)
28. Too-tight T-shirts that come up over your navel
29. Piercings
30. Brothel creepers
31. Tattoos
32. Raccoon eye makeup
33. *Blade Runner* or *Clockwork Orange* gear
34. Peg-leg pants, straight jeans
35. Skinny ties
36. Those satin baseball jackets
37. Patches (old T-shirts with band logos cut up to patch other T-shirts or jeans)
38. Leather jacket (to be max punk, tricked out with chains and extraneous zips and clips)
39. Basic hardcore (jeans or shorts, T-shirt, hoodie, shaved head/cropped hair)
40. Military surplus gear
41. Trousers with a "diaper" flap in back (like pj's)
42. Zippers anywhere, particularly useless ones
43. Broken nose
44. Padlock necklace, and padlock worn around crotch
45. Garters over jeans

46. Self-mutilation scars (cutting yourself, carving words, cigarette burns)
47. Bullet belts
48. Shirt buttoned the wrong way
49. Stilettos
50. Fingerless black lace gloves

39 PUNK FASHION DON'TS!

1. Natural fibers
2. Twin sets
3. Visible butt crack
4. Getting your colors done
5. Birkenstocks, etc., or any OTC orthopedic footwear
6. Smocking
7. Smocks
8. Letter jackets
9. Embroidered Mexican shirts
10. Monograms (yours)
11. Flower prints
12. Polo shirts, any shirt with a crocodile logo
13. Bushy beards
14. Ultrasuede
15. Major bell-bottoms, a.k.a. flares (Sorry, the comeback is jive.)
16. "Punk" clothes from Neiman's or Barneys
17. Turquoise jewelry
18. Mullet cuts
19. Bling (unless you're an Italian contessa)
20. Tie-dye
21. Shag haircuts

22. Down vests (Same goes for down coats, down booties, down gloves. We don't care if you live in Maine—it's better to get frostbite than look this uncool.)
23. Workout clothes
24. French manicure
25. After-ski wear
26. Diane Feinstein/Margaret Thatcher wear, such as blouses buttoned up to the neck with a big bow
27. Sideburns (exceptions made for psychobilly)
28. Salon tans
29. BVDs (especially colored)
30. Shorts with white socks pulled up on men (especially desperate with sandals)
31. Pantyhose with tummy-firming elastic (Pantyhose are unhip unless crotchless or garter-belt style.)
32. Bathing suits with skirts
33. Fanny packs
34. Sheepskin coats
35. Peasant blouses
36. Any item of clothing that announces itself (like a T-shirt that says "DKNY" or "Banana Republic"
37. Murses, or man purses
38. Toupees
39. Cell phones as fashion accessories (No. You look like a pathetic, lonely person, even though the Martians are speaking to you through your silver fillings and you're under oath to reply.)

TISH & SNOOKY'S TOP 10 BEST-DRESSED PUNKS

In the beginning, there were Marlon Brando and James Dean, who paved the road of punk fashion (which to some small minds is a contradiction)! We like this psycho-biker bad-boy look mixed with the fashions of the tail end of '70s-era glam. In order of appearance, here is our list of best-dressed punks!

1. Iggy (the Stooges)

Shirtless (why gild the lily by wearing a shirt?), and sometimes almost pantsless! The first time we saw him at the Electric Circus, his pants consisted of two pant legs and a belt! They were accented by an elegant pair of red nylon panties.

2. Wayne/Jayne County (Wayne County & the Electric Chairs)

Jayne started the whole ripped-up-fishnet look! She wore them not only on her legs but also on top! She showed us how to make a hole in the crotch, stick our heads through it, punch our fists through the feet, and—presto change-o!—the perfect punk top for the price of a pair of 14th Street pantyhose!

3. Richard Hell (Television, Richard Hell & the Voidoids)

Richard is the inventor of the DYI punk haircut and T-shirt to match.

4. Patti Smith

Patti rocked the down-and-dirty androgynous sex goddess look that screamed, "I don't dig this FUCKIN' SHIT!"

5. Debbie Harry (Blondie)

Debbie's look—punk/trash/glam goddess in tons of bad-girl black eye shadow—is reminiscent of the mod-a-go-go '60s!

6. Tish & Snooky (performers)

Hey! It's our list! And besides, our ripped-up nuns' drag with stockings and garters and xxxtreme eye makeup made the look legendary.

7. Johnny Thunders (New York Dolls, the Heartbreakers), the Ramones, and the Dictators

These guys all favor(ed) the classic bad-boy look: black leather MC jacket, T-shirt, and jeans. It's *still* our fave look for guys!

8. Helen Wheels (rocker, scene-maker)

Tough, black-leather lady with a heart of gold! If you didn't know how sweet she was, you would have run from this petite yet threatening-looking bodybuilder. We don't think her fans ever knew that she made those sexy little outfits herself!

9. Johnny Rotten (Sex Pistols)

He brought color to the stage with his spiky neon orange hair. Safety pins, chains, and various tchotchkes embellished the thrift-shop blazers framing the all-time classic "Seditionaries Destroy" shirt.

10. Siouxsie Sioux (Siouxsie & the Banshees)

Oh, the fabulosity! She created her own sort of Theda-Bara-on-acid look. Her raven black hair is still a fave look for today's punks. We would bet that she went through at least three black eye pencils a week back in the day!

Sisters Patrice (Tish) and Eileen (Snooky) Bellomo were born in Manhattan and bred in "da Bronx." They are well known for being members of the original Blondie band as well as for being guest backup singers for countless luminaries including the Dictators, U.K. Squeeze, the Blues Brothers, Robert Gordon, Ronnie Spector, and Freddy Scott (just to name a few!). Their legendary tuchases won them the coveted title of "Best Asses in NYC" from the world's foremost authority on the subject, John Belushi. In 1977 they opened Manic Panic, the first and all-time greatest punk boutique in the USA. Their products are now sold in more than 50 countries worldwide! Tish & Snooky are currently working on their scathing, tell-all exposé about life in the early punk days. No one will be spared!

16 PUNK FASHION VICTIMS

1. Johnny Rotten (Sex Pistols), part 1

Johnny Lydon created one of his first controversies before the formation of the Pistols, by walking down London's Kings Road wearing a Pink Floyd T-shirt with "I HATE" scrawled in black ink above the logo. He occasionally strolled into Malcolm McLaren & Vivienne Westwood's SEX shop. Lydon's brash T-shirt, along with what was to become his trademark stare, caught Steve Jones's eye, and he asked him to audition for the band. (Rotten trivia: The "Lydon Stare" is partly cultivated and partly the result of an extremely severe childhood bout of meningitis, which kept young Johnny hospitalized for months.)

2. Brody Dalle (the Distillers)

The singer caused a stir when she broke up with her punk husband Tim Armstrong of Rancid. Armstrong is a hardcore Alcoholics Anonymous twelve-stepper, who put a lot of pressure on his Australian wife to conform to his sobriety standards. She soon got together with Josh Homme of Queens of the Stone Age. It must have been a relief for Brody to get away from the militant AA environment: Queens of the Stone Age sometimes dress in all white for performances, each band member representing a line of cocaine or a rail of speed.

3. Bryan Gregory (the Cramps)

The bassist wore "nuns," a.k.a. chicken bones, every day. An early, controversial shirt in London's SEX shop was a T-shirt with "P-E-R-V" spelled out in bones.

4. Shane MacGowan (the Pogues)

MacGowan described early punk wear in Britain in *A Drink With Shane MacGowan*: "Catholic punks like Johnny Rotten and myself used lots of crucifixes and stuff, and images like that. Catholic imagery lends itself beautifully, along with bondage gear and mod clothes and rocker clothes and '40s baggy pants . . . pink pants and stuff . . . [T]he whole thing put together was just like classic punk gear. Crucifixes, and upside-down crucifixes, and rosary beads, and . . . well, I was the first one to wear rosary beads and berets, the Spanish Civil War look."

5. Johnny Rotten (Sex Pistols), part 2

Legs McNeil wrote of Rotten, backstage at the Pistols' final Winterland concert, "He looked like a duck on crack, except that he wore a long overcoat, so that he actually resembled a French duck on crack."

6. Jason Ringenberg (Jason & the Scorchers)

Ringenberg told author Clinton Heylin, "I was a hillbilly punk rocker in those days [1981]. I'd wear a priest's robe onstage and a cowboy hat. . . . Warner had this hair stuck [across] his face; Jeff wore a Mohawk and his pants backwards. Perry had cigarette burns all over his arms. It was a punk rock band."

7. Mick Jones (the Clash)

Some of the friction that led to the Clash's breakup had to do with Jones's demands that a cigarette be placed in his mouth before he went on stage. Rock star.

8–11. Butthole Surfers

The Surfers' first road trip—in 1984—across America was not in a van, but in a '71 Chevy Nova, which pulled a U-Haul trailer. They squished into the car—singer Gibby Haynes is 6'5"—and traveled with a female pit bull named Mark Farner of Grand Funk Railroad. Band member Jeffrey "King" Coffey had, according to author Michael Azerrad. "a nose ring and an outgrown purple Mohawk that was lapsing into dreads," and consequently got beat up in a fast-food restaurant outside of Dallas. Paul Leary wore "a sideways Mohawk done in cornrows and dyed hot pink." Teresa Taylor (a.k.a. Teresa Nervosa) "let her hair grow into dreads, although she eventually shaved off all the dreads except for three that popped out of her head at random spots, and those were dyed brilliant red." (See Punk Hairdo List, No. 1, the FUYH-do.) Said Coffey, "Gibby had a fucked-up geometric haircut that was just . . . fucked up."

12. Robert Quine

Quine told Legs McNeil and Gillian McCain how Richard Hell gave him a makeover, after inviting him to join his band. Said Quine, "Instead of wearing these button-down shirts that I always wear, to accommodate Richard I would wear a T-shirt under my sport coat, but he'd shred it. Once we were in a cab going to CBGB, and he set my T-shirt on fire. It was one of those flammable materials and it went quite out of control. It was a major thing to put it out. I grew the beard for him. I let him give me a haircut, but that never happened again. He took what little hair I had, and created bald spots all over, which I didn't appreciate. I'd never been treated in such a way in grocery stores in my life."

13. Johnny Rotten (Sex Pistols), part 3

In John Lydon's autobiography, *Rotten: No Irish, No Blacks, No Dogs*, he offers an astute description of bandmate Sid Vicious' fashion faux pas: "Sid was an absolute fashion victim—the worst I'd ever known. It was appalling. Everything about him was wrong. He'd buy these ridiculous *Vogue* magazines to study them and copy people. It was just terrible. . . . He couldn't quite grasp that the idea wasn't to follow, it was to lead. . . . He'd wear nail gloss and think of himself as being very dainty. . . . He'd wear sandals in the snow with no socks when he wanted to show off his nail varnish. It was a Dave Bowie thing. After I ribbed him too much about that, he went out and got a Marc Bolan perm. . . . [He would] hang upside down in the oven to get his hair to stand up like Bowie's. . . . Nothing he wore ever really suited him. It was as if the clothes wore him."

14. Richard Hell (Television, Richard Hell & the Voidoids)

In *Please Kill Me*, Bob Gruen, Richard Hell, and Richard Lloyd tell the story of a notorious T-shirt. Said Gruen, "The first time I saw Richard Hell, he walked into CBGB wearing a white T-shirt with a bull's-eye painted on it, and the words 'Please Kill Me' written on it. That was one of the most shocking things I had ever seen." Hell says, "I don't remember wearing the T-shirt. I do remember forcing Richard Lloyd to wear it. I was too much of a coward." Lloyd does recall being brave enough to wear it, and being disturbed by "these fans [who] gave me this really psychotic look—they looked as deep into my eyes as they possibly could—and said, 'Are you serious?'"

15. Patti Smith

William Burroughs' assistant James Grauerholz remembered Patti Smith onstage in 1978 at a New York avant-garde "summit meeting" in honor of Burroughs: "She was in her own world. She was wearing her new fur coat, which was very odd—one of those things where punks get money and then they revert to type. I mean, she was from where? Bergen, New Jersey? She said, 'This coat cost $10,000. I sleep in it. I live in it. I haven't taken this off in . . .' So she was showing off this fur coat, and I don't know for a fact, but I believe that her hands were in her pockets, and she was doing something funny down there."

16. Joey Ramone (Ramones)

In *Please Kill Me*, Joey Ramone's early sartorial tastes are discussed. Said his brother, "Joey really got into the glitter thing. He was stealing all my mother's jewelry, her clothes, her makeup, and her scarves, which created even more fights between them. . . . That was another reason I didn't like glitter—it created more fights at home."

Joey used to hitchhike "completely decked out," as he put it. "I used to wear this custom-made black jumpsuit, these like pink, knee-high platform boots"—Joey was 7' in platforms—"all kinds of rhinestones, lots of dangling belts and gloves. I got rides, but that was my first time experiencing queers."

ARTURO VEGA'S FAVORITE ROCK 'N' ROLL LOGOS AND T-SHIRTS

1. The Ramones' Eagle Logo

One of the best rock band logos ever. Why? Because it worked! It not only got the intended effect, but it continues to do so. In a society like ours that has such a high regard for visuals, a strong image is essential. When I designed this piece of appropriation art for the Ramones' second album in 1976, I was looking for something to erase the cartoon image the band was being tagged with. I wanted something that would represent the band and made them look as powerful as their music. I had already used an eagle on the design of their first album, so all I had to do was to improve on that. The inspiration came when we went to Washington, D.C., for the first time—I saw all the eagles on those government buildings and I knew what to do. My next goal was to paint a backdrop the band could play in front of, and that worked well too. Everyone saw the eagle backdrop on the stage, bought the T-shirt, and left like walking billboards for the Ramones

2. The Rolling Stones' Tongue

Like everything that came from the Stones back when they were great, this logo is nasty, raunchy, aggressive, sexy, wild, provocative, and sticky all over. The creator—Ruby Mazur, not Andy Warhol, as many people believe—managed to capture all these elements that were actually part of the band's persona and give them form in a genuine Pop-art masterpiece.

3. The Beatles' Apple

Like almost everything that came from the Beatles, their apple logo has the power of something fundamental, basic, archetypal, primal, and natural. When you took a bite of their rock 'n' roll apple, the doors of both heaven and hell opened wide; then it was up to you to start making decisions that could lead you one way or another. That was the way things were when rock was alive and relevant, before ringtones and sponsored tours.

4. The Voidoids' Handwriting

This is definitely one of the first examples of DIY ingenuity applied to rock graphics and fashion. Richard Hell, formerly of Television and the Heartbreakers and then a Voidoid, was the first artist/musician to explore the punk aesthetic. He simply wrote the name of the band in ink on a T-shirt—and not just any shirt, but a ripped and torn plain white tee with holes, and yes, he was the first human being I ever saw with dirty (it was dirt and sweat that did it, not gel) spiky hair sticking up.

5. Black Flag's Bars

This great punk logo doesn't give you anything—it makes you question everything. A black hole fractured by getting slammed too many times.

6. Kiss' Kiss

Kiss was never a favorite band of mine, but I think that turning the "ss" of their name into storm-trooper-style lightning bolts completely and effectively altered the word, transforming a sappy and potentially embarrassing name into a symbol of power with lots of sex appeal.

7. Motörhead's Metal Monster

Motörhead are an all-time favorite band of mine with the only image in all of heavy-metaldom that I really like. This makes me believe that yes, it is the power of a band's music that seduces you into accepting everything about them. Mmmm, kind of like a great lover.

8. The Grateful Dead's Skulls and Flowers

On the other hand, no amount of gracious, whimsical dancing bears or beautifully accessorized flowery skulls could make me fall for this band. Because of these images I have been tempted (without succumbing) to wear one of their shirts more than once, and still nothing could make me want to endure more than a minute of this band's music.

9. The Misfits' Skull

This is a 100 percent appropriated item. It has evolved over the years, but it was originally used by the band exactly the way it appeared on the posters of a certain horror movie. A stroke of genius, it anticipated the current skull craze.

10. Animo's (Other) Eagle Logo

Animo is a new band, so to see this logo you are gonna have to go to their MySpace page, that ridiculous place where bands exist these days. It's another appropriated image—this time, a certain beer company lends the unintended hand. But if this is a promise of good times to come, go for it, have a cold one, keep on wearing rock T-shirts, be well, stay sick, and thank you for paying attention.

Arturo Vega is the Ramones' creative director and designer of their indelible logo, which graces quite possibly the most popular T-shirt of all time.

12 DUDES WHO WORE DRESSES ONSTAGE

1. Philo Cramer (Fear)

Guitarist Cramer wore dresses while performing, in order, in the words of singer Lee Ving, "to get those big boneheaded jocks all riled up" and "throw those bozos into states of mass homosexual panic." Ving adds, "How could anyone be offended by a band whose guitar player is in a dress offering people in the audience a dollar to be his friend?"

2. Captain Sensible (the Damned)

The Captain favored ballet tutus and female nurse wear—did he know Gary Floyd of the Dicks, who favored both of these ensembles?

3. Gary Floyd (the Dicks)

The Dicks and the Big Boys were popular Austin, Texas, hardcore bands who played together regularly—the singers were in drag for most performances. The cover of a 1983 issue of *Maximumrocknroll* featured a picture of Dicks vocalist Gary Floyd—who was extremely fat—wearing a Mohawk and a muumuu, with the title "The Dicks Are a Commie Faggot Band?!" Another drag incarnation featured Floyd dressed up like a nurse with chocolate frosting in his underpants.

4. Iggy Pop (the Stooges)

Among the singer's many transgressions was dressing in drag. He was fond of wearing a ballet tutu, and on one such occasion he went home after the show with a rich girl (he's said to be fond of them, too) to her parents' house. He later observed that it was weird in the morning with her mom, eating breakfast in his tutu. His extensive girly wardrobe included a maternity dress and a gingham frock, which he wore with a ladies' straw hat.

5–7. New York Dolls, minus 1

These glam-punk icons—particularly tall, hulking bassist Arthur Kane—wore dresses regularly. However, guitarist Johnny Thunders held out: although he wore makeup, platform shoes, and women's tops, he steadfastly refused to wear a dress.

8. Jeffrey Lee Pierce (the Gun Club)

L.A. scenestress Pleasant Gehman had this to say about singer Pierce, in *We've Got the Neutron Bomb*: "Jeffrey was into this sick combo of looking like Marilyn Monroe and Elvis at the same time. . . . [P]art of the Marilyn thing came from Debbie Harry. . . . [O]ne Halloween . . . he was wearing a kind of smoking jacket, and his hair was bleached white. . . and he wanted me to put this '50s kind of Marilyn Monroe outfit on him."

9. Bob Stinson (the Replacements)

Author Steve Blush wrote, "I saw 'em in '82—where guitarist Bob Stinson, wearing a dress and dripping mascara, drunk to the point of crying, repulsed the sparse crowd of straight edge types."

10. The Big Boys

Called the Kings of Austin, Texas, hardcore, the Big Boys were the "first punk-funk group" according to Steve Blush. Two-hundred-and-fifty-pound gay front man Randy "Biscuit" Turner wore tattered dresses onstage, wrote Blush, "which wasn't just unhip—it was downright distressing."

11. GG Allin

Allin started dressing in drag in school—his 11th-grade school picture portrays him in women's clothes.

12. Kurt Cobain (Nirvana)

Cobain loved wearing dresses, all kinds, on- and off-stage, to interviews and around the house. He told the *L.A. Times*, "Wearing a dress shows I can be as feminine as I want. I'm a heterosexual . . . big deal. But if I was a homosexual, it wouldn't matter either." A dress of Cobain's was featured in a 2003 Metropolitan Museum of Modern Art exhibit, "Bravehearts: Men in Skirts," along with dresses, skirts and worn by Sean Connery, Mel Gibson, David Bowie, Boy George, and Keanu Reeves, among others. After Cobain's death, his wife, Courtney Love, decided to auction off most of his clothes, including the yellow prom dress her husband wore to the set of *Headbangers Ball*. It is not known what price it fetched.

Bob Gruen's

TOP 10 MOst Photogenic PUNK Rockers

You cannot take a bad photo of:

1. Debbie Harry
2. Paul Simonon
3. Sid Vicious
4. Joan Jett
5. Joey Ramone
6. Joe Strummer
7. Johnny Thunders
8. Iggy Pop
9. Supla
10. Soo Catwoman

Bob Gruen's name is synonymous with classic rock 'n' roll photography. His images have graced the pages of countless books and magazines, and his album cover photography is unparalleled. Gruen recently published books on both the Clash and Sex Pistols, with many candid and never-before-seen shots of both groups. In 2005, he directed the spectacularly sleazy New York Dolls documentary All Dolled Up.

23 PUNK HAIRDOS

You're about to read about all kinds of amazing, authentic punk hairstyles. However, despite our intensive, official research, the most meaningful hairstyle you can have, the one that sends the loudest message, is your own. And remember, creating good hair can be time-consuming—listen to music! See chapter 2 for lists of drinking and drug songs.

1. Basic Mohawk, a.k.a. the Mohican

Shave both sides of the head and leave a strip of hair in the middle. It can be wide or thin, like a skinny tie, flat or really tall. Aaron Studham, a 17-year-old kid from Utah, made the Guinness Book of World Records in 2007 for having the World's Highest Mohawk. It's 25 or 26 inches (60 cm), took Mr. Studham five to six years to grow, and takes 45 minutes to an hour to put up. Says Studham, "It's a real icebreaker with the girls."

2. The Bowl Cut

Favored by the Ramones, this cut looks like you put a salad bowl on your head, then trimmed around its edges.

3. Skinhead

Shave it.

4. The FUYH, or FUH

The Fuck Up Your Hair (FUYH), or, simply, Fucked-Up Hair (FUH), is the No. 1 way you can make a punk fashion statement. The FUH wearer is always the punk with style. The cut is achieved by grabbing handfuls of your hair and randomly slashing and burning. Take a razor and mess it up more. (For a better look, always shave and hack against the grain.) Even though some stylists say that if you want colored hair, you should dye it before cutting, we say, Go for it! FUH artists take acrylic colors and paint them at random: house paint is cool, too. Then they take super-glue (remember, don't wear gloves!) and make anti-liberty spikes by mashing it down and forcing it up at random. (Remember, try this at home.) Once you've mastered this most challenging of styles, you can go to . . .

5. Liberty Spikes

Named after the Statue of Liberty (you do the math), this 'do involves picking up hunks of hair, applying egg whites or something similar (see Punk Hair Tips), to make them stand up aggressively all over your head. You can do this with all your hair, or shave in between the spikes.

6. Dreadlocks and Dreadhawks

Okay, this is a reggae thing, but punks do it. Making dreads is a complicated affair involving braiding many individual clumps of hair. You can make your dreads into liberty spikes or 100 other styles. It's probably a good idea to sniff glue while making dreads, to pass the time. Or, if you're an old-school punk, take the Ramones' advice: Carbona, not glue.

7. Fan

This popular style, which originated in Britain, can also be described as "charged." Shave the sides of your head; force the remaining hair up and laminate it (with the toxin of your choice), so that it resembles a fan going from your forehead to the back of your neck. An early "charger" was Wattie Buchan of the Exploited.

8. Fauxhawks

These are uncool, and are associated with pop punks. Fauxhawks are for hippies or stars like David Beckham. The fauxhawk, which is usually dyed a natural color, like blond or black, is basically a short Mohawk made without shaving the head, and often without the aid of hair gel. This is so you can comb it out and look normal at your day job. Popular with emos. Don't be a pussy.

9. Slanthawk

This is a diagonal hawk that crosses from one side of the neck to opposite side of the brow.

10. Chelsea Hawk and Chelsea Style

Often worn by girls, the Chelsea hawk is the same as a Mohawk but features a fringe in front. The Chelsea Style is a completely shaved head with fringe in front.

11. 270-Degree Hawk

You need to have passed math to do this one. The 270 is a fan Mo that looks like the basic model but forms a 270-degree angle. Be sure you get the angle exactly right. Measure it. You're a square if its 280! This look requires a thicker strip of hair than the basic model in order to stick out in front. Pay attention to the rules. This isn't a quiff we're talking about.

12. Beaver

The beaver is a short, thick strip of hair in the middle with the sides skinned down. Sports guys wear it, not rockers.

13. Bi-Hawk, or Twin Tins; and Tri-Hawk

Put on a compilation CD—this is gonna take a while. Again, kids, remember to self-medicate appropriately! Raid your parents' bar. Bi-hawks and tri-hawks have two or three strips of hair running from neck to forehead, respectively, shaved in between. Band-Aids look weird on your head, so use gaffer tape to be cool when you cut yourself.

14. Reverse Mohawk, or Antihawk, HawkMo, Skunk, Highway, Nohawk, or Polish Mohawk

Do the math. Shave a line down the middle of your head and leave hair on either side. The hair can be made into spikes or can lie down and die. *[Authors' note: We do not endorse the use of the term "Polish Mohawk," which is, of course, totally racist.]*

15. Sidehawk

Shave the back of your head; then lay a strip of long hair horizontally across from ear to ear. Leave the bangs on. Spike it. This is not to be confused with the extremely cool combover, worn by men with male pattern baldness.

16. Crosshawk

The crosshawk is a combination of a fan and a fanned side-hawk that come together to form a cross. There are variants too arcane to explain here, known as the H-hawk and the A-hawk. Do your homework if you must know.

17. Death-hawk, or goth-hawk

These wide hawks are worn kinda loose, or very loose—in tendrils—backcombed but not fanned or spiked. Associated with rockers and goths.

18. Glowhawk

The glowhawk is a riotously colored, brightly hued thing of beauty to behold.

19. Blowjob Handles

These are ponytails coming out of the sides of your head.

20. Horror-Punk Look

Dye your hair blue-black or black, like a goth; then spike up a Mohawk and shape it like a horn in front.

21. Devilocks

This legendary look was created by a member of the Misfits, circa 1979. To create a devilock, leave the sides and back of your hair short, and the front long. Comb front hair forward, then gather together, with the aid of gel or pomade (whatever works best for you) so that it forms a spike that hangs in front of your face.

22. Mollet

A variant of the mullet, the mollet is possibly the worst hairstyle ever created. A mullet is short in front—sometimes a crew cut—

and longer in the back. No one has ever looked good in a mullet, including David Bowie. The mollet is a Mohawk in front that branches out to a mullet in back. President James K. Polk kinda wore a mollet.

23. Mini-Mo

Ouch! This 'do doesn't go from nape to forehead—it sits on the middle of your head. Terrible. *[Authors' note: Wouldn't you rather wear a FUH-'do?]*

13 NOTABLE NONPUNK MOHAWK WEARERS

1. Mr. T
2. Robert de Niro, as Travis Bickle in *Taxi Driver*
3. Cedric the Entertainer
4. Chad Johnson, wide receiver for the Cincinnati Bengals
5. Brian Bosworth
6. Jazz saxman Sonny Rollins (wore a Mohawk in the '50s)
7. Chuck Liddell, martial artist and UFC light-heavyweight champion
8. Shannon Moore, a professional wrestler in ECW
9. Maddox Chivan Jolie-Pitt, adopted son of Angelina Jolie and Brad Pitt
10. Finnish hockey team Ässät (most of the team had Mohawks during the 2005–2006 playoffs)
11. Darrent Williams, cornerback for the NFL's Denver Broncos
12. P. Diddy, rap entrepreneur and owner of Bad Boy Records
13. Sly Stone (wore a blond Mohawk at the 2006 Grammy Awards)

5 PUNK HAIR CARE TIPS

This helpful list is brought to you by free-makeup-tips.com. The author advises that "these tips are for longevity in styles, but be warned that it doesn't come out for about a week."

1. Gel
For the little freaks out there, gel is your starting point. A good kind of gel is a big tub of something called La Bella. It only costs about $4.50—beware of cheaper rip-offs!! Use the blue and green ones—they are the only ones that don't smell really bad.

2. Hair Spray
White Rain and Freeze Frame are both great brands. Use loads and loads.

3. Egg Whites
These really stink, so don't use them without hair spray. Slowly make a hole in the egg with a knife or whatever, and let the clear translucent goop creep out; when you start seeing bright yellow—stop! *Do not use the yolk!*

4. Knox Gelatin
This stuff works perfect for about a week, but it stinks like crazy! It is pure protein, so it will attract flies if you get it wet. *[Authors' note: We think the Fly is a great look.]* Mix the gelatin powder with water and nuke it for 45–50 seconds. You can find this stuff at the store for like three bucks, and it is the best.

5. Elmer's Glue
This stuff works for people with fine hair or those with curly hair. Pour some onto your hand, grab a hunk of hair, pull and twist upwards. Do not just do one or two spikes—do six or seven. Elmer's glue makes for A-1 pimpin' liberty spikes!

[Authors' note: Other chic hair specialists recommend using super-glue, for a balls-out fashion statement.]

HEIDI MINX'S 6 ESSENTIALS FOR THE DOMESTIC PUNK

So, you grew up. That doesn't mean you gave up being innovative as hell, and DIY is still so thick in your veins your doctor thinks it's your blood type. After all those years of having to wing things—do them on the lam—there are some tried-and-true around-the-house fixes that should be topping your list . . . and that won't send you running to the store.

1. Peroxide and Bleach

Shit. There's hair dye in the tub. So you don't have to worry anymore that it's your mother's house—it's yours. But maybe you just don't want your friends to know that nowadays you're covering your gray. The quickest way to get semi-permanent and even permanent hair dye off the counters and tiles is bleach, as in your hair bleach. Dab a bit of the leftover on the offending colored spot and presto—in seconds, it's gone. That lovely color-stripping 40-volume peroxide isn't just for hair. It works wonders on bloodstains, too. If you get blood on white fabric, try blotting it with some crème 40-volume before you chuck it in the wash. It removes stuff Shout can't touch.

2. Safety Pins

You used to use them to pierce your ears and hold your pants together. They are still an indispensable item. Smaller ones are great for taking back curtains, or even holding busted buttons on your pants. Kilt pins are great to replace busted belt loops. Always have one on your key chain—you never know when you'll need it!

3. Vinegar

Thank God Heinz is slow at catching on and you can still get a gallon of this wonder stuff for a ghetto-low price. Put some in a bowl near a window and it helps eliminate odors. Throw it in with a load of wash and it stops colors from bleeding. Cat pee somewhere in retaliation for a late night out? Douse the offending area and rinse with cool water. Wanna clear the street grime off your windows? Spray them with vinegar cut with a little warm water and use your old newspaper to wipe them sparkling clean. Moving? Gotta try and clean up years of "sticker décor"? Yes, here's another use for vinegar: put vinegar on the sticker and let it soak in for a few minutes. The sticker can easily be removed (or you can warm up the sticker with a hair dryer and peel it away slowly and carefully).

4. Rubber Cement = Quick Creeper-Sole Repair

Creepers rock. Unfortunately, when they wear, they get those stupid holes deep in the soles. A quick fix is to pour rubber cement into the holes and let it dry.

5. Elmer's Glue

You used to use it to put up your hawk, now you can use it to decorate! Whether you use regular Elmer's or the "designer version," Mod Podge, there is positively nothing you can't do with this stuff. That crappy dresser you found on the street becomes a custom piece of art, even if you just MP on some newspaper scraps. Grab a Sharpie, make some cool drawings, add some stickers, old postcards, fliers, ticket stubs—anything. Let it set and you've got a custom piece with all your memories!

6. Razor Blades

They used to be an "anti-fashion: statement. Today they're on emo tees all over the mall. Don't ditch your stash, though—they're super helpful when you're decorating. Blades designed for straight razors are best—you don't have to worry about that other edge bearing into your thumb! If you can't find tape when you're painting around the windowsills, let the paint dry, then scrape it away. Pegging your own pants? Razor blades make the *best* seam rippers, quicker and more accurate than the real thing. They're also super handy for cutting out all the cool stuff you want to stick on that furniture you want to redo with Elmer's!

Heidi Minx runs Franky & Minx, a punk rock 'n' roll–inspired clothing and accessories line, with her tattoo-artist partner, Elvis. She is also cohostess of Punk Rock Domestics, a DIY "Punk Martha Stewart" Web site with Kamilla Vanilla, formerly of the HorrorPops.

DR. JAMES BROWN'S 8 WORST SETS OF PUNK ROCK TEETH (AND RECOMMENDED TREATMENT)

1. Shane MacGowan (the Pogues)

By far the obvious choice to head this list, MacGowan is almost as famous for the horrific condition of his teeth as he is for his work as Pogues' front man. An up-close glimpse of the plaque-encrusted incisors jutting from his swollen and bleeding gums has no doubt turned the stomach of many a stage-side spectator. Mr. MacGowan's is the mouth that inspired the song "Shane's Dentist" by Mojo Nixon.

Recommended treatment: Extraction of all remaining teeth, followed by placement of four titanium dental implants per arch and fabrication of full upper and lower implant-supported dentures. Two different sets of removable dentures would be made; one set would give Shane a new, healthy and natural-looking smile for everyday use, while the other, replicating his old devastated dentition, would be available for use during performances to give a new generation of fans a truly authentic Pogues experience.

2. Lemmy Kilmister (Motörhead)

The dental woes of the Motörhead bassist and front man have gone largely unnoticed by the public perhaps because one's attention is drawn more immediately to his intimidating facial hair and moles the size of cantaloupes. But drug use of the kind

and frequency to which Lemmy has freely admitted often wreaks dental havoc and has turned his mouth into a real "damage case."

Recommended treatment: Extraction of all nonrestorable teeth, including entire upper dentition, followed by bilateral sinus-lift surgery and bone augmentation where necessary. Placement of eight to ten titanium dental implants to support a 14-unit nonremovable upper prosthesis. Restoration of the lower arch would involve endodontic therapy (root canal) and porcelain fused to metal crowns where applicable, and implant-supported crowns to replace missing teeth. Finally, an acrylic night guard, or NTI (nociceptive trigeminal inhibition) device, would be custom fabricated for use while sleeping to prevent damage to Mr. Kilmister's expensive dental work and oral structures from the sleep bruxism this intense rocker would no doubt otherwise engage in.

3. Dee Dee Ramone (Ramones)

Perhaps the prototypical punk rocker, Dee Dee, along with Joey and Johnny, fell victim to a sort of reverse Spinal Tap curse wherein only the drummers are spared untimely deaths. Long before that, however, his teeth fell victim to his taste for Chinese rock. Like Lemmy's, Dee Dee's dental rehab would be expensive and complex.

Recommended treatment: See No. 2, Lemmy Kilmister.

4. Darby Crash (the Germs)

If the Germs front man hadn't offed himself with an intentional heroin overdose the day before John Lennon was shot, he might well have been suicidal after learning of the process he'd have to undergo to get his teeth fixed. Darby's dramatically flared upper front teeth and anterior open bite might have been caused by tongue-thrusting or thumb-sucking as a kid, but the multidisciplinary approach necessary for putting them back where they belonged would not have been child's play.

Recommended treatment: Extraction of two maxillary bicuspids (one right, one left) followed by one to two years of orthodontic therapy (braces) to move the front teeth back into their proper position. This would still leave Darby with an open bite, unable to bring his upper and lower front teeth into contact. This would be corrected with a LeFort osteotomy, a surgical procedure whereby the entire upper jaw is sectioned and repositioned; and, if necessary, a similar procedure on the lower jaw, known as a sagittal split osteotomy.

5. Tommy Frenzy (Tuff Darts)

Frenzy replaced Robert Gordon early on as front man for CBGB stalwarts Tuff Darts. The Darts had a song in their repertoire called "Your Love Is Like Nuclear Waste" and, judging by the cover of their album, the same comparison could be used to describe Tommy's teeth. His maniacal grin proudly bares for all to see a mouthful of badly discolored and decaying choppers.

Recommended treatment: Where only minimal decay has formed, simple fillings will be placed, but on the more severely broken down teeth—the upper incisors and canines, for example—root canal therapy will be necessary, followed by the placement of porcelain, or porcelain fused to metal crowns. The first in the list that won't require the removal of any teeth, this case would nonetheless keep Tommy's dentist in fresh toupees and Members Only jackets for some time.

6. Johnny Rotten (Sex Pistols)

So named because of the apparent condition of his teeth, Rotten, one might argue, should be higher on the list. In fact, the Pistols-era Johnny Rotten was a right punter in the tooth decay department compared to many of his punk rock contemporaries. While he probably had no more cavities than the typical British youngster, his dull, possibly tetracycline-stained front teeth would have fueled the illusion of a mouth brimming with decay.

Recommended treatment: Excavation of all carious lesions, followed by fillings, with perhaps a few teeth requiring root canal therapy. An in-office whitening procedure would be followed by the placement of six or eight bonded porcelain veneers on both the upper and lower anterior teeth.

Honorable Mentions

7. Cheetah Chrome (Dead Boys)

Regardless of the oral health of the Dead Boys' lead guitarist, I feel compelled to suggest a course of dental treatment that might have elevated his stature from that of merely "guitar-slinging ginger kid with the coolest name in punk rock" to that of "timeless entertainment icon" along the lines of Elvis, Liberace, or Flavor Flav.

Recommended treatment: Fabrication of all-metal semiprecious alloy crowns on all upper and lower anterior teeth polished to a high sheen and featuring elongated, big-cat-like fangs, or "feline canines." So Mr. Chrome makes the list not because of what was, but because of what might have been.

8. Unknown Hinson

This guit-tar pickin' hillbilly vampire (think Johnny Paycheck meets the Cramps) has but two teeth and, to the uninitiated, perhaps even fewer punk rock credentials. But he describes himself as "ever womern's dream and ever jealous husband's nightmare," and if that's not punk rock, then I don't know what is.

Recommended treatment: Wouldn't change a thing.

In the 1978 movie The Buddy Holly Story, *there's a scene in which Buddy, just moments before an appearance on the Ed Sullivan Show, replaces the lost crown on his front tooth with a chewed piece of bubble gum. This was a pivotal moment in the life of the young James Brown of Lindenhurst, Long Island, who realized then that a life at the confluence of dentistry, rock 'n' roll, and, to a lesser extent, sugary treats was not only possible, but necessary. A 1988 graduate of New York University College of Dentistry, Dr. Brown currently plays guitar with NYC zombie-rockers the Scared Stiffs, and counts among his patients numerous punk rock stars with famous smiles.*

CHAPTER 4

JEAN BEAUVOIR OF THE PLASMATICS' 5 FAVORITE ACTS OF ONSTAGE DESTRUCTION

1. Blowing up cars onstage: first the hood, then, with additional charges, the doors, trunk, and a whopper on the front seat, taking out all the glass! Helmets and face shields a must!

2. Smashing guitars and basses into bits. A lucky audience member gets a unique souvenir!

3. Shooting the speaker cabinets with a 12-gauge shotgun that actually ignites the dynamite carefully placed in the cabinets! Juicy . . .

4. The same shotgun aimed at the ceiling unfastening a huge lighting truss! Never know where it lands! Beware—broken bulbs can add to the blazing mess.

5. Let's not forget those chickens, saved from a slaughter-house—only to get to tour with the most outrageous band in the world! Cages held by two little knots unraveled by the

gunshot. Rock 'n' roll/voodoo chickens get to run around for the rest of the set, truly enjoying a series of glamorous punk rock eves! Voodoo chickens, aaah! A familiar sight from my childhood in the old country!

Jean Beauvoir, the blond-Mohawked maniac bass player of the Plasmatics, was born of Haitian parents in Chicago. He was the leader of a junior high school rock band at age 13, which led to his playing dances and clubs throughout the New York area. Not withstanding his tender age, he was recruited to be musical director for Gary U.S. Bonds. Soon after this, he became the youngest lead singer of the group the Flamingos, they of "I Only Have Eyes for You" fame. He moved out on his own and headed to the Big Apple at the tender age of 15. After a reading an ad in a local paper, he was recruited for what was to become the Plasmatics. He changed his image to suit the part, and the Plasmatics went on to take over the world. Since then, Jean has worked with Little Steven & the Disciples of Soul as well as releasing solo albums, and has been instrumental in production and co-writing ventures with artists such as Kiss, the Ramones, 'N Sync, John Waite, Deborah Harry, Lionel Richie, the Pretenders, Carol Davis, Nile Rogers, Nona Hendryx, Desmond Child, Jim Vallance, and many more.

JOHNNY ROTTEN'S 22 PICKS, CIRCA 1977

On July 16, 1977, at the height of the Sex Pistols' fame, Johnny Rotten made an appearance on the late Tommy Vance's Saturday evening Capital Radio show. He arrived with a pile of albums, from which he chose 22 songs that represented some of his favorite music. The selection was hugely controversial and unexpected. Many thanks to U.K.'s Chrome Books, whose editors did the research to make this list possible in the fascinating book *John Lydon: Stories of Johnny, Compendium of Thoughts on the Icon of an Era*, edited by Rob Johnstone.

1. "Sweet Surrender"—Tim Buckley
2. "Life Is Just Beginning"—the Creation
3. "Rebel Rebel"—David Bowie
4. "Jig a Jig"—the Chieftains
5. "King Tubbys Meets Rockers Uptown"—Augustus Pablo
6. "Doing Alright with the Boys"—Gary Glitter
7. "Walls"—Fred Locks
8. "I'm Not Ashamed"—Culture
9. "Born for a Purpose"—Dr. Alimantado
10. "Back from the Dead"—Bobby Byrd
11. "Revolution Blues"—Neil Young
12. "Men of Good Fortune"—Lou Reed
13. "The Institute of Mental Health Is Burning"—Peter Hammill
14. "Jah Wonderful"—Aswad
15. "The Blimp"—Captain Beefheart & the Magic Band
16. "Eastbourne Ladies"—Kevin Coyne
17. "Janitor of Lunacy"—Nico
18. "Is It Because I'm Black?"—Ken Boothe
19. "Legs Larry at the Television Centre"—John Cale
20. "Fleance"—Third Ear Band
21. "Halleluwah"—Can
22. "Legalize It"—Peter Tosh

DID I PASS THE AUDITION? 8 POSSIBLE LEAD SINGERS FOR THE SEX PISTOLS

1. Steve Jones

Jones was originally the singer for the Swankers (sometimes known as the Strand), the band that became the Sex Pistols with Glen Matlock and Paul Cook. In the spring of '75, the band pushed out founder Wally Nightingale, and Jones moved to guitar.

2. Midge Ure

Pistols' manager Malcolm McLaren had his eye on Ure, who later joined Ultravox. Ure declined the invitation to become a Pistol without comment.

3. Sylvain Sylvain

When the New York Dolls were on the decline, McLaren came to New York to give them new clothes and a new image. "He wasn't our manager, he was our haberdasher," said David Johansen. The boys were outfitted in red leather and vinyl, given copies of Mao's *Little Red Book*, and performed under a poster of a hammer and sickle. The experiment failed. McLaren then began to woo Sylvain to front the Pistols, even sending him photo-booth pics of the lads and noting, "This one we're thinking of calling Johnny Rotten." McLaren wrote Sylvain a seven-page letter (now in the Cleveland Rock and Roll Hall of Fame) enticing him to join. Said Sylvain in 2005, "The Sex Pistols were supposed to be my band. I'm still waiting for the plane ticket."

4. Richard Hell

Singer, poet, and fashion icon Hell had just left Television when McLaren—who was obsessed with Hell's deconstructed look—made overtures to him to be the Pistols' vocalist. Hell was interested, but Cook and Matlock refused because they insisted on an English front man.

5. Johnny Thunders

Author Gavin Edwards, whose life work is setting straight rock 'n' roll rumors, wrote a book titled *Is Tiny Dancer Really Elton's Little John*? In it he states that Johnny Thunders, then recently of the New York Dolls, was approached by McLaren to be the Pistols' front man. Regrettably, no more information is available.

6. Nick Kent

Kent, a musician and well-known rock journalist for *NME*, was a favorite of McLaren's to front the Pistols. However, according to Kent, there was no chemistry among them, and the idea was dropped.

7. John Lydon

Lydon had never sung before but was an impressive presence down the Kings Road with his chopped-off green hair and "I Hate Pink Floyd" T-shirt. He stopped into Malcolm McLaren and Vivienne Westwood's SEX shop occasionally, and Steve Jones allegedly suggested to McLaren that Lydon audition.

Said Rotten, "I knew practically none of the records inside Malcolm's jukebox because it was all that awful '60s mod music that I couldn't stand. The only song that I could cope with was Alice Cooper's 'Eighteen.' I just gyrated like a belly dancer."

Witnesses report that his gyrating/singing also consisted of shouting, mumbling, spasming, and striking hunchback poses. According to Rob Johnstone, the band members had their doubts, but McLaren wanted Lydon. According to band member Paul Cook, he and Matlock thought Lydon was perfect, and it was McLaren who was freaked out by John. Whatever the truth, the rest is history.

8. Sid Vicious

In Jon Savage's *England's Dreaming*, the author recounts two occasions when Vicious was considered as front man—before John had auditioned (though this story is unconfirmed, and there are more accounts of Lydon bringing Vicious into the group). However, in version one, Sid was thrilled by his mate John, and happy just to be a fan and part of the scene.

Second time around: After the Pistols combusted, McLaren wanted Vicious to replace Rotten as the singer. McLaren, typically, had not paid enough attention to Sid's mental and physical decline—now that Sid had Nancy and heroin—and the maestro's plans came to naught.

REVEALED! THE 5 ACRONYMS AT THE END OF "ANARCHY IN THE U.K."

Ever wonder what Johnny Rotten was on about at the end of "Anarchy in the U.K."? What do all those initials mean?

1. The U.K.

We all know that one: it's the United Kingdom, the major villain of the piece.

2. The IRA

"Is this the IRA? I thought it was the U.K.!" You probably know that one, too. The Irish Republican army was on the Republican side in Ireland's civil war—anti-British, pro-unification.

3. The UDA

In the second verse, Lydon continues, "Is this the UDA? Is this the IRA? I thought it was the U.K.!" The IRA and the UDA were the main paramilitary armies fighting in Northern Ireland.

4. The MPLA

"Is this the MPLA?" This is for rock 'n' roll Mensa grads. This group took control of Angola, one of Portugal's African colonies, during a 1975–76 civil war. The Movimento Popular de Libertação de Angola (the Popular Movement for the Liberation of Angola) remains in power today. In the final verse, Mr. Lydon screams, "Is this the MPLA? Is this the UDA? Is this the IRA? I thought it was the U.K.!"

5. NME

And when Rotten sings, "I use the NME," it's a homonym for the *New Musical Express*, at the time Britain's hippest weekly musical paper, very up on punk rock.

PAUL CRIPPLE'S 10 HEAVY METAL BANDS SUITABLE FOR PUNK ROCK CONSUMPTION

1. Motörhead—"Iron Fist," "Ace of Spades," etc.

2. Led Zeppelin—Because they were considered heavy metal in 1971, and because of "Communication Breakdown"'s simple three-chord structure.

3. Jimi Hendrix—Just because the intro to "Astro Man" sounds so very thrash to me.

4. Black Sabbath—First four albums are completely suitable for punk!

5. David Bowie—*The Man Who Sold the World* is heavy, hard, and very punk . . . but the song "The Man Who Sold the World" isn't, even if Nirvana did cover it.

6. Van Halen—The Atomic Punk! Need I say more . . . or less?

7. Alice in Chains—Yeah, their music is considered grunge, but they bought it from punks.

8. Jethro Tull—The live version of "Dharma for One" has so much punk in it, my hair sticks up without the help of any Dippity-do (I mean, when I did have hair). That's punk!

9. Metallica—*Ride the Lightning,* bitches! And then they lost their punk.

10. Megadeth—The first album . . . yeah, punks dig it!

You can replace anyone of these bands (except Jethro Tull) with King Diamond, Slayer, or Venom . . . but that's my story and I'm sticking with it.

Paul Cripple plays guitar for New York's beloved peace-punk thrash band, Reagan Youth. He says, "You can blame me for taking the DIY sound of Reagan Youth's first album and forsaking that for the heavy, heavy sound of 'Red metal' we perfected on 'Jesus Was a Communist.' Black metal, speed metal, death metal, etc., etc., and let's give a warm and hearty toast to Red metal . . . Comrades!"

5 RAMONES "I DON'T WANNA" SONGS, 5 RAMONES "I WANNA" SONGS, AND ONE HONORABLE MENTION

5 Ramones "I Don't Wanna" Songs

1. "I Don't Wanna Be Learned"
2. "I Don't Wanna Be Tamed"
3. "I Don't Wanna Die in the Basement"
4. "I Don't Wanna Get Involved with You"
5. "I Don't Wanna Walk Around With You"

5 Ramones "I Wanna" Songs

1. "I Wanna Be Sedated"
2. "I Wanna Be Well"
3. "I Wanna Be Your Boyfriend"
4. "I Wanna Live"
5. "Now I Wanna Sniff Some Glue"

Honorable Mention

"I Wanna Be Your Joey Ramone" by Sleater-Kinney

9
RAMONES

Tribute Bands from Around the World

1. Carbona Not Glue (Scotland)
2. The Cretins (Sweden)
3. The Joeys (Australia)
4. The Ramouns (Germany)
5. Ne Luumaet (the Netherlands)
6. The Vindictives (the Netherlands)
7. Acid Eaters (the Netherlands)
8. The Cabrones (U.S.)
9. Gabba Gabba Heys (U.S.)

MONTE A. MELNICK'S GOOD, BAD, AND UGLY RAMONES GIGS

The Good

The Estadio Monumental Antonio V. Liberti, better known as El Monumental, or River Plate Stadium, is a stadium in the Belgrano district of Buenos Aires. It's the biggest stadium in Argentina. On March 16, 1996, the band sold more than 52,000 tickets. On the bill that day were Super Uva, Dos Minutos, Attack 77, Die Toten Hosen, and Iggy Pop, with the Ramones closing the show. I remember Eddie Vedder of Pearl Jam came down to Buenos Aires to hang out with the band and he was running around with his video camera shooting everything. This was one incredible show for everyone.

The Bad

In March 1977, the band played the Rocker Club in Aberdeen, Washington. Aberdeen is a small town located on the pacific coast about 100 miles from Seattle. This show was on the band's first tour of the Northwest. The Rocker Club was a hardcore rock 'n' roll lumberjack bar (bear in mind, this was 1977). At that time, the Ramones' set was only 20 minutes long (about 30 songs), so the club was really pissed off when we finished so fast. After the set the club management demanded we play some more or we wouldn't get paid, so the band played the same set again. Needless to say, the lumberjacks had no idea what the Ramones were playing.

The Ugly

The Ramones opened up for Black Sabbath in San Bernardino, California. It was December 1978, and the crowd didn't want to hear anyone but Black Sabbath. This was a very hardcore heavy metal crowd. This show was long before the days of searching everyone before they got into the venue. They let in people with bottles of booze and other objects. After polishing off their booze, the Sabbath fans promptly tossed the empty bottles at the Ramones. After only playing a few songs and dodging the bottles and various other lethal paraphernalia, the band walked off the stage.

Monte A. Melnick served as the Ramones' tour manager from their early club days in the '70s at CBGB to their farewell gigs in 1996. He is the author of On the Road with the Ramones, *an informative and entertaining look at the band from someone who was there with them from the beginning to the end. He is now the Audio Visual Associate at the New York Hall of Science in Flushing Meadows–Corona Park, Queens, New York.*

TOMMY RAMONE'S 10 FAVORITE OLD-TIME MUSIC ARTISTS

1. The Carter Family
2. Uncle Dave Macon
3. The Skillet Lickers
4. The Monroe Brothers
5. The Stanley Brothers
6. Flatt & Scruggs
7. Charlie Pool
8. Dock Boggs
9. The Stoneman Family
10. Tommy Jarrell

Tommy Ramone began his musical career as Tommy Erdelyi, an engineer at the Record Plant. Born in Budapest, Hungary, and raised in Forest Hills, Queens, New York, he co-founded the Ramones with Johnny, Joey, and Dee Dee, and participated in the birth of punk and indie rock, working as the band's drummer, producer, and manager. He has also produced recordings by the Talking Heads, Redd Kross, and the Replacements. He currently performs, with partner Claudia Tienan, in the critically acclaimed progressive bluegrass duo Uncle Monk.

KID CONGO POWERS' TOP 10 GUITARISTS

Top ten guitar stylists I could listen to forever....

1. Bo Diddley
2. Poison Ivy (the Cramps)
3. Marc Bolan (T.Rex)
4. Lydia Lunch (Teenage Jesus & the Jerks)
5. John Lee Hooker
6. Pat Place (the Contortions/Bush Tetras)
7. Link Wray
8. Hasil Adkins
9. Nafloyd Scott (James Brown)
10. Aurelio Valle (Calla)

Kid Congo Powers was a member of the Cramps, Gun Club, and Nick Cave and the Bad Seeds and was once described by Time Out *magazine as the coolest looking guy in New York. He currently fronts Kid Congo Powers and the Pink Monkey Birds.*

JEFF AMENT OF PEARL JAM'S 8 BEST PUNK ROCK BASS PLAYERS

1. Dee Dee Ramone (Ramones)

He wrote some the best songs of all time and he was committed to rocking the shit hard, even though he didn't have a lot of technique. Did I mention that he looked cooler than James Dean?

2. Bruce Foxton (the Jam)

Absolutely the Paul McCartney of the punk world. Foxton wrote some of the best bass lines from that time, and he sang harmony on most of the hits. Wicked punk mullet, too!

3. Jah Wobble

PiL's *Second Edition* is one of the funkiest punk records, and most of the songs revolve around Wobble's fretless ramblings.

4. J.J. Burnel (the Stranglers)

The absolute best tone ever. "Peaches" has it all: great line, tone, and super lyrics.

5. Rainy (Discharge)

Insane, meth-riddled bass. "Warning" makes me wanna break shit.

6. Klaus Flouride (Dead Kennedys)

We got to play with the DKs back in the day, and Klaus was a great player who wrote great parts. He set the bar high early on for me. So many good bass lines: "Holiday . . . ," "Bleed for Me," and "I Am the Owl."

7. Chuck Dukowski (Black Flag)

The most visceral player I've ever seen wringing so much pain out of his bass. "Damaged" has a lot of cool shit going on in the low end. And he wrote some great lyrics.

8. Mike Watt (Minutemen)

Prolific and a rule breaker, punk rock to the core. The early Minutemen shows were some of the best from that era. He's another great bassist/songwriter whose style has never been copied . . . still doing it.

Punk rock died around '85, so that's all I got.

Jeff Ament is a founding member of Mother Love Bone and, more importantly, Pearl Jam—one of the biggest rock bands of the last two decades. Jeff knows you can only destroy the system from the inside out.

J MASCIS' 10 FAVORITE FUZZ BOXES

1. Big Muff Lamb's Head
2. Superfuzz
3. Shinei Fuzz Wah
4. Fuzzface
5. Big Cheese
6. Fuzz Factory
7. Jordan Bosstone
8. Fender Blender
9. Vox Tone Bender 3 Knob
10. Foxx Tone Machine

J Mascis is a founder of western Massachusetts' first and best hardcore band, Deep Wound. In the '80s and '90s, Mascis found fame and fortune as front man for Dinosaur Jr. He plays his guitar very loud.

GILBY CLARKE'S 10 BEST PUNK ROCK GUITAR SOLOS

I know—there aren't supposed to be guitar solos in punk rock. But, like everything else, that's not entirely true. Here are my faves, in reverse order

10. "We Want the Airwaves" (Ramones)—Johnny Ramone wore his guitar lower than anybody.

9. "Search & Destroy" (Iggy & the Stooges)—A few Les Pauls were destroyed on this track.

8. "Neat, Neat, Neat" (the Damned)—Brian James does his best Chuck Berry.

7. **"Chatterbox" (New York Dolls)**—Johnny Thunder does his best Chuck Berry.

6. **"Did You No Wrong" (Sex Pistols)**—Steve Jones told me he cut the SP tracks with a Vox AC30, the same amp the Beatles used.

5. **"White Girl" (X)**—Just Billy Zoom and his Gretsch.

4. **"Running with the Boss Sound" (Generation X)**—The bass holds one note throughout the solo. Why hasn't anybody else done this? Perfect.

3. **"Stay Free" (the Clash)**—Mick Jones was imitating Mick Ronson here, and killing it.

2. **"Beat Her with a Rake" (the Weazels)**—And make her pay for her mistake.

1. **"Kick out the Jams" (MC5)**—Wayne Kramer destroying a Strat, the best-sounding out-of-tune guitar ever!

Gilby Clarke was raised in the birthplace of rock 'n' roll, Cleveland, Ohio. All he ever wanted to do was play guitar in a loud rock 'n' roll band. He got that chance when he joined the most dangerous band of its era: Guns N' Roses. Gilby survived the mammoth Use Your Illusion *tour, which lasted two and a half years; epic MTV videos (with overblown budgets that could fund a third-world country); and recording sessions that lasted years. When the band disintegrated, Gilby went a solo, recording five records after GNR. He also played guitar for Slash's Snakepit, Heart, DKT/MC5, and Nancy Sinatra. He has produced many artists, including the Bronx, L.A. Guns, and one of his childhood heroes, Alice Cooper, in his home studio, Redrum Recording. Most recently, Gilby, Tommy Lee, and Jason Newsted formed a new band for the Mark Burnett–produced show* Rock Star Supernova.

MICHAEL DAVIS OF THE MC5'S TOP 10 MOTOWN FAVORITES

1. "Contract on Love" (Stevie Wonder)

The Hammond B3 organ track of Earl Van Dyke is about the funkiest, butt-movin' sound I ever heard as a 15-year-old, and pushed me into an absolute transcendental teenage mind warp. The background vocals aren't too shabby either.

2. "Look What You've Done" (Smokey Robinson & the Miracles)

The ultimate teenage love ballad à la C, A minor, F, and G. What makes this one so special besides the incredible timbre of Smokey's voice and the harmony of the Miracles is the luscious guitar part and the signature bass/guitar turnaround at the end of each stanza. James Jamerson and Eddie Willis invent a notation which, though simple, conveys the essence of the Motown sound yet to come. This track was done circa 1959.

3. "What's Going On?/Mercy Me" (Marvin Gaye)

The masterpiece song written and performed by Marvin Gaye, on which he is accompanied by the entire Motown session players group, as well as members of the Detroit Lions football team and other personal friends. What can you possibly say about this incredible song? Not only does it reach into the very pit of every issue new and old concerning human existence, it embodies the quintessential performances of every person who played on this recording. It is an absolute wonder, and bares the soul of everything true. This song can bring tears to your eyes for all the right reasons.

4. "One More Heartache" (Marvin Gaye)

The rhythm section of James Jamerson and Richard "Pistol" Allen (or Benny Benjamin on drums) shows the world what this groove is all about, what Motown is all about. This is more than a record. This is a machine that is unstoppable.

5. "I'm Wondering" (Stevie Wonder)

On this song, Jamerson becomes the force that shapes bass playing for the next 25 years. No one has ever played like this before. The synch between his mostly improvised bass notes and the drummer's work is astonishing, captivating, and above all, moving. The Motown sound has come to the table. I could pick dozens of songs that exemplify Jamerson's talent and technique, but I defer to this one because it is a personal favorite, and Stevie's harmonica adds icing to the cake.

6. "Love Is Here (And Now You're Gone)" (the Supremes)

Awesome backup vocals; heavenly tone, superior arranging. One of the slickest, most beautiful productions of all time. Probably produced by Gil Asky—I don't have these tunes in front of me, so I don't know the credits for certain. Unforgettable!

7. "Papa Was a Rolling Stone" (the Temptations)

The story of every black kid in the world. The incredible use of the various lead vocalists is pure genius, like each kid in the family is asking the questions.

8. "You Keep Me Hanging On" (the Supremes)

" . . . And there ain't nothin' I can do about it." Oowch!

9. "Bernadette" (the Four Tops)

I could pick many Four Tops songs, and I'm sure there are others I prefer but can't recall at this moment. I choose "Bernadette" just because it rings with lust and gut-busting passion. I don't know who Bernadette is, but I know what he's talkin' about. Once again, James Jamerson steps up and delivers a bass line unparalleled.

10. "Love's Gone Bad" (the Underdogs)

Motown's white-boy band of the mid-'60s. I knew the bass player of this band. He was an eccentric fellow, but a good bass player, although not a good enough bass player to play on this session.

In fact, the entire band on the session are the regular Motown session people. Only the lead vocals are done by an actual band member. Nonetheless, it's a good track—maybe not a great track, but one I like to listen to anytime. I have to include it just for its anomaly value.

Michael Davis is a bassist, songwriter, singer, record producer, painter. Born June 5, 1943, in Detroit, Davis earned his icon stripes as the bassist in legendary proto-punk band the MC5. After the spontaneous combustion of that band, Davis spent some time doing time at the "Drug Farm" in the federal penitentiary in Lexington, Kentucky. Upon his release, he was recruited into Detroit avant-artiste noise-cum-punk band Destroy All Monsters by a pal, Stooges axeman Ron Asheton. Because being a rock icon doesn't necessarily mean that the bills get paid, Davis now tours with the reconstituted version of the MC5 known as DKT; produces records; crashes motorcycles; designs rock merchandise; hangs out at skate shops, skate parks, and hospital emergency rooms with his sons; and has launched a nonprofit foundation to support music educa-tion in public schools, called Music Is Revolution. Because he lives in Southern California, he now has a surfer accent.

JAYNE COUNTY'S TOP 10 BEST SONGS OF ALL TIME

10. "Blame It on the Bossa Nova"—Steve Lawrence and Eydie Gorme!!!
9. "Sunshine Superman"—Donovan
8. "Lookin' Thru Gary Gilmore's Eyes"—the Adverts
7. "Dirty Water"—the Standells
6. "Sandy"—Ronnie & the Daytonas
5. "Feel Like I'm a Fixin' to Die Rag"—Country Joe & the Fish

4. "With God on Our Side"—Bob Dylan

3. "I Ain't Marchin' Anymore"—Phil Oaks

2. "Play With Fire"—the Rolling Stones

1. "Universal Soldier"—Buffy Sainte-Marie & Donovan

Jayne (formerly Wayne) County and her band the Electric Chairs came to prominence during the first wave of New York City punk with the declaration of promiscuity, "If you don't wanna fuck me, then baby, fuck off!" You can read about her feud with Handsome Dick Manitoba in Legs McNeil's Please Kill Me.

AMY GORE'S TOP 5 WEIRDO GIRL-GROUP FAVES

1. "Egyptian Shumba" (the Tammys)

Bizzaro, toe-tappin', otherworldly pop overloaded with girly screams. Great stuff from girls who can't help themselves—they just wanna Shumba.

2. "Camel Walk" (by Ike Turner, as performed by the Ikettes)

What does it mean? It doesn't matter—it's easy to do, baby.

3. "Terry" (Twinkle)

She is untrue; he dies in a motorcycle accident after finding out. She begs him to wait for her in heaven. What makes her think they are going to the same place? Bitch!

4. "Tie Me Tight" (Bob Kayli)

Not a true girl-group song (yet—check my next record), this minimalist R&B ballad by Berry Gordy's brother is laced with S&M references and animalistic bravado. Hot!

5. "Daddy You Gotta Let Him In" (the Satisfactions)

Dad, he's just a Hells Angel on the lam who needs somewhere warm to park his bike. Please?

Amy Gore is the singer and guitarist of Detroit garage outfit the Gore Gore Girls.

JESSE MALIN'S TOP 10 FAVORITE PUNK SONGWRITERS (AND TOP 10 '80S HARDCORE BANDS)

1. Joe Strummer/Mick Jones (the Clash)
2. Joey Ramone/Dee Dee Ramone (Ramones)
3. Paul Weller (the Jam)
4. Johnny Thunders/David Johansen (New York Dolls)
5. Paul Westerberg (the Replacements)
6. Ian MacKaye (Minor Threat)
7. Pete Shelley (Buzzcocks)
8. Leonard Graves Phillips/Stan Lee (the Dickies)
9. Charlie Harper/Nicky Garrett (U.K. Subs)
10. Jimmy Zero (Dead Boys)

Top 10 '80s Hardcore Bands

1. Bad Brains
2. Black Flag
3. Dead Kennedys
4. Circle Jerks
5. Reagan Youth
6. The Germs
7. Murphy's Law
8. S.O.A.
9. D.O.A.
10. The Mob

Born in Flushing, Queens, Jesse formed his first band, Heart Attack, in 1981 and released the hardcore 7" God Is Dead *on Damaged Goods Records. The band put out two other releases and broke up in 1984. Jesse went on to form a band called Hope that never put out any records and then formed D Generation with Howie Pyro and Danny Sage in '91. After three major-label releases, including the critically acclaimed* No Lunch, *Jesse in 2002 released his first solo album,* The Fine Art of Self Destruction, *followed by* The Heat *and his most recent album,* Glitter in the Gutter. *Jesse continues to tour all over the world and currently resides in NYC.*

LENNY KAYE'S "ZIONUGGETS": 25 ORIGINAL REGGAE ARTYFACTS

I was introduced to reggae in the earliest seventies by Andy Paley, who had brought back a few hand-pressed 45s from Montego Bay, including the Maytals, Ethiopians, and F. McKay tracks included herein, ensnared by their sense of doo-wop harmony and jigsaw rhythms and hooks; the patois made it seem even more musical, and spoken Jamaican is one of the most beautiful English slanguages to have evolved into its own dialect.

Traveling to England, I found a whole subcult awaiting, a genre obsessive's dream, replete with back-alley marketplace stalls and arcane labels and mad visionaries smokin' de spliff, *mon*: all emblazoned with a message of righteous peace and love and the conquering Lion of Judah. My kind of record collecting. Spurred by the charismatic figure of Marl-I and the roti-western of *The Harder They Come*, reggae became the soundtrack of choice to a punk parallel universe, the mirror-mirror *hongin' on de wall*, one rebel music jamming with an other.

In this, the last great decade of the blessed 45, I would travel to the Caribbean enclaves of Brooklyn and roam record stores, asking to hear the latest batch of singles and selecting the ones that viscerally appealed. The music was paradoxically sweet and firebranding, love songs holding their own with declarations of rasta illuminatus, biblical images of retribution and the world's ending surrounded by falsetto harmonies and gospel call-and-response.

In light of the splendor of Jah music, this playlist is hardly comprehensive, let alone comprehensible. The interior styles vary widely and with little reason, though much rhyme. Some of my most *respecting* artists and their work—Tapper Zukie and Ijahman Levi and Ras Michael with his Sons of Negus and Burning Spear—can't be distilled onto a CD-length collection of red, green, and golden oldies. But the bass, it *drive de car, mon. . . .*

1. "Tonight"—Tommy McCook & the Supersonics
2. "Book of Rules"—the Heptones
3. "Picture on the Wall"—Freddy McKay
4. "A Peculiar Man"—the Gaylads
5. "Soldeering"—the Starlites
6. "Scare Him"—Toots & the Maytals
7. "Power Pressure"—Cornell Campbell
8. "Think"—the Marvels
9. "Maccabee Version"—the Ethiopians
10. "Revolutionary Dream"—Pablo Moses
11. "I Man a Mafia"—Lloyd Parks
12. "Space Flight (To Venus and Mars)"—I Roy
13. "Fade Away"—Junior Byles
14. "No Jestering"—Carl Malcolm
15. "In a Dis a Time"—the Itals
16. "Silver Words"—Ken Boothe
17. "Screaming Target"—Big Youth
18. "Chase the Devil"—Max Romeo
19. "Right Time"—the Mighty Diamonds
20. "Roast Fish and Cornbread"—Lee "Scratch" Perry
21. "Cherry Oh Baby"—Eric Donaldson

22. "Two Sevens Clash"—Culture
23. "Rasta Pon Top"—Twinkle Brothers
24. "Three Wise Men"—Earth & Stone
25. "Satta a Massa Ganna"—the Abyssinians

As a musician, writer, and record producer, Lenny Kaye has been intimately involved with the creative impulse that marks the music. He has been a guitarist for poet-rocker Patti Smith since her band's inception more than 30 years ago, and is the coauthor of Waylon, *the life story of Waylon Jennings. He has worked in the studio with such artists as Suzanne Vega, Jim Carroll, Soul Asylum, Kristen Hersh, and Allen Ginsberg, as well as his own solo muse. His seminal anthology of '60s garage rock,* Nuggets, *has long been regarded as defining a genre.* You Call It Madness: The Sensuous Song of the Croon, *an impressionistic study of the romantic singers of the 1930s, was published by Villard/Random House in 2004. He is currently on tour with Patti and Her Band celebrating the release of their album of classic covers,* Twelve, *and wrote this somewhere between Dresden, Germany, and San Severino Marche, Italy, in June/July of 2007.*

STEVEN BLUSH'S 10 MOST INFLUENTIAL PUNK BANDS

In alphabetical order . . .

1. Bad Brains

Their mind-blowing multiculti punk/reggae fusion should've been bigger than U2, but in the end, their greatest achievement was encouraging young punks to smoke pot.

2. Black Flag

Greg Ginn's fierce DIY ethos and atonal guitar shred—along with Henry Rollins' shaved-head-and-tattoos assault—forever changed the face of (un)popular music.

3. The Clash

Their now-legendary albums include the absolute best (*The Clash*) and worst (*Cut the Crap*)—and, as such, have inspired untold generations of mediocre MTV-friendly "punk."

4. The Dictators

The Bronx's most important contribution to humanity. Their melodic, hard-edged rock sounded the genesis of the modern pop-punk formula. Manitoba's "Jew-fro" ushered out the '70s.

5. The Germs

Darby Crash and crew transformed suburban boredom, aesthetic nihilism, and lack of musicality into an art form. Darby's death signaled the dawning of a new era.

6. Minor Threat

The most important band in the history of Washington, D.C. Ian MacKaye's militant straight-edge vision and zealous indie principles defined American hardcore.

7. The Misfits

Glenn Danzig's incorporation of horror, schlock, and Jersey rock into punk continues to inspire—kids today know Misfits songs like kids of yore knew Led Zep.

8. Ramones

Now that "Hey! Ho! Let's go!" has been reduced to an advert and sports chant, let's never forget their revolutionary influence. Joey remains the heart and soul of NYC punk.

9. Sham 69

Jimmy Pursey's skinhead-friendly working-class chants ("If the Kids Are United," "Borstal Breakout") spurred the rise of testosterone-fueled hardcore—so blame him.

10. Television

TV's original lineup with Richard Hell and Tom Verlaine sowed the seeds of modern music; Verlaine's artistic affectation was the inspiration for decades of god-awful indie rock.

Steven Blush has written three books on the subject of rock— American Hardcore: A Tribal History; .45 Dangerous Minds; *and* American Hair Metal*. Blush's writings have appeared in more than 25 publications, including* Spin, Details, Interview, *the* Village Voice, *and the* Times Of London*. For 15 years, he published the cult music magazine* Seconds, *and he currently serves as a contributing editor at* Paper*. Blush is also writer/producer of the Sony Picture Classics–distributed documentary film* American Hardcore, *inspired by his book of the same name.*

JOHN HOLMSTROM'S 10 MOST TRULY OFFENSIVE PUNK ROCK SONGS, AND 10 THAT ARE NOWHERE AS OFFENSIVE AS THEY SEEM

A lot of recent punk rock has been gratuitously offensive—it's not the kind of stuff that destroys a band's career or gets the band kicked off its record label. So let's toast these pioneers who really pissed a lot of people off . . . and paid the price:

1. "Beat on the Brat" (Ramones)

A woman (and ex-Ramone fan) once said to me, "I loved the Ramones until I heard that Joey wrote this when he was at the beach and a nearby baby was crying so loud that he wanted to hit it with a baseball bat! Before that, I always assumed he was being ironic and that 'Beat on the Brat' was a statement against child abuse! But once I learned he was being serious . . ." Yes, another Ramones fan bites the dust. Sorry, Suzy and Sheena! But don't lose your sense of humor: Joey never actually hit a baby with a baseball bat. He was just expressing what a lot of us nonparents feel. Honest, your cute, bawling baby doesn't sound as adorable to the rest of us as you might think. Ramones' runners-up for this list: "Blitzkrieg Bop" (an ode to Holocaust victims), "Now I Wanna Sniff Some Glue" (banned in Scotland!), "Carbona Not Glue" (removed from their third album after a lawsuit) . . . Hell, there are so many Ramones lyrics to choose from, you could make up another Top Ten list with 'em. Sick humor is like that.

2. "Belsen Was a Gas" (Sex Pistols)

Yeah, right, but sorry, Rotten apologists. This song, from *The Great Rock 'n' Roll Swindle*, is not ironic. A song making fun of victims of the Holocaust is about as offensive as it gets (although at the time it was released, most scenesters in New York were still upset with "New York," which made fun of our precious Dolls). Besides, Sid Vicious is credited with the songwriting, and he was no Glen Matlock. "Bodies," which tries to say something about abortion, might top this list if anyone could understand the lyrics.

3. "Bullet" (Misfits)

The assassination of President John F. Kennedy is regarded by many Americans as the most tragic event of the twentieth century. So the Misfits' confused song lyrics that mix together JFK widow Jacqueline Onassis, Kennedy's skull, fellatio, and other sex acts has to be as offensive as anything ever written.

4. "A Little Bit of Whore" (Johnny Thunders)

This song has to have the most vile, disgusting, hateful, antifemale lyrics ever written. Well, except for most recent rap lyrics, but since Thunders' music predates rap by several years, it's beyond 99 percent of the worst misogynist "gangsta rap" lyrics. Its premise—

that "there's a little bit of whore in every girl"—demeans every single woman in the world. Ironically, this is also why so many women adored Johnny—he was such a bad boy. Besides, Bebe Buell covered it, and . . . Oh, never mind.

5. "Golden Showers" (the Mentors)

Senator Al Gore and his wife, Tipper, read the lyrics to the Mentors' "Golden Showers" during the 1985 PMRC Senate hearings in Washington. Somehow, these lyrics, centered around a sex act perpetrated on a seemingly underage girl and involving acts of urinal and fecal defecation, were found to be not only disturbing and disgusting but also highly amusing. (This is a typical response to truly offensive material. One person blanches, the other giggles.) As a result, the "smell my anal vapors" lyric became the most unforgettable of the proceedings. Thank you, Al Gore, for trying to stop global warming by preventing lyrics that mention "anal vapors."

6. "Jesus" (Feederz)

They recorded a more infamous song ("Jesus Entering from the Rear," featured on Alternative Tentacles' *Let Them Eat Jellybeans* compilation), but the title track from the Feederz' first recording, a 1980 four-song EP, *Jesus*, is arguably more offensive, because it was their first, so their later anti-Jesus stuff was inspired by it. Lyrics like "You're just a worthless corpse, you're just a pile of shit" are probably more offensive than most Bible Belt types can handle in one lifetime. Non-Christians are often offended by some of their other songs: "Fuck You," which (some say) encourages violence against women, and "Ever Feel Like Killing Your Boss," which encourages murder. But hey—they're from Arizona, so obviously their brains have been baked by the hot sun. What's *your* excuse?

7. "Anal Cunt" (GG Allin)

Where do you start with an "artist" like GG Allin, whose songs are the most foul, degrading, and disgusting ever recorded?

A "musician" whose stage act climaxed when he defecated on stage and then threw his doody at the members of his audience? Whose most popular songs include "I'm Gonna Rape You," "Legalize Murder," "Fuckin' the Dog," "I Wanna Piss on You," and "I'm a Cunt Suckin' Cannibal?" Allin's "Anal Cunt" is about sex with a corpse. It's certainly not the first punk rock song about sex with a corpse (Alice Cooper recorded several, and even simulated necrophilia onstage during his stage act), but it's described in such graphic detail here that . . . Forgive me while I barf. An honorable mention for offensive lyrics must go to the band named after this song, the legendary Anal Cunt.

8. "Toilet Love" (Wayne County & the Electric Chairs)
Transsexual rock star Wayne/Jayne County was one of the few early-1970s glam rockers who was actually homosexual, to say nothing of transgendered. Many of Jayne's songs attempt to offend by glamorizing perverted sex and scatology. Since her song "Toilet Love" was performed in the early 1970s, when it was still possible to shock people with this stuff, and the very idea of a transgendered person expressing him- or herself was enough to make the average person's jam drop to the cellar, we must pay tribute to Sweet Jayne here. . . . She also often simulated eating crap from the crapper during her stage act. (Unlike GG Allin, Jayne faked it and used dog food that looked like excrement.)

9. "California Pipeline" (Murphy's Law)
This song, from Murphy's Law's second record, *Back with a Bong*, is seemingly the least offensive song on this list—until at the very end, when singer Jimmy Gestapo yells "Ronald Reagan / He's our man / If he can't do it / No one can!" and then punctuated it with "America rules!" At the time, during a very politically correct, anti-Reagan atmosphere in the music industry, it was career suicide. Leader singer Jimmy has pretty much disavowed his politics from that era and has blocked the lyrics from appearing on the Web. But that this kind of thing would result in a band being blackballed just shows how far we have to go to achieve

true "freedom of expression" in this country. *Back with a Bong* is one of the best punk records from the 1980s, yet certain people have put the band on a blacklist because they don't agree with the band's politics. . . . Who are the hypocrites now? And who are the fascist bastards? Free Murphy's Law! (Hey, lighten up, okay? Don't burn this book! Hey, it was just a joke!) So obviously, the song was very offensive!!!

10. "Al-Queda Detonator" (the Nihilistics)

This song is so offensive—toward Muslims—that it should be banned forever. Otherwise it could get us all killed! It begins with an Arabian melody, then gets interrupted abruptly by gunshots, then goes into lyrics that promise to kill Muslims and Arabs. Tch, tch. Is this really how Americans reacted after 9/11? Anyhow, the song lyrics are so offensive, even the Nihilistics (who try hard to be as offensive as possible) haven't posted the lyrics on their Web site yet. I guess they're afraid suicide bombers are going to start going to their live shows!

10 Punk Songs That Are Nowhere Near as Offensive as They Seem

1. "Dead Babies" (Alice Cooper)

In 1971, the Alice Cooper Band released their fourth album, *Killer*, which caused a worldwide outrage due to the song "Dead Babies," which involved a stage show which featured the band's lead singer chopping up a cute little Betsy Wetsy doll with a hatchet and place-kicking its body parts into the audience afterwards. Alice Cooper sold millions of records, appeared on *Creem* magazine's cover as their 1974 "Punk of the Year," provided the blueprint for "shock rock" and punk rock, and inspired bands like the Sex Pistols (whose singer, one J. Rotten, auditioned by lip-synching "I'm Eighteen"), the Ramones (Joey was an unabashed A.C. fan), the Damned, and countless others. But the actual lyrics involve neglectful parents who allow their infant to grab aspirin from the medicine cabinet. So it's actually a warning, and not about gratuitous violence. Oh well, too bad. We liked the song better before we knew that!

2. "Back to Africa" (the Dictators)

Although they are too often written out of the official "punk rock" histories, the Dictators helped create the punk rock movement in New York. Their first album, *The Dictators Go Girl Crazy*, cemented the how-to-be-a-punk-band formula:

> a. Dress in jeans and sneakers—not fishnet stockings, silk dresses, and lipstick.
> b. Play loud, fast rock 'n' roll.
> c. Be obnoxious, brash, and shocking.
> d. Write lyrics about cars and girls, not sex and drugs.
> e. Drink Coca-Cola for breakfast.

They stuck to the formula only too well, since the song titles from that first LP ("Master Race Rock," "Two Tub Man," "I Live for Cars and Girls") have to this day placed them on some kind of secret PC blacklist. The irony is that the most "offensive" song title from that album, "Back to Africa," is also their most politically correct. It's about a white guy who loves a black girl so much that he wants to "go back to Africa" to better understand her culture. This blacklist against the Dictators remains one of mainstream rock culture's stupidest, most grievous, evil and least reported crimes against society. Thank you, you fucking hippies, for being as stupid as we know you are. That truly is offensive.

3. "God Save the Queen" (Sex Pistols)

Yes, this is the most banned song in England, land of the queen-worshippers (the band and the head of the royal family). But the truth is: the entire controversy over this record was manufactured, phony, and designed to sell records so as to prop up the then-failing U.K. record industry. It was a "wink-wink" conspiracy by Malcolm McLaren and the English press to sell newspapers and Sex Pistols records. Not that this was necessarily a bad thing to do so, since it promoted the greatest music of all time (punk rock), but let's face facts: punk rock was created in the U.S. by the New York City band Television (who quit on it way too early), and the Sex Pistols, who released their first single in the U.K. at the end of 1976, were latecomers to the punk scene who based their sound and style on Television. Heck, the Saints earned the late, great U.K. music newspaper *Sounds'* "Single of the Year" for their recording "Stranded"/"No Time" in 1976, and if that isn't punk rock, then nothing is. Sample "God Save the Queen" lyric: "We love our queen! God Saves!" Johnny Rotten even admitted years later that, yes, he does love their queen!

4. "Frankie Teardrop" (Suicide)

Ninety-nine percent of punk rock fans have never heard of Suicide, much less listened to their music. But this two-man band, who were the first combo in the world to advertise themselves as "punk rock" in 1974, forged the concept of minimalism in punk rock, and wrote the most brutal and uncompromising lyrics ever recorded. Lead singer Alan Vega would provoke fistfights in the audiences of their shows, and Martin Rev provided the simple drumbeat that punk bands would later copy—even though Rev used a drum machine. Suicide's music still sounds scary, brutal, and beyond honest to this day.

5. "White Riot" (the Clash)

The Clash were the first punk band to introduce politically correct lyrics to punk rock. Their first album included "White Riot," dedicated to solidarity with the civil rights movement. But the National Front, a racist, right-wing hate group popular in England in the 1970s, sometimes didn't get that connection and took the song title at face value. The Clash song "I'm So Bored with the USA" is actually offensive, since they dismiss the plight of US Vietnam vets' heroin addiction in the first verse (as if Vietnam vets aren't human beings), but since the rest of the lyrics are just typically leftist and anti-American enough, the counterculture embraced the group, resulting in lots of favorable coverage in *Rolling Stone* and other hippie magazines. Smooth move! And anyhow, the Clash didn't really hate America—New York was like Joe Strummer's second home! So there's a two-for-one.

6. "White Minority" (Black Flag)

Another song lyric that on the surface appears to reference "white pride," Black Flag's early anthem, which appeared on their 1980 EP *Jealous Again*, is actually a statement on the impotence of it. As a result, serious political correctness officially began to take root in punk rock, as Black Flag toured everywhere and spread the gospel of punk.

7. "Kill the Poor" (Dead Kennedys)

Left-wing California punk band the Dead Kennedys (whose name is enough to offend most of America) successfully followed the Alice Cooper/Dictators formula of shocking song titles with PC lyrics. As a result, their songs, like "Holiday in Cambodia" and "California Über Alles," rarely offended anyone—most people were in on the joke by then. So songs like "Kill the Poor" were properly viewed as political statements and not as "how-to's." On the other hand, if Bon Jovi recorded the same lyrics . . . who knows?

8. "Fresh Flesh" (Fear)

This has appeared on several lists of "most offensive punk rock songs," but there's nothing truly offensive about it. It's a bit perverted, even a bit sexy, but it's so nonspecific that it can't truly be considered offensive. It's not sexist or racist; it offends no racial or political groups; it tackles no difficult issues. . . . It's basically white bread. But never fear, Fear are a great punk band—just not a great, offensive punk band.

9. "Kill All the White Man" (NOFX)

Probably no band in the world represents punk rock's genuflection to the leftist, PC world better than NOFX. Its leader,

Fat Mike, set up punkvoter.com, a Web site that claims to be "progressive" but is in fact unabashedly leftist and anti-Republican, and his label, Fat Wreck Chords, released the compilations *Rock Against Bush* (Vols. 1 and 2). Johnny Ramone, who is unabashedly pro-America and right wing, could not qualify as punk rock in Fat Mike's world. "Kill All the White Man" might be the safest punk song ever (except for every other song in NOFX's library). So here's a call-out to NOFX, the band that started emo (worse than disco) and all other "pop punk" bands—grow some balls!

10. "I Wanna Be Black" (Lou Reed)

The "Godfather of Punk" (a stupid, misleading title that he unfortunately shares with Iggy Pop) recorded this song on 1979's *Street Hassle*. It's an orgy of invective (seemingly against black people), but a careful reading reveals that it's actually a clever send-up of what is now called "whigger" culture, in which white, middle-class college students ape the most offensive aspects of black culture. Although, Reed's antiblack rhetoric is so strong that it could make you second-guess whether he's being politically correct or truly hateful toward blacks. Then again, you could do this with every "offensive" or "nonoffensive" song on this or any other list. It's not up to a committee or even this book of lists to judge whether these songs are truly offensive or not. Almost all of them are supposed to make you think, so you can decide for yourself. Please do so.

108 PUNK ROCK SUBGENRES

1. Hardcore
2. Anarcho-punk
3. Garage punk
4. Anti-folk
5. 2-tone

6. Death country
7. Glam punk
8. Pigfuck
9. Oi!
10. Horror punk
11. Riot grrrrl
12. Skate punk
13. Hillbilly punk
14. Ska
15. Spaz punk
16. Chaos punk
17. Tardo punk
18. Psychobilly
19. Crust punk
20. Dance punk
21. Jazz punk
22. Cyberpunk
23. Cowpunk
24. Straight edge
25. Synth punk
26. Celtic punk
27. Queercore
28. Taqwacore
29. Douchecore
30. Scum punk
31. Punk blues
32. New Wave
33. Punk pathetique
34. Gothabilly
35. Post-hardcore
36. Gaelic punk
37. Punkabilly
38. Punk polka (popularized by the band Polkacide)
39. Neo-punk
40. Neo-hardcore
41. Ironic retro garbage

42. Street/gutter punk
43. Christian pop punk
44. Nazi punk
45. Noise punk
46. Emo
47. Screamo
48. Mall punk
49. Surf punk
50. Slowcore
51. Sadcore
52. Country punk
53. Paisley Underground
54. Roots punk
55. Grunge
56. Prog punk
57. Crassobilly
58. Peacock punk
59. Peace punk
60. New Romantic
61. Grindcore
62. Rockabilly voodoo
63. Pop punk
64. Goth
65. Metal punk
66. Power trash
67. Rebop punk
68. Power violence
69. '77 style
70. U.K. '82
71. Wave punk
72. KBD (Killed by Death)
73. Jap punk
74. Nardcore
75. Proto-punk
76. Youth crew hardcore
77. Krishnacore

78. Psychobilly
79. Post-punk
80. Bandana thrash
81. Jangle punk
82. Lo-fi
83. Hippie punk
84. Ska punk
85. Ska-core
86. Death punk
87. Art punk
88. Acid punk
89. Political punk
90. Thrashcore
91. Disco punk
92. C86
93. DIY
94. Basement punk
95. Cali punk
96. Punk 'n' roll
97. Metalcore
98. Punksploitation
99. Power pop
100. Mathcore
101. Indie punk
102. Action punk
103. Soul punk
104. Lounge punk
105. Power lounge punk
106. Swedish enema punk
107. Third-wave trad ska revival
108. No Wave

List compiled by the Backbeat Punk Rock All-Stars.

CLIFF MOTT'S FAVORITE PUNK COVER VERSIONS

1. "Walk on By" (Burt Bacharach/the Stranglers)

Burt Bacharach's songbook proved to be a rich and enduring vault to pry open for punk and New Wave types like Elvis Costello, the Tourists, and the White Stripes. However, the dark underbelly of the Brill Building was never rubbed as menacingly as here, where the plea to walk on by morphs into a threat.

2. Tie: "California Sun" (the Rivieras/Ramones) and "Stepping Stone" (Paul Revere & the Raiders/Sex Pistols)

The '60s roots of punk are displayed here and demonstrate the split between the U.S. and U.K. punk brands. The Pistols pick a pop hit that properly displays their snooty teenage pessimism, while the Ramones present their sunny (and yet snotty) teenage optimism.

3. "I Fought the Law" (Bobby Fuller Four/the Clash)

U.K. class-warfare rockers dust up their manifesto by digging into '60s pop Americana and turn up a dark gem. The furious approach amps up the song's shadows (including an unresolved murder) and helps cement the band's outlaw status.

4. "Take Me to the River" (Al Green/Talking Heads)

For sheer youthful chutzpah, this inexplicably soulful cover of an Al Green cut must be given high notice—more so because these art nerds (from RISD, no less) go on to display a genuine flare for geek-funk.

5. "Neat Neat Neat" (the Damned/Elvis Costello)

Elvis Costello covers the Damned almost simultaneously, and punk nearly laps itself!

Honorable Mentions

Mary Tyler Moore theme, (Paul Williams/Hüsker Dü); "Satisfaction" (the Rolling Stones/Devo); *Gigantor* theme (???/the Dickies); "Help!" (the Beatles/the Damned); and . . . "My Way" (Francis Albert Sinatra/Sid Vicious). DUH!!!!!!!

Cliff Mott is the official artist for the Official Punk Rock Book of Lists.

5 PUNK BANDS COVER THE MONKEES' "(I'M NOT YOUR) STEPPIN' STONE"

1. The Sex Pistols
2. The 101ers—This first incarnation of the Clash decided to perform "Steppin' Stone" after Joe Strummer saw the Sex Pistols do it. Said Strummer of the experience, "It took my head off."
3. Johnny Thunders & the Heartbreakers
4. The Klitz—"Steppin' Stone" was performed by this all-girl Memphis band with the Yiddish-sounding name.
5. Minor Threat covered "Steppin' Stone," taken from the Pistols, unaware that it was originally a Monkees song.

9 TERRIFYING COVERS THE REPLACEMENTS JUST LOVED TO PLAY

The Replacements were notoriously debauched in so many wonderful ways. Among these was a perverse desire to disappoint the audience. If they knew they would be playing to a roomful of A&R types, they would only play covers while shit-faced drunk—thus clearing the house. When they had a gig for country music folks, they invariably played kick-ass punk rock—thus clearing the house. Their manager devised a strategy: "Don't Tell the Boys if There's Anyone to Impress in the Audience." A typical night of misanthropic cover tunes went like this:

1. "Taking Care of Business"—Bachman Turner Overdrive
2. "20th Century Boy"—T.Rex
3. "Polk Salad Annie"—Tony Joe White
4. "It's a Heart Beat, It's A Love Beat"—the DeFranco Family
5. "Breakdown"—Tom Petty
6. "Iron Man"—Black Sabbath
7. "Jailbreak"—Thin Lizzy
8. "Kansas City Star"—Roger Miller
9. "If Only I Had a Brain" from *The Wizard of Oz*, sung by the road manager for extra effect

LITTLE STEVEN'S TOP 10 GARAGE PUNK BANDS

1. Pretty Things
2. Them
3. The Easybeats
4. The Stooges
5. New York Dolls
6. Dictators
7. Paul Revere & the Raiders
8. Sonics
9. Love
10. Tie: The Birds, the Wailers, the Shadows of Knight, the Troggs, the Music Machine, Blues Magoos, the Electric Prunes, the Kingsmen, Count Five, Richard & the Young

Lions, the Leaves, the Seeds, the Remains, the Standells, the Knickerbockers, the Amboy Dukes, Chocolate Watchband, the Premiers, the Gants, Syndicate of Sound, ? & the Mysterians, Golliwogs, 13th Floor Elevators, Rationals, Nazz, the Unrelated Segments, the Swingin' Medallions, the Sir Douglas Quintet, Choir, the Castaways, and Apostolic Intervention

Steven Van Zandt (born November 22, 1950) is an American musician, songwriter, arranger, record producer, actor, and radio disc jockey, who frequently goes by the stage names Little Steven or Miami Steve. He is best known as a member of Bruce Springsteen's E Street Band, in which he plays guitar and mandolin, and as an actor on the television drama The Sopranos, *on which he plays Silvio Dante.* Little Steven's Underground Garage *is an internationally syndicated weekly radio show that reaches more than 1 million listeners every week.*

14 PUNK BANDS THAT SNUCK ONTO *THE SOPRANOS* SOUNDTRACK

1. Link Wray
We say Link is a punk, and we should know. After all, this is *The Official Punk Rock Book of Lists*. His signature tune, "Rumble," was once banned from radio for being too menacing. No wonder it showed up in the very first episode of this series.

2. Dropkick Murphys
Ass-kickers from Boston pop up in Episode 5 with "Cadence to Arms."

3. Rocket from the Crypt

Episode 5 was a real firecracker, all right. R from the C score with "Eye on You."

4. Jon Spencer Blues Explosion

So nice they made it twice: first with sleazoid grinder "Lap Dance," in Episode 21, and again in Episode 40, with "Do You Wanna Get Heavy"—not their most aggressive moment, but just being there rates high.

5. Johnny Thunders

The Prince of New York's finest ballad, "You Can't Put Your Arms Around a Memory," oozed into Episode 24. In Episode 74, his version of "Pipeline" played during a cannoli-eating contest.

6. Elvis Costello

Maybe he hit the mainstream, but he's still a punk to us. "High Fidelity" sounded in Episode 27, "Mr. Ruggerio's Neighborhood."

7. Greg Ginn

According to his MySpace page, Black Flag axeman Ginn is "unquestionably the most influential guitarist to emerge from the late-'70s/early-'80s U.S. hardcore/punk movement." He humbly appears up on Episode 29 with "Never Change, Baby."

8. The Ramrods

Detroit ass-kickers go all spooky on Episode 34 with a turn at "Ghost Riders in the Sky."

9. Keith Richards

Keith is a punk rocker. And if his solo stuff is good enough for *The Sopranos*, it is good enough for us. "Make No Mistake" is on Episode 35.

10. Swingin' Neckbreakers

Finally, a band from New Jersey! The Neckbreakers do their thing on Episode 41 with "You."

11. Nashville Pussy

Southern pot munchers' "Drive" is featured in Episode 46.

12. The Chesterfield Kings

How come we are starting to think Steve Van Zandt had something to do with this? Garage rock champs peel off "Mystery Trip" in Episode 57.

13. Blondie

"Dreaming" is definitely not punk, but hey, it's Blondie, right? Episode 66.

14. Joan Jett & the Blackhearts

Joan Jett rules. You got a problem with that? You can hear her sing "Little Drummer Boy" in Episode 77.

List compiled and annotated by Mike Edison.

CAPTAIN SENSIBLE'S "TOP 20 RECORDING SESSIONS THAT I WISH I'D ATTENDED"

1. "A Day in the Life" (John Lennon)

Okay, I'm starting with John Lennon's melancholy masterpiece from *Sgt. Pepper*, which I have chosen because I would love to have seen George Martin telling the orchestra to forget everything they had ever been taught as classical musicians about control and technique and the like, and instead to go completely berserk at the end and improvise like fuck during the song's manic, ascending crescendo.

2. "It's Not Unusual" (Tom Jones)

Tom Jones's sensational performance on this song is literally dripping with testosterone. He is totally going for it—right up to the end bit with those ludicrous ad libs. What fun.

3. End of the Century (Ramones)

It would also have been a giggle to have seen that megalomanic Phil Spector pulling a gun on the Ramones when they questioned the relative benefits his over-the-top production techniques were having on their gnarled lo-fi punk sound.

4. "All Along the Watchtower" (Jimi Hendrix)

On this track, Jimi Hendrix is a magician making his guitar sound like it comes from another planet. How *did* he make that wonderful noise? I wish I could time-travel and find out.

5. "You Really Got Me" (the Kinks)

Apparently, Dave Davies had some peculiar amplifier that he'd messed around with the insides of, which provided the distortion for the glorious caveman riff that drives this proto-punk song along and that some folk say was the first-ever appearance of heavy metal. It must've been pretty radical at the time.... I'd like to have seen the studio engineers' (who all wore white laboratory coats at the time) faces when he wheeled in his hot-rodded amp, plugged in, and made *that* noise!

6. "Cherry Red" (Groundhogs)

I'll never forget seeing the determinedly unshowbiz Groundhogs on TV's *Top of the Pops* in the early '70s performing this frenetic number that could possibly be described as "blues on speed." At the time, this band were the best power trio on the planet.

7. "Have You Got It Yet" (Pink Floyd)

At the end of Syd Barrett's time as leader of Pink Floyd and when his behavior was getting increasingly "psychedelic," he attempted to teach the band a song that was ever changing. Poor

old Roger Waters would repeatedly learn what Syd was show-ing him, only to be told that it *wasn't* like that at all, but like *this*. This apparently went on for ages, with Syd asking the others, "Have you got it yet?" Oh, to have had *that* filmed and up on YouTube!

8. "Who'll Read the Will" (the Lollipop Shoppe)

This tune by '60s garage merchants the Lollipop Shoppe (also known as the Weeds) is a fine example of a band going mental in the studio.

9. "Son of a Preacher Man" (Dusty Springfield)

Dusty is really living the lyric here.

10. "Who's That Lady" (Isley Brothers)

Oh, to have been in the studio when Ernie Isley plugged his guitar into his fuzz box for the first time. And what a fabulous combination it made, as you can hear on this amazing recording of the wonderful Isley harmony soul sound and that wild, soar-ing, freaked-out guitar. Terrific stuff.

11. The Name of the Game (Abba)

The two couples that made up Abba attending recording ses-sions while their relationships were disintegrating made for a distinctly emotional album of tearjerkers, including classics like "The Name of the Game," "One of Us," and "The Winner Takes It All." This could also be the reason that Fleetwood Mac's *Rumours* is by far their best thing they did post–Peter Green. Oh, and the 5th Dimension recorded an album full of songs by Jimmy Webb written when *he* was going through a relationship split, which includes passionate material like "Carpet Man" and "Paper Cup."

12. "Tutti Frutti" (Little Richard)

The world had seen nothing like Little Richard when he appeared on a music scene that still belonged to crooners like Frank and Bing. To have witnessed the session where the "Georgia Peach" opened his mouth and screamed those immortal words, "A wop bop a loo bop," etc. . . . I'd imagine that those present in the control room would've been somewhat gobsmacked!

13. "A Concise British Alphabet" (Soft Machine)

The pop music songwriting formula of the day was thrown out of the window by Soft Machine's Robert Wyatt, who decided to just simply sing the letters of the alphabet over a quick piece of quirky jazz on the band's wonderful first album, interestingly entitled *Soft Machine 1*. Truly a band that only ever did their own thing, and to hell with the (non)commercial consequences!

14. "Don't Stop Me Now" (Queen)

Freddy Mercury going crazy on this impassioned plea to be allowed to party must've been a sight to see. And if anyone knew how to have a "good time," it was Freddie!

15. In a Silent Way (Miles Davis)

Davis assembled a right bunch of creative mavericks to record with here and single-handedly invented a whole new interpretation of jazz. This no-limits, fusion vibe must've upset a fair old few purists in its time.

16. "The Great Banana Hoax" (the Electric Prunes)

The Prunes always "went for the weird," and there are certainly some strange guitar sounds driving this self-penned psychedelic garage gem along. It is difficult to tell if some noises in the song are voice, guitar, drums, or whatever. What a band!

17. Live at Leeds (the Who)

In my estimation, either this or *Grand Funk Railroad Live* is the greatest stage recording ever made. The Who were incredible at the time, and every note played is gold dust, with each member in total control of his respective brief, and the end result was a hugely powerful whole.

18. "Shadows Breaking Over My Head" (the Left Banke)

Garage band invites piano player's dad and friends to recording session to add some string quartet arrangements—shock horror! If you've not heard them before, check out the Left Banke, as they created something wonderful and unique during their brilliant but all-too-brief existence.

19. Pet Sounds (the Beach Boys)

The appalling and sartorially challenged Mike Love whining and bleating about Brian Wilson's incredible new collection of songs would've been fun to witness. This bearded buffoon was apparently demanding that the likes of "God Only Knows" and "Good Vibrations" were scrapped in favor of a return to their tried-and-tested surf-with-Chuck-Berry-riffs sound. What a pillock!

20. Things Your Mother Never Told You (Wayne County & the Electric Chairs)

Wayne County and Co. dramatically changed their musical direction on this dark and moody prog-tinged record. What *was* this punk band on, one wonders, to have produced such amazingly psychedelic material as this? Superb stuff!

Captain Sensible was (and still is) a member of U.K. punk group the Damned, who kicked up a bit of a stink with their chums the Clash and the Sex Pistols back in 1977. They are still touring—mad fools!

3 WHINY SINGERS AND THEIR PUNK ROCK COVER RECORDS

1. *Chipmunk Punk* was released in the summer of 1980 as a crass attempt to cash in on the booming punk rock trend. The jury is still out on whether or not Billy Joel, Tom Petty, Linda Ronstadt, and Queen qualify as punk.

>   a. "Let's Go"—the Cars
>   b. "Good Girls Don't"—the Knack
>   c. "How Do I Make You . . . ?"—Linda Ronstadt
>   d. "Refugee"—Tom Petty
>   e. "Frustrated"—The Knack
>   f. "Call Me"—Blondie
>   g. "You May Be Right"—Billy Joel
>   h. "Crazy Little Thing Called Love"—Queen
>   i. "My Sharona"—the Knack

2. *Pink Panther Punk* is undoubtedly the best of the rash of punk-sploitation records released in 1981 as in an attempt to cash in on the genre's fleeting commercial success. Covers of mainstream hits from Pink Floyd, Billy Joel, the Doobie Brothers, and Blondie, plus a few original power-loungers and interludes beg the musical question, It's pink, but is it punk?

>   a. "Scene from *The Pink Panther*"
>   b. "Another Brick in the Wall, Part 2"—Pink Floyd
>   c. "Panther on the Prowl"
>   d. "Still Rock & Roll to Me"—Billy Joel
>   e. "It's Punk!"
>   f. "What a Fool Believes"—Doobie Brothers
>   g. "Call Me"—Blondie
>   h. "Rock & Roll Panther"

3. *The Spaghetti Incident*—Guns n' Roses' 1993 punk covers record—was the final nail in the GNR coffin and to date

remains the last thing they've released. The CD version features an unlisted bonus track: Axl's take on the Charles Manson–penned "Look at Your Game, Girl." There are no Billy Joel covers on the record.

    a. "Since I Don't Have You"—the Skyliners

    b. "New Rose"—the Damned

    c. "Down on the Farm"—U.K. Subs

    d. "Human Being"—New York Dolls

    e. "Raw Power"—the Stooges

    f. "Ain't It Fun"—Dead Boys

    g. "Buick Makane/Big Dumb Sex"—T.Rex/Soundgarden

    h. "Hair of the Dog"—Nazareth

    i. "Attitude"—Misfits

    j. "Black Leather"—the Professionals

    k. "You Can't Put Your Arms Around a Memory"—
       Johnny Thunders

    l. "I Don't Care About You"—Fear

    m. "Look at Your Game, Girl"—Charles Manson

List compiled by Aaron Lefkove.

OH, NO! IT'S TIM WARREN'S TOP 10 THINGS THAT DOOMED PUNK ROCK!

1. David Bowie

Let's keep things civil without expounding further. . . . Ah, fuck civility! Wrongness at its most wrong. Foppery in vocals and designer clothing, never mind the androgyny circa Ziggy: eyeliner, mascara, spandex, lipstick. Ain't Pat Benatar scary enuf without it having to be a DUDE with that shit on? Prince in Victoria's Secret gear? Bowie's fault! The Cure? Bowie's fault! All those bad Iggy recs? Bowie's fault! Marilyn Manson? Bowie's fault! Depeche Mode? Bowie's fault! Jagger and Bowie doing that gawdawful Motown cover? Blame 'em both!

2a. Prog Rock

Just HOW de heck'd King Crimson et al. ad nauseam wrangle their unrockingness BACK INTO that which Johnny Ramone's buzzsaw guit did tear asunder?????

2b. Psychedelic Rock

Ditto! Mind-expansion via noodling guitar trickery: no thanks! Just WHAT THE FUCK is so cool about this bullshit "freak folk" nouveau-hippie crap? That entire new "industry margin" could really "save the earth, man" by NOT pressing their crap and creating more greenhouse gasses and pollution via the manufacturing of their gawdawful CDs and LPs and just buy up alla the Donavan and Incredible String Band etc. albs sitting unwanted in every Goodwill and Salvation Army used bin! (Spinal Tap nailed both 2a and 2b spot-on: The Stonehenge segment! The flower-people segment! Can ya NOT see just how retarded and pompous that crap is?)

3. The Beatles

The slickery that the Fab Four castrated primal R&R with is to blame for all pathetic whiney "indie-rock" pap.

4. Classic Rock

Ditto as per No. 3. Further: those without a sense of SHITTY BAD "ROCK" HISTORY are doomed to forever vomit up crap-influenced punk rock/indie-rock/etc. Irony, my ass—you tards just LOVE this shit, dontcha?

5. Heavy Metal

Thanks fer speedcore, etc., and special "thanks" fer that "wicked" overly active double-kick-drum-sounding, gag-inducing style of "punk" as purveyed by bands associated with No. 8.

6. Radio and MTV

Sucked . . . always . . . and it'll keep folks dumb forever. "Oh, but what about College Radio?" What, other than it serving as a "springboard" to a job at a major label?? That's what killed college radio, nimrods. Instead, please use a DIVING board and SPRING into the empty swimming pool at McCarren Park at a "hip" gig by some whiny twee motherfucking acoustic-guit-strumming shoegazer band!

7. English Rock Media

Kee-rist . . . the Alarm??? The Beautiful South??? Spear of Destiny??? The Stone Roses??? Big Country??? The Happy Mondays??? Balaam & the Angel??? The Smiths??? The Cult??? The House Martins??? The Style Council??? I never had the misery of actually HEARING sech turdery, so mebbe I missed out on the greatest thing since sliced bread . . . (hah!) . . . but to have this shit trumpeted as the be-all and end-all of "The Future of Rock"? There IS a place in hell reserved fer ye whore bastids. . . .

8. Epitaph Records and the Bands Associated With All That Slicked-up West Coast Teen-Friendly Crap

Next time yer accosted for change by some suburban mallbrat in disguise as a 1981 U.K. crusty punk, just say, "Thank you, Rancid," then beat the fucker unconscious, grab his studded leather jacket and nose-jewelry, and hit the pawn shop, collect your $100, and go have a great steak dinner!

9. The Success of Nirvana

Not to blame the band necessarily—but who coulda ever foreseen the gazillion shitty bands and record labels that formed in the aftermath of Nirvana's hitting the big time, never mind alla the slack-assed "hipster" generation that make Williamsburg the proper area fer any upcoming ground-zero-style attacks.

10. Disco

How else are ya s'posed to NOT include it when mosta today's "post-punk" bands soak up Gang of Four recs as inspiration—and it was those clowns that stated that the group CHIC was their biggest inspiration? Thanks, dweebs, fer dooming us to many more years of SHIT "post-punk" bands!

Tim Warren is the lunatic behind hate-fueled Crypt Records. Crypt changed the world with legendary garage-rock comp Back from the Grave *and slabs of greatness from such sick phenoms as the Gories, Jon Spencer Blues Explosion, Raunch Hands, Oblivians, Pagans, New Bomb Turks, Nine Pound Hammer, etc., etc. Or as Tim says, Crypt is "a wee cult label/record store/mail-order outfit around since 1983 that sells wee amounts of records, so why get a stick up yr ass if you don't like what you've just read? By the time ya ever read this, I'll have most likely folded the pathetic American 'arm' of Crypt and returned to Europe, where primal roots R&R urgh is appreciated. America: Drown with Bush."*

CHAPTER 5

SEX AND RELIGION

DEBBIE HARRY'S LIST OF "PEOPLE I'D LIKE TO FUCK"

First, let me say that my list could be a lot longer—a *lot* longer—but for the sake of not belaboring the subject, here's a list of people I'd like to fuck:

1. Kate Moss (Who wouldn't?)
2. Hugh Hefner (Who hasn't?)
3. Lady Bunny (Too bad I'm not gay, or black.)
4. Marilyn (Manson or Monroe—either one would do nicely.)
5. David Walliams (My computer says yes.)
6. O.J. Simpson (He just kills me.)
7. Justin Timberlake (It's obvious.)
8. Jack Nicholson (Some sexy fun . . .)

If anyone feels left out and that they should be on my list, remember this is just the tip of the iceberg. Contact Dick Manitoba for further info or a date.

Debbie Harry is the singer of Blondie.

PORN STAR JOANNA ANGEL'S 10 PUNK ROCKERS I WOULD LOVE TO CAST IN MY NEXT FEATURE

1. Debbie Harry (Blondie)

Although I want the Debbie Harry from the '80s (not the one now, no offense). Okay, I mean if Debbie Harry came banging on my door, begging me to put her in a porno, I damn well wouldn't say no, but that's not gonna happen. Debbie Harry in her prime was like, by far, the most attractive human being to ever walk the planet—and I mean attractive like she was sexy, awesome, hot, and talented . . . and there just aren't enough girls like that in porno these days.

2. Travis Barker (Blink 182)

I have always wanted to have sex with Travis Barker—way before I owned a porn company or even thought about owning a porn company. As the years went by, it started to become clearly obvious that this was never going to happen, so I began fantasizing about casting him in a porno, and this sort of kind of felt more realistic. Then I realized that *this* probably wasn't going to happen, and I was like, Eh, whatever. But then one day I saw that Travis Barker had his own reality TV show, and I got really pissed. It is far more degrading to have a reality TV show than to be in a porn. I still haven't given up. One day I will find a way!

3. Joan Jett (Joan Jett & the Blackhearts)

I would like to cast Joan Jett in a porno because she would kick the ass of whatever guy (or girl) she was in the scene with, and that would be pretty cool to watch.

4. Beau Beau (Avail)

Watching Beau Beau have sex probably wouldn't be the most erotic thing ever, but it would probably be fun to watch. In fact, maybe I don't want him to have sex. He should do in one of my

pornos what he does in Avail; he should just dance and play air guitar around the people banging. That would be awesome.

5. Jerry Only (Misfits)

It just seems like everyone in the world is making money off the Misfits except me. People who have never even heard a Misfits song are responsible for capitalizing off of all sorts of Misfits paraphernalia; and I—a real, true Misfits fan—have yet to cash in on any of this, so I think I deserve it.

6. Billie Joe Armstrong (Green Day)

Green Day was the first punk rock band I ever listened to. They hold a special place in my heart. Even though some of their newer albums aren't that great, I still own them all and love them all. One time I was at a bar, and as soon as I got there all these people were like, "Dude! Billie Joe from Green Day was just here! It was crazy." And another time, I was at my friend Tim Armstrong's house, and as soon as I got there he was like, "Oh, Billie Joe just left . . . you missed him." And stuff like this has happened a few other times in my life where I just miss Billie Joe. If I cast him in a porno that he agreed to do, that means I would actually get to meet him and not just almost get to meet him—and I kinda wanna shake his hand and give him a hug and thank him for turning me into the derelict that I am. I know that sounds lame, and a porno might not be the right way to get this message across, but I think it is worth a try.

7. Kathleen Hanna (Bikini Kill, Le Tigre)

I just want to see her in a porno of mine because I am pretty sure she would be damn good in bed. I can just tell.

8. Dennis Lyxzén (International Noise Conspiracy, Refused)

This is out of the goodness of my heart. Dennis is a smart guy who's really nice and really talented, and I think he deserves to get laid by a hot porno chick—even if it's just once. I know for a fact that hot porno chicks don't hang out at, like, vegan restaurants and anarchist communes, so if he isn't in one of my movies, it might never happen to him.

9. Matt Skiba (Alkaline Trio)

Skiba is a catch. He's cute, he is in a good band, he's a good dancer, and he wears nice clothes. There need to be more dudes like that in porn—or just *a* dude like that in porn. I elect Skiba to raise the bar on porn dudes. Maybe other people with his attractive qualities will follow in his footsteps.

10. Nico (the Velvet Underground)

Lou Reed got all the attention in the Velvet Underground, and Nico was always sorta cast in his shadow somewhere. I know she is dead and all, but if I could resurrect her, I would like to give her an outlet in which to shine, and porno is really the only vehicle I have to do that. I bet Lou Reed would try to weasel his way into the porno with her, but I wouldn't let him.

Joanna Angel is the founder of alt-porn giant Burning Angel, where she has written, directed, and starred in numerous films. Angel took home the award for "Most Outrageous Sex Scene" at the 2006 Adult Video News Awards for her performance in Re-Penetrator.

4 PUNKS WHO HAD SEX ONSTAGE (AND ONE DIY JOB)

1. Sid Vicious (Sex Pistols) . . . with "a Blonde"

According to Jon Savage, author of *England's Dreaming*, Vicious got lucky during the Sex Pistols' infamous American tour. It was at their fourth show, in Baton Rouge, Louisiana, that "during the set, Sid started having sex with a blonde who came up onstage." The Pistols had refused to let Nancy Spungen, a.k.a. "Nauseating

Nancy," the love of Sid's life, travel with them. Sid was devastated, but boys will be boys.

2. Stiv Bators (Dead Boys) . . . with a Waitress

In Legs McNeil and Gillian McCain's book *Please Kill Me*, one can read the details of Mr. Bators' first onstage fellation. Dead Boys producer Genya Raven put a waitress (name unknown) up to a naughty prank. Raven talked the young lady into going across the street from Max's Kansas City where a Dead Boys show was in progress, to pick up some treats at a deli. Raven instructed the girl to buy whipped cream and give Stiv a big surprise when he began to sing "Caught with the Meat In Your Mouth." Said Raven, "The waitress didn't fellate Steve (sic) to the point of coming, because the guy had to sing. I didn't want him to get off-key. So I said, 'Don't go that far.' Poor guy." Years later, Stiv bragged to *Search & Destroy* magazine that he had received several onstage blowjobs during his artistic career.

3. Gibby Haynes (Butthole Surfers) . . . with Friend-of-the-Band Kathleen Lynch, a.k.a. "Ta-Dah, the Shit Lady"

The full story of Ms. Lynch, her stage frolics, and the origin of her nickname, can be enjoyed in Michael Azerrad's *Our Band Could Be Your Life*. The PunkNotes version:

In 1986 the Butthole Surfers played at New York's Danceteria. Lynch jumped onto the stage from the audience, pulled down her pants, and Haynes "stuck his thumb up her ass . . . for like a half hour or 45 minutes," explained an onlooker. The pair proceeded to have sex onstage, a romantic interlude captured on video. Said band member Paul Leary, "Her legs are up in the air and there's Gibby pumping butt in the strobe lights and the smoke. It's really fuckin' hideous, man." Lynch never formally joined the band; however, she frequently got naked and "performed" with them. "She didn't speak for an entire year," wrote Azerrad, "a practice [band member] Coffey believes had a spiritual basis, like fasting."

4. GG Allin

Allin regularly attempted to rape both female and male members of his audience. He was not known to have succeeded, though he did score when he begged for fellatio. It must have been a lively experience for his partners, as Allin was usually covered in blood and feces.

And One DIY Job

5. Patti Smith . . . with Herself

In *Please Kill Me*, several people are quoted as watching chanteuse Smith "fiddling around down there" or "doing something to herself with her hand" while onstage. In one notable case she was wearing a $10,000 mink coat (circa the mid-'70s—adjust for inflation) and rhapsodizing about how she "lived in it and slept in it."

4 PUNKS WHO MADE IT AS MALE HUSTLERS, AND ONE WHO ALMOST DID

1. Dee Dee Ramone (Ramones)

Dee Dee turned tricks in NYC to support his heroin habit. He wrote the famous—or infamous—song about hustling in New York, "53rd & 3rd." He claimed the tune was largely autobiographical.

2. Richard Lloyd (Television)

Before joining Television as lead guitarist, the fetching Lloyd is reputed to have been a hustler in Los Angeles and New York. In *Please Kill Me*, scenester Duncan Hannah is quoted as saying, ". . . his hair looked like an Easter chick. He was really pretty."

3. Jim Carroll

The lanky, blond Carroll is perhaps best known for his autobiographical writing. In *The Basketball Diaries* he describes his years as a lapsed Catholic, a heroin addict, a basketball wonder . . . and a teen prostitute.

4. Billy Rath (the Heartbreakers)

Billy Rath took Richard Hell's place as bass player in the Heartbreakers in 1976. Rath had just returned from Florida, where he'd been working as a gigolo.

And a punk who almost did . . .

5. Sid Vicious

According to Jon Savage, author of *England's Dreaming*, Sid Vicious flirted with hustling before joining the Sex Pistols. Uncertain about his sexuality, he later slept with and made out with a few older male friends . . . but without consummation.

6 Punks Who Were Altar Boys

1. Johnny Thunders (New York Dolls, the Heartbreakers)
2. Jim Carroll
3. Stiv Bators (Dead Boys)
4. Johnny Blitz (Dead Boys)
5. Jimmy Zero (Dead Boys)
6. Cheetah Chrome (Dead Boys)

TOOLS OF THE TRADE: 5 NOTORIOUSLY WELL-ENDOWED PUNKS (AND 2 HONORABLE MENTIONS)

1. Dee Dee Ramone (Ramones)

2. Jon Langford (the Mekons)

3. Johnny Thunders (New York Dolls, the Heartbreakers)

Thunders was once stopped by police who believed he had contraband in his pants. When he unzipped and showed what he had, the cops arrested him for indecent exposure.

4. Iggy Pop (the Stooges)

Iggy's member is so big it's reputed to "need its own zip code."

5. Smutty Smith (Levi & the Rockats)

A band member said, "He's hung like a horse—there's a reason they call him Smutty."

Honorable mentions

1. Darby Crash (the Germs)

Crash had a famously tiny Johnson.

2. Mark McGrath (Sugar Ray)

McGrath (whose band's first album was vaguely punk, before they became a pop band) is possibly only the rock star to brag about having a small willy—Howard Stern not being a real rock star, of course.

7 PUNKS WHO WHIPPED IT OUT (OR JUST GOT NAKED)

1. Iggy Pop (the Stooges)

Iggy loved to whip it out onstage and anyplace else. He once pulled out his dick and showed it to Jim Morrison's wife, Pamela. She said, "Put that toy away." He also liked to wear dresses with nothing underneath, and pull up the dress to freak people out. Pop spent a good part of his onstage career with his pants around his knees.

2. Matt Lukin (Mudhoney)

Mudhoney toured as support for Sonic Youth, and the bands jammed together on "I Wanna Be Your Dog" as their encore. Lukin would hobble onstage holding a tambourine with his pants around his ankles. As a bandmate told author Michael Azerrad (*Our Band Could Be Your Life*), "[Lukin] discovered his body and started getting completely naked."

3. Don Bolles (the Germs)

When singer Darby Crash met Rob Henley, an adorable surfer punk, he fell in love and decided to make Henley the band's new drummer, even though Henley didn't know how to play. Crash sought an excuse to replace drummer Don Bolles. Darby was in the closet about his sexual preference, and Bolles frequently teased him about being gay. According to author Brendan Mullen, Darby "accused [Bolles] of disloyalty and of embarrassing the Germs by frequently appearing in public naked." Bolles particularly upset Crash by appearing onstage in dresses. Crash got someone else to tell the drummer he was fired. Observed Bolles, "Darby was so heavily narcotized he was apparently unable to see the irony (in this)."

4. Henry Rollins (Black Flag)

According to Thurston Moore, in an interview in *Punk Planet*, "Henry was growing his hair long, kids saying, 'Get a haircut,' and him reaching down and pulling his dick out and saying, 'I'm going to grow my hair down to here before I satisfy you.' When he said that, I don't know what he was thinking but to me that meant, 'Everything's going to break apart right now.' It was great—it did!"

5. Lux Interior (the Cramps)

Lux is never shy and shows every bit of his private parts onstage as often as possible. Occasionally, a complaint would be made to a police officer. On one such occasion, a fan objected to the sight of Lux's family jewels. By the time the cops showed up, the jewels were back in storage, leaving Poison Ivy to play the beleaguered wife. "Officer, I am *so sorry*. I can't imagine what got into him—I assure you, this has never happened before!" Recalling the not-so-untypical incident, Ivy shrugs and says of her ploy, "It worked every time."

6. Shane MacGowan (the Pogues)

In *A Drink with Shane MacGowan,* MacGowan muses on the results of friction within the Pogues: "I used to go into a rage some nights. . . . If I entered into this rage, everything was all right. . . . [I]t would be a dynamic gig, but if I was feeling self-pity and sadness, then I'd just drink myself stupid. . . . I could forget the words for the whole set, I could fall over on stage, I could suddenly find myself standing on the stage with my trousers around my ankles—that happened to me a few times."

7. GG Allin

Where to even begin?

ROBERTA BAYLEY'S TOP 5 PUNKS I WOULD LIKE TO SHOOT FOR *PLAYGIRL*

1. Iggy Pop
2. Tadanobu Asano
3. Peter Wolf
4. Michael Hutchence
5. Dave Vanian

Roberta Bayley is best known for documenting the New York punk scene in the mid-'70s, working as Punk *magazine's chief photographer. She has done album covers for the Ramones, Richard Hell, and Johnny Thunders' Heartbreakers. She has also curated numerous photography exhibitions, including "The Cool and the Crazy" and "Bande à part: New York Underground 60's 70's 80's," and is author of the book* Blondie Unseen: 1976–1980, *published in 2007.*

BEBE BUELL'S 10 SEXIEST PUNKS THAT HAVE GRACED GOD'S GREEN EARTH

1. Iggy Pop (the Stooges)

In his youth there was no one sexier in that animal kind of way. Jim was "primal" and had the best upper body in rock 'n' roll. Still does.

2. Debbie Harry (Blondie)

"The face" . . . need I say more?

3. Richard Hell (Richard Hell & the Voidoids, etc.)

He used to make the girls swoon with that Marlon Brando kind of "who gives a fuck" attitude. Dangerous and deadly.

4. Joan Jett (Joan Jett & the Blackhearts)

She picked up where Suzi Quatro left off. Even bald she is gorgeous.

5. Patti Smith

Patti looked more like Keith Richards in the '70s than most men. When she put on a suit and loose tie, she oozed sex appeal that was genderless.

6. Joe Strummer (the Clash)

He had a movie-star aura that made him shine as an entertainer. It was kind of like seeing James Dean in a band. He also had a sexy pointy Dr. Spock ear that I found irresistible.

7. Elvis Costello (Elvis Costello & the Attractions)

If Humphrey Bogart had started a band, perhaps? Elvis had a wonderful Arthur Miller, smart-boy sexiness. The topper is his flat feet and the shoes that house them.

8. Johnny Thunders (New York Dolls, the Heartbreakers)

Thunders was the Italian Stallion . . . in more ways than one.

9. Chrissie Hynde (the Pretenders)

Chrissie wears tight black jeans better than anyone I know. Her voice makes the skin on my arms tingle.

10. Stiv Bators (Dead Boys)

Stivvy was one of those guys that had more charm than a cunning fox. He was the best dancer I've ever known. I always thought he looked like a sexy "imp."

"Legendary beauty" Bebe Buell has been part of the NYC music and fashion scene since she landed there in 1972. Often called "the Queen of the Rock Chicks," she is a rock 'n' roll singer, an avid patron of the arts, a former model and Playboy *centerfold (Miss November 1974), an animal rights activist, the mother of actress Liv Tyler, and the author of the New York Times best-seller* Rebel Heart: An American Rock and Roll Journey *with Victor Bockris (2001). She still performs with the Bebe Buell Band across the U.S. and Europe and shows no signs of slowing down anytime soon. Another book and TV show are in the works.*

AMY WALLACE'S 13 BEST "PUNK" SONGS TO MAKE OUT TO*

1. "You Can't Put Your Arms Around a Memory"—Johnny Thunders
2. "Violent Love"—Lee Brilleaux/Dr. Feelgood
3. "Nighttime"—as performed by Alex Chilton
4. "Can't Hardly Wait"—the Replacements
5. "Love Comes in Spurts"—Richard Hell & the Voidoids
6. "The Broad Majestic Shannon"—the Pogues
7. "Crazy"—Patsy Cline
8. "Volaré"—as sung by Jonathan Richman
9. "Volaré"—as sung by Alex Chilton
10. "Misty Morning Albert Bridge"—the Pogues
11. "I'll Be Your Mirror"—the Velvet Underground, as covered by the Hitmakers
12. "After Hours"—the Velvet Underground
13. "You Can't Put Your Arms Around a Memory"—Johnny Thunders

*This list changes every day, just like luv. . . .

Amy Wallace is the coauthor of The Official Punk Rock Book of Lists.

9 POPULAR CHRISTIAN PUNK ROCK BANDS

1. The Crucified
This Fresno, California, band gained popularity in the late 1980s and early '90s. They were among the first pioneers of Christian hardcore, taking musical inspiration from numerous metal and punk bands such as Minor Threat.

2. Ninety Pound Wuss
This band, from Port Los Angeles, Washington, is often described as "chaos punk" or "spaz punk." They broke up after the release of their third album. Explained vocalist Jeff Suffering, "We had a rough tour, and nobody wanted to continue playing in the Christian music industry."

3. Crashdog
One of the first Christian punk bands, Crashdog was active primarily in the 1990s. They were among the first such bands to write overtly political, liberal songs, as well as Christian tunes. They are currently on "indefinite hiatus."

4. The Altar Boys
These pioneers of Christian rock formed in 1982, influenced by the Southern California punk scene. Breaking away from the traditional mold of religious rock, their lyrics are precise and specific about their faith.

5. Undercover
Undercover released its first album in 1982. Short, three-chord songs, tattoos, ripped jeans, and Mohawks classified them as punk. They performed punk versions of traditional hymns such as "Holy, Holy, Holy," shouted vocals—"God rules!"—and wrote songs such as "Jesus Is the Best." In 1986 they wrote "Pilate," from the guilt-ridden POV of Pontius Pilate, describing his grief at having crucified Jesus.

6. Hawk Nelson

Hailing from Peterborough, Ontario, this popular band has won numerous awards. Their album *Letters to the President*, released in 2004, marked their major-label debut.

7. Relient K

Formed in 1998 in Canton, Ohio, Relient K named themselves after guitarist Matt Hoopes' Plymouth Reliant K car.

8. Flatfoot 56

Formed in the year 2000, this Chicago band fuses Christian punk rock with Oi! Because they use highland bagpipes, they have also been classified as a Celtic punk band.

9. Dropkick Murphys

A Celtic punk band from Massachusetts, they blend Oi!, Irish music, and hardcore. Their nonstop, worldwide touring, and their famous Boston St. Patrick's Day shows have helped them create a devoted following. Among their influences they cite the Pogues, the Clash, and AC/DC. Their name was taken from a rehab center.

GABBA GABBA OY VEY! 22 NICE JEWISH PUNKS

1. Lou Reed (the Velvet Underground)
2. Mick Jones (the Clash)
3. Robert Quine (Richard Hell & the Voidoids)
4. Richard Hell (Richard Hell & the Voidoids)
5. Sylvain Sylvain (New York Dolls)
6. Joey Ramone (Ramones)
7. Tommy Ramone (Ramones)

8. Nancy Spungen (Sid Vicious' girlfriend)
9. Daniel Rey (the Martinets; producer)
10. Lenny Kaye (Patti Smith)
11. Genya Raven (Goldie & the Gingerbreads; producer)
12. Danny Fields (journalist)
13. Malcolm McLaren (impresario)
14. Jonathan Richman (Jonathan Richman & the Modern Lovers)
15. Handsome Dick Manitoba (the Dictators)
16. Andy "Adny" Shernoff (the Dictators)
17. Scott "Top Ten" Kempner (the Dictators)
18. Ross "the Boss" Funicello (the Dictators)
19. Stu "Boy" King (the Dictators)
20. Chris Stein (Blondie)
21. Alan Vega (Suicide)
22. Martin Rev (Suicide)

26 QUEERCORE BANDS WITH COOL NAMES

1. Black Fag (U.S.)—This is a queercore Black Flag cover band.
2. Cunts with Attitude (U.S.)
3. Deep Dickollective (U.S.)
4. Fagbash (U.S.)
5. Family Outing (U.S.)
6. Full of Shit (U.S.)
7. Gay Deceivers (U.S)
8. Gay for Johnny Depp (U.S.)
9. God is My Co-Pilot (U.S.)
10. Hyperdrive Kittens (U.S.)
11. Jean Genet (U.K.)
12. Kitty Kill (U.S.)
13. Lesbians on Ecstasy (Canada)

14. Lesbo Pig (U.K.)
15. Limp Wrist (U.S.)
16. The Little Deaths (U.S.)
17. Lucifag (U.S.)
18. Mourning Sickness (U.S.)
19. Oi-Gays (U.S.)
20. Panty Raid (U.S.)
21. Pom Pom Meltdown (U.S.)
22. Puta (U.S.)
23. Shitting Glitter (U.S.)
24. Sister George (U.K.)
25. Slutarded (Canada)
26. Youth of Togay (U.S.)

3 PUNKS WHO WERE TOUCHED BY GOD OR OTHERWISE HAD MYSTICAL EXPERIENCES

1. Mick Jones (the Clash)

Having left the band London SS, Jones was considering getting together a group called the Mirrors. Said Jones, "I was just going up the stairs one day and God hit me on the head with a mallet and said, 'You be in a group, you cunt. . . . It's the way you get ideas across faster than anything else. You don't wanna waste 10 hours doing a painting, which may flop . . . you just go out and do it.'" From this epiphany, the Clash was born.

2. Patti Smith

Smith was raised a Jehovah's Witness, renounced her faith at a young age, then accidentally got pregnant. She decided to give the baby up for adoption, with the single stipulation that it be raised Catholic. When she became a rock star, her fame became synonymous with the phrase, "Jesus died for somebody's sins, but not mine."

During a performance where she was doing her whirling dervish act perilously close to the edge of the stage, all the while talking to God, she fell and injured herself very seriously. Her recovery was slow and painful, and when she returned to the stage she was wearing a neck brace. She viewed the fall as an omen and renewed her Catholicism, reading Bible verses aloud before some of her songs.

3. Shane MacGowan (the Pogues)

It's difficult to say whether this item belongs under the list of Mental Breakdowns or Mystical Experiences. They're so often similar, and Shane was raised a good Catholic boy, so we've decided to leave it here. One night Shane took a section of blotters of acid—"I don't know how many, but it was very strong." In short, he imagined that the Third World War was beginning, that Ireland had become the ruler of the world, and that he was Ireland's diplomatic attaché to the world's powers. "I got out the vodka and the caviar for the Russians. Not real caviar. What I had around. Lumpfish roe. The summit meeting was at my flat. . . . [W]e decided to divide world power up between the blacks and the Irish. And in order to demonstrate the USA's cultural redundancy, I ate my *Beach Boys Greatest Hits* album. Kathy [the friend whose flat Shane was staying in] knocked on the door and my mouth was covered in blood. I said, 'Go away, can't you see I'm involved in the future of the world here?' I woke up and I thought the Third World War had happened and I was in Vienna. . . . And it gradually dawned on me that I was in London and the Third World War hadn't happened. Then I realized I'd eaten my Beach Boys record."

CHAPTER 6

ARTS AND SEIZURES

TV PARTY TONIGHT! 11 GREAT PUNK TV PERFORMANCES AND DEGRADING SITCOM PORTRAYALS, WITH APOLOGIES TO BILL GRUNDY

1. *Quincy, M.E.,* "Next Stop Nowhere"

Other than *Suburbia*, punk's abject nihilism was never captured as succinctly as in this episode of *Quincy, M.E.* Quincy has to find a wayward teen who has been falsely accused of murder but could unwittingly be with the real killer. Features the fictional band Mayhem—in cliché garb that falls somewhere between Mad Max and Lords of the New Church—and their rawkus nugget, "Get Up (I Wanna See You Choke)."

2. Fear on *Saturday Night Live*

When John Belushi booked Fear on SNL, no one knew that it would lead to the first nationally broadcast full-scale punk rock riot. Legend has it that John Joseph of the Cro-Mags is the first person seen diving off the stage. Ian MacKaye, John Brannon, and Harley Flannagan follow suit. Yeah, New York's all right if you like saxophones. . . .

3. Public Image Limited on *The Tomorrow Show* with Tom Snyder

John Lydon and Keith Levene's appearance on *The Tomorrow Show* with Tom Snyder ranks as one of the most uncomfortable talk-show moments in history, even for a show famous for uncomfortable talk-show moments (Tom to Charles Manson during a jailhouse interview: "Get off the space shuttle, Charlie!") A belligerent Lydon attacks Snyder and denounces rock 'n' roll (and punk), all in the same breath. Keith Levene bums cigarettes from the chain-smoking host, who was rumored to have blown up during commercial, screaming, "Why the fuck did you come on a talk show if you didn't want to talk?!" Another fine PiL moment is the band's mimed performance of "Poptones" on *American Bandstand.*

4. *CHiPs,* "Battle of the Bands"

Ponch and Jon have to stop a gang of renegade punks from ruining the Battle of the Bands. After a spectacular chase and car crash, Ponch races inside the Battle to save the day with his inspirational rendition of Kool & the Gang's "Celebration."

5. Elvis Costello on *Saturday Night Live*

Booked as a last-minute replacement for the Sex Pistols, Elvis Costello & the Attractions caused a stir during their 1977 appearance on *SNL* when Elvis stopped the band at the top of their hit, "Less Than Zero," screaming, "Stop! Stop! I'm sorry, ladies and gentlemen—there's no reason to do this song here." The band then went into "Radio, Radio." Producer Lorne Michaels was so impressed, he banned Elvis from the show for next 12 years.

6. The Dickies on *CPO Sharkey*

Don Rickles is hardly the first name one associates with punk rock. But in 1978 *CPO Sharkey*'s "punk episode" showed the dapper Don pogoing with a bunch of liberty-spiked punks as the Dickies performed "Hideous." Alice Bag and Kid Congo Powers also make cameos in the audience, which was made up of Masque regulars.

7. GG Allin on *The Jerry Springer Show*, *Geraldo*, and *Morton Downey Jr.*

Littleton, New Hampshire's least favorite son will go down in infamy for his antics both onstage and off. Fortunately, a handful of talk-show appearances (and nonappearances) will preserve GG's legacy for future generations. The night before he was to appear on conservative talk-show host Morton Downey Jr.'s show, Allin trashed his hotel room. Due to the resulting arrest, Allin was unable to attend the taping, which prompted an animated discussion from Downey and the audience. GG's appearance on *Geraldo* was different matter entirely. When asked why he felt the need to defecate in front of a live audience, he replied, "My body is the rock 'n' roll temple and my flesh, blood, and body fluids are the communion."

8. Patti Smith on *Wonderama*

Another odd pairing is punk rock and children's television. Patti Smith appeared on the Sunday morning kids' show *Wonderama* to perform the Bruce Springsteen–penned "Because the Night." Kids in the audience each received a Lender's Bagelette necklace and a Patti Smith single.

9. Punk Chips Ahoy Commercial

Nothing screams, "Smash the system!" quite like a giant Claymation chocolate-chip cookie flanked by members of the Casualties bouncing down the street shouting, "Oi! Oi! Oi!"

10. *The Muppet Show* with Debbie Harry

Episode 509 of *The Muppet Show* ranks as one of the strangest, right next to the one featuring Alice Cooper's performance of "Welcome to My Nightmare." Debbie Harry hosts, and does a commanding duet with Kermit the Frog on "Rainbow Connection" as well as the Blondie hits "Call Me" and "One Way or Another."

11. *Bosom Buddies*, "Double Date"

The screwball antics of sometimes–drag queens shift into high gear when a real-life punk rocker with purple hair is thrown into the mix. Kip's first date with Sonny is made all the more uncomfortable when Ruth's niece and Henry's date Cicilly turns out to be a Beki Bondage look-alike that goes by the name Andrea Pus. Hijinks ensue. There's a good reason why Tom Hanks has kept *Bosom Buddies* from ever going into syndication.

6 MEMORABLE QUOTES FROM THE *QUINCY, M.E.* PUNK EPISODE

The *Quincy* punk episode is a holy grail among tape traders and punk rock historians. The episode features a band that's a dead ringer for the Germs—and some of the greatest dialogue this side of *Dragnet*.

1. ADRIAN MERCER: You're not really saying that music can kill, are you?

    QUINCY: Yes, I am. I believe that the music I heard is a killer. It's a killer of hope. It's a killer of spirit. The music I heard said that life was cheap and that murder and suicide was okay.

2. DR. EMILY HANOVER: She comes home and she finds her daughter burning cigarette holes in her arm. Shredding her

clothes to bits, taking pills, and locking herself in her room listening to that violence-oriented punk rock music that does nothing but reinforce all those bad feelings!

3. Dr. Emily Hanover: You tell a vulnerable kid over and over again that life isn't worth living, that violence is its own reward, with the kind of intensity this music has, and you just might convince her.

4. Club promoter: Maybe you want to take over as the opening act? You paint a target on your head and I'll arrange it.
   Quincy: I want to find an innocent girl.
   Club promoter: You won't find anybody innocent here.

5. Random punk: If I knew where that girl was, I sure as hell wouldn't tell a cop! Because that's all you are, man, is a dog without a uniform!

6. Molly: C'mon, your face needs some PUNKING UP!

List compiled and annotated by Aaron Lefkove.

UNCLE FLOYD'S FAVORITE PUNK BANDS (THAT APPEARED ON HIS SHOW)

1. Ramones
2. Barney Rubble & the Cunt Stubble
3. Fats Deacon & the Dumbwaiters
4. Dead Boys
5. Phoebe & the Females
6. Joey Miserable & the Worms
7. Connie & the Linguistics
8. The Stickmen

9. The Rebel Rousers

10. The Chuckleheads

"Uncle" Floyd Vivino produced and hosted his own "kids'" show in the New York–New Jersey area from 1974 until 2001. During its 6,000-plus episode run, the Ramones, Misfits, Dead Boys, Pussy Galore, Agnostic Front, and bands too numerous to name were guests on The Uncle Floyd Show, *which taped on the same set as* Romper Room. *Uncle Floyd has made his living as a comedian and piano player in burlesque, and for 40 years has worked the Catskills and Pocono mountain resorts. He also has his own weekly Italian-language radio show.*

CHRIS STEIN'S 10 FAVORITE MOVIE WEAPONS

This sounds like its an easy task: Forget about it, as the fella says—it's really tough! James Bond films alone qualify as a whole subcategory. The field is dominated by many current films where the issue is "forced"—that is, there is an effort made to deliver bigger, weirder, etc., weapons. Despite my enjoying a great many of these modern offerings (for example, Gogo Yubari's chain-ball device from *Kill Bill: Vol. 1*), there is some subtle element lost in the overthinking that has gone into their creation. Here are some of my favorites:

1. The "kris" blade switchblade from the original Henry Fonda version of *Twelve Angry Men*. This represents a bygone era, when one could walk into a "novelty" store on Times Square and come out with one of these things. The one in the movie has a great dragon or serpent motif on the handle, if I remember correctly.

2. Dirty Harry's .44 revolver. In spite of being relatively lo-tech these days, its influence and cache can't be denied.

3. Travis Bickle's forearm pistol. The bit where he makes the slide out of a drawer pull is inspirational. Who thought of that?

4. The ankh pendant knife from *The Hunger*. This is the ultimate piece of goth jewelry. I have seen many versions of it over the years, most of them too ornate.

5. Similarly, the crucifix gravity knife from the Willie Nelson western vehicle *Barbarosa* is a great objet d'art that I have never seen reproduced.

6. Oddjob's deadly derby from *Goldfinger*. What can one say here? I know I must have read the book, but I can't recall whether this thing was thought up by Fleming. The idea that this dude could cut someone's head off with his hat brim is somehow oddly convincing, though.

7. The *Blade Runner* gun. There is a whole cult that surrounds this particular film prop. There are Web sites devoted to its study, as well as expensive models of it. The Plager Katsumate Series-D might be the first "signature" non-ray-gun gun created for a film—it undoubtedly falls into some sort of "first" category. It has been followed by all manner of (mostly sci-fi-) related firearms, e.g., the pulse rifles from the *Alien* series, etc.

8. The flying guillotine, from the *Flying Guillotine* series of martial arts films. How can any mayhem enthusiast not love the flying guillotine? It rocks! Possibly related to the derby, perhaps, but still its own thing.

9. There's no getting around it: Freddy's glove from *The Nightmare on Elm Street* franchise is dumb but still a great thing. I've seen a really high-end version built around a Willie G. motorcycle glove, made by knife maker Pat Crawford

10. Finally, from a more recent film, I was really taken with the gun from *Sympathy for Lady Vengeance*, the third in the *Vengeance* trilogy by great Korean director Chan-wook Park.

This is a really elegant homemade two-shot pistol that is worked into the film's plot nicely. As far as a contemporary offering, it is in its own genre and away from the forced nature of many similar modern Hollywood screen weapons.

After looking back, I see that I avoided lightsabers, phasers, and the like. I guess I am a classicist!

Noted musician, producer, and photographer Chris Stein is the guitarist and a founding member of Blondie. As a producer, he has worked with the Gun Club and Iggy Pop, among many others.

MICK FARREN'S PUNK MOVIE LIST

1. *Taxi Driver*

"Are you looking at me?" Martin Scorsese's alienated, isolated, and ultimately homicidal Travis Bickel—as played by Robert De Niro at his most magnificent—was released just as punk was finding its feet in its Doc Martens, and provided not only the perfect antihero for the new movement, but also a unique haircut as De Niro shaved a Mohican into his scalp as his personality disintegrated.

2. *Apocalypse Now*

Francis Ford Coppola's indictment of a war conducted on Jimi Hendrix and LSD, and the metaphoric journey up the river to where the Heart of Darkness was waiting—in the awesome persona of an atavistic and bloated Marlon Brando—resonated with all those punks too young to have been drafted to Vietnam, but who wouldn't have minded (in their dreams) tripping through the jungle with an M16. The film also gave the Clash the classic song title "Charlie Don't Surf."

3. *Texas Chainsaw Massacre*

The cult horror movie that told the bloody tale of how five friends visiting grandpa's house are hunted down by a chainsaw-wielding killer and his family of grave-robbing cannibals offered the same kind of scare-the-squares shock that punk would adopt a year or so later. In the malignant and monstrous character of Leatherface, director Tobe Hooper made it abundantly clear that no punk icon could ever be too extreme.

4. *The Wild One*

As the bike-gang hoodlum leader Johnny Strabler, Marlon Brando established the uniform of black leather jacket and beat-up blue jeans that would serve as a template for every malcontent greaser from Eddie Cochran to Sid Vicious to the Ramones to mass murderer Perry Smith from Truman Capote's *In Cold Blood*, and on to an endless line, generation after generation, of rebels and renegades. And, of course, the film posed the classic square's question, and supplied the equally classic punk answer.

"Johnny, what are you rebelling against?"

"What have you got?"

5. *Belle de jour*

Catherine Deneuve's rebellion in Luis Buñuel's erotic masterpiece was a little different to that of Travis Bickle or the leather-jacketed Marlon. Here, Deneuve plays a frigid housewife staging a one-woman insurrection against the social and sexual constriction of middle-class values, morals, and conventions by willingly and willfully offering herself for humiliation and debasement by working as a prostitute during her otherwise suffocating afternoons. The vicious young pimp, played by Pierre Clémenti—with his gold teeth, walking cane, and long leather coat—became a Rimbaud-style icon for the more cosmopolitan punks of a decade later.

6. *Sid & Nancy*

The complaint has always been that it "wasn't really like that," and the film version of the short but intense—and heavily drugged—relationship of Sex Pistol Sid Vicious and his girlfriend Nancy Spungen may not have been historically correct in every visual detail in the recreated subworlds of London and New York at the end of the 1970s. But it faithfully recreated the basic ethos of early punk and, if nothing else, director Alex Cox proved that doomed lovers could come in every conceivable style.

7. *A Streetcar Named Desire*

Marlon again, this time as Stanley Kowalski—soaked to the skin, T-shirt shredded, screaming for Stella in rage, anguish, and frustration. Tennessee Williams' play was a revolution in itself, first on the Broadway stage, and then on the screen, but the single image of Brando in his ripped T-shirt, reproduced by Richard Hell almost three decades later, was the total foundation for the look of punk.

8. *The Hills Have Eyes*

A family on vacation in the desert, close to an abandoned cold war–era nuclear test site, stray away from the safety of the highway; their vehicle breaks down; and they become the prey of one malevolent family of inbred mutant cannibals. Released in 1977, at exactly the same time that the mass media was trumpeting the horror of the new punk phenomenon, Wes Craven's bloody low-budget horror classic couldn't help but become a both a cult film and a metaphor for the times.

9. *Natural Born Killers*

Mickey and Mallory Knox are Oliver Stone's concept of second-generation punk—the future of a world with no future. These figurative children of Sid Vicious and Nancy Spungen are not doomed outlaw lovers; they are murderous outlaw lovers, riding the imaginary and highly psychedelic Route 666, slaughtering at random, as a slavering and wholly unprincipled mass media turn them into folk heroes of reality TV.

10. *Kiss of Death*

Richard Widmark, as the psychotically giggling murderous sociopath Tommy Udo, who enjoys killing old ladies in wheelchairs while looking so hep and super-sharp in striped suit, black shirt, and white tie, is perhaps rivaled only by James Cagney as Cody Jarrett in *White Heat* as the very first film-noir inkling that something like punk would ever, some day, become part of the popular culture.

JIM JARMUSCH'S 25 PRE-PUNK FILMS WITH "PUNK ATTITUDE"

The following 25 pre-punk films, in my opinion, have "punk attitude," whatever that means (with respect and apologies to Don Letts). These are in no particular order, and of course there are many, many more. So if you don't get the connection, I suggest you make your own damn list.

1. *Zero for Conduct* (Jean Vigo, 1933)
2. *Towers Open Fire* (William S. Burroughs & Antony Balch, 1963)
3. *Breathless* (Jean-Luc Godard, 1960)
4. *Monkey Business* (The Marx Brothers, directed by Norman Z. McLeod, 1931)
5. *Gun Crazy* (Joseph H. Lewis, 1950)
6. *Un Chien Andalou* (Louis Buñuel, 1929)
7. *The Wild One* (László Benedek, 1953)
8. *Accattone* (Pier Paolo Pasolini, 1961)

9. *Johnny Cool* (William Asher, 1963)

10. *Freaks* (Tod Browning, 1932)

11. *Beware of a Holy Whore* (Rainer Werner Fassbinder, 1970)

12. *Tokyo Drifter* (Seijun Suzuki, 1966)

13. *Rebel Without a Cause* (Nicholas Ray, 1955)

14. *Chant d'Amour* (Jean Genet, 1950)

15. *Beat Girl* (a.k.a. *Wild for Kicks*) (Edmond T. Gréville, 1960)

16. *Le Samouraï* (Jean-Pierre Melville, 1967)

17. *Saturday Night and Sunday Morning* (Karel Reisz, 1960)

18. *Point Blank* (John Boorman, 1967)

19. *Scarface* (Howard Hawks & Richard Rosson, 1932)

20. *Danger: Diabolik* (Mario Bava, 1968)

21. *Pickup on South Street* (Samuel Fuller, 1953)

22. *The Tenth Victim* (Elio Petri, 1965)

23. *Performance* (Donald Cammell & Nicolas Roeg, 1970)

24. *A Clockwork Orange* (Stanley Kubrick, 1971)

25. *Faster, Pussycat! Kill! Kill!* (Russ Meyer, 1965)

Born in Akron, Ohio, director Jim Jarmusch lives and works in New York. His films include Permanent Vacation *(1980),* Stranger than Paradise *(1984),* Down by Law *(1986),* Mystery Train *(1989),* Night on Earth *(1991),* Dead Man *(1995),* Year of the Horse *(1997),* Ghost Dog: The Way of the Samurai *(1999),* Coffee and Cigarettes *(2003),* Broken Flowers *(2005) and the short film "Int. Trailer. Night." (2002).*

LEEE BLACK CHILDERS' "TOP 10 MOVIES THAT MADE ME AN ALCOHOLIC"

In the ever so polite parlance of today's society, "I am a recovering alcoholic." In the language of my day, "I am a drunk on the wagon." Either way, I have realized that all those "watchdogs" that blame the popular media for all forms of juvenile delinquency are apparently, in my case, perfectly correct. Although morally anemic and certainly amusing entertainment, those movies that graphically depict the horrors of alcohol abuse are not truly suitable here. Therefore, there is no need for *Valley of the Dolls* or *I'll Cry Tomorrow* or *The Days of Wine and Roses*—too easy. Instead, I have compiled a list of films that truly create an intoxicating (sic) image of booze—one suitable for underage consumption.

1. *Dumbo*

The fabulously psychedelic "pink elephant" sequence of a drunk Dumbo and mouse, followed instantly by the singing crows as a hangover, is a mischievous masterpiece.

2. *All About Eve*

Practically any Bette Davis movie will do, but in this case, she employs her very dry martini with all the skill of an expert knife thrower.

3. *The Thin Man*

This is the drinking man's guide to a hilarious marriage, starring William Powell and Myrna Loy as detectives Nick and Nora Charles. Sample dialogue:

NORA: As a matter of fact, my husband is working on a new case right now.
REPORTER: What case?
NORA: A case of scotch.

4. *Some Like It Hot*

Nothing is as glamorous as a silver flask slipping deliciously from Marilyn Monroe's garter.

5. *From Russia with Love*

"Shaken, not stirred"—a phrase that has entered our language to imply sophistication and devilish charm.

6. *China Seas*

Or any of the movies where lovable drunks are impervious to harm. In this case, Robert Benchley is aboard a small ship in a typhoon, blissfully unaware of a runaway grand piano that repeatedly just misses crushing him to death.

7. *The Maltese Falcon*

Sydney Greenstreet to Humphrey Bogart: "You begin well, sir. I distrust a man who says 'when.' He's got to be careful not to drink too much, because he's not to be trusted when he does."

8. *Cat on a Hot Tin Roof*

Paul Newman demonstrates how to be supremely sexy while loving and desiring his booze more than he does Elizabeth Taylor.

9. *The Razor's Edge*

Liquor as the seducer. The Scene: Paris, the Ritz, after dinner. The cast: Anne Baxter as Sophie, hopeless drunk trying to go straight. Gene Tierney as the evil and selfish rival for Tyrone Power's affections. Clifton Webb as Elliott Templeton, amoral sophisticate.

Tierney: Oh, Sophie, I have to go out for about half an hour.
     Will you be a dear and tell Uncle Elliott that his case of
     Żubrówka has arrived? I've put it right here by the window.

     Sophie's eyes glaze. The next day her body is fished out of the Seine!

10. *Titanic*

Any of the many versions of this story always features industrialist George Widener gallantly dressed in full evening dress with his valet at his side and his fine brandy in his hand as he meets the rising, and deadly, water.

Honorable Mention

Anything by Ernest Hemingway with Ava Gardner in it.

Naturally, I have chosen films from my youth; you may find any number of more contemporary examples, such as the "Green Fairy" number from *Moulin Rouge*. Equally valid lists could be compiled to highlight drugs, smoking, sex, rock 'n' roll, or prostitution. Please keep in mind that I do not consider any of these lifestyle choices in the least wrong.

Lee Black Childers was a regular photographer on the scene at Andy Warhol's Factory, Max's Kansas City, and CBGB; his shots of David Bowie, Iggy Pop, the Ramones, and the New York Dolls have achieved iconic status. Childers can still be found today snapping pics of the next wave of up-and-coming rockers and rollers.

RICHARD MELTZER'S BEATNIK ROOTS OF PUNK: A READING LIST

1. Ray Bremser, *Black Is Black Blues*

A supreme asshole and fuckup shamelessly scams the forgiveness of the gal he loves for having been such an asshole and a fuckup.

2. William Burroughs, *The Last Words of Dutch Schultz* (U.K. edition)

This is the literal source of Throbbing Gristle. *Note*: The U.S. edition has snazzy pics but doesn't contain the verbatim text of Dutch's final sputterings.

3. Gregory Corso, *An Accidental Autobiography*

Forty years of groovy/nasty/hilarious letters from the brattiest of beatnik brats—he fucking knew *how*.

4. Diane di Prima, *Dinners and Nightmares*

Lydia Lunch slept here. Featuring a recipe for "menstrual pudding."

5. William Everson, *Man-Fate*

God equals pussy, see? And pussy of course equals God. What else is there to say?

6. Bob Kaufman, *Does the Secret Mind Whisper?*

The hottest (and coolest!) ten-page run-on sentence you ever saw.

7. Jack Kerouac, *Big Sur*

This is *the* great now-I-begin-to-die novel. Try as he might, Jack can't stop drinking. Demons, demons, demons . . .

8. Philip Lamantia, *Narcotica*

Terrific photo-pics of Phil shooting smack, then showing off his veins, *smiling*.

9. Jack Micheline, *River of Red Wine*

Okay, so this guy from the Bronx is named Harvey Silver—who would he *rather* be? And what, specifically, would he like as his calling card?

10. H. D. Moe, *Tuba Petunia*

Can "anyman" write poetry? Dunno. But "babbling armpits gothic carnival / quantum ochone ywis jhwh / tomb beehives determined surprise / ottering umlauts" is proof enough that David Moe sure can.

11. Peter Orlovsky, *Clean Asshole Poems & Smiling Vegetable Songs*

You don't believe that's the real title? 'Tis! With unintentional misspellings *galore*.

12. Lew Welch, *Ring of Bone*

After writing his masterpiece, "Song of the Turkey Buzzard," Lew split for the deep woods to shoot himself and be EATEN BY VULTURES. Wow. Too bad his stepson was Huey Lewis.

13. John Wieners, *The Hotel Wentley Poems*

Razor blades scrape my soul . . . therefore I am.

A towering figure of Anglo-American cultural etc., Richard Meltzer is the father of rock criticism, the uncle of pizza criticism, and the second cousin of sumo criticism. He's written lyrics for Blue Oyster Cult, fronted the punk band Vom, and authored 27 books, including The Night (Alone), A Whore Just Like the Rest, Tropic of Nipples, *and* The Count of Monte Cristo. *He hopes he's getting paid for his list ('cuz you never know, eh?).*

GARY LUCAS'S 5 PUNK LITERARY GENIUSES

1. Wyndham Lewis

Brilliant English modernist painter, polemicist, poet, playwright, and novelist, Lewis was the founder of the Vorticist art movement (housed appropriately enough originally in the Rebel Art Centre in London) right before World War I. He is the author of *The Apes of God*, a savage satire on the pretensions of the Bloomsbury middlebrow poetry and art clique, and also of provocatively titled nonfiction such as *The Jews: Are They Human?*—an attack on anti-Semitism.

2. Jim Thompson

Thompson is the American noir-pulp author/avatar of experimental and transgressive men's magazine serial classics such of *The Killer Inside Me*, *Savage Night*, and *The Grifters*—poet of the small-time con, the hot-sheets motel, the cheap blond floozy, the seamy underside of the American dream

3. Terry Southern

Ultra-black humorist; droll prankster; taboo breaker; and outrageous, guffaw-inducing artist, Southern is the author of *Candy* (with Mason Hoffenberg), *Dr. Strangelove*, *Blue Movie*, and of course, the unforgettable short story "The Blood of a Wig" with its unspeakable riff on the Kennedy assassination

4. J. G. Ballard

Ballard conjures dystopian waking nightmares in the guise of science fiction, offering Burroughsian glimpses into the yawning chasm of the coming global technological clusterfuck/meltdown. He is never better than in his seminal, unsurpassed fusion of sex and metal titled *Crash*.

5. Boris Vian

This French jazz poet, trumpet player, singer, and writer achieves a position at the top of the (slag) heap for *I Spit on Your Grave* (original French title: *J'irai Cracher sur vos tombes*) a pastiche of hard-boiled American noir fiction written under the pseudonym of Vernon Sullivan that caused Vian to pay a fine of 100,000 francs for the 100,000 copies sold of this allegedly obscene, twisted, neo-Faulknerian misogynist masterpiece of miscegenation and malicious mayhem in Mississippi.

Gary Lucas is a New York guitar hero whose psychedelic pyro-technics, barbed-wire bottleneck, and beatnik musings can be heard with his band Gods & Monsters, which also features Billy Ficca from Television and Ernie Brooks of the Modern Lovers (and, more recently, Jerry Harrison from Talking Heads). Gary was also a member of Captain Beefheart's Magic Band, which places him in a rarefied stratum, indeed.

7 PUNK ROCK BANDS THAT PAY HOMAGE TO—OR TRASH—LESTER BANGS

Lester Conway Bangs (1948–82) was a wacky, fucked-up brilliant music writer and musician.

1. Bangs is mentioned in R.E.M.'s 1988 hit, "It's the End of the World as We Know It (And I Feel Fine)."

2. The Dillinger Four mention Bangs in the song, "Our Science Is Tight."

3. The Ramones reference Bangs on their album *Pleasant Dreams*, in the beloved track "It's Not My Place (In the 9 to 5 World)."

4. Ghost of Lester Bangs is a Long Island, New York, punk band.

5. The song "Lester Sands" appears on the Buzzcocks' 2003 self-titled CD. "Sands" is a reference to Bangs, whose criticism is described as "a drop in the ocean."

6. Baltimore band the Slumlords wrote a track entitled "Lester Bangs" on their 2006 CD *On the Stremph*. Lyricist Jeff Perlin sings about the music industry, "Lester Bangs, be glad you're dead, 'cause all this shit we're being fed."

7. Horseshoe wrote a song called "Lester Bangs," which is on their album *King of the World*. The chorus is, "I hate you almost as much / As I hate me."

WAYNE KRAMER'S LUCKY 13 RECENT READINGS

These *are* the fun books.

1. Christopher Hitchens, *God Is Not Great*
This book is even more strident than Sam Harris on the evils of religious dogma.

2. Charles Olson, *The Collected Poems of Charles Olson*
The archetype for all postmodern poetry.

3. Michael Shermer, *The Science of Good and Evil*
Answers for some of my big questions.

4. Michael Shermer, *Why People Believe Weird Things*
More answers to why folks act so nuts in this world.

6. J. M. Coetzee, *Waiting for the Barbarians*
Just superb prose.

7. Sam Harris, *The End of Faith*
The heavyweight champion of reason.

8. George P. Pelecanos, *King Suckerman*

Pelecanos, along with Elmore Leonard, is one of our greatest living crime writers.

9. William James, *The Varieties of Religious Experience*

The first book to scientifically study issues of faith.

10. Norman Cantor, *In the Wake of the Plague: The Black Death and the World It Made*

How sixteenth-century ignorance and superstition decimated most of Europe.

11. Pun Plamondon, *Lost from the Ottawa: The Story of the Journey Back*

My dear brother's epic journey from orphan to White Panther to Native American elder.

12. Rafael Alvarez, *The Wire: Truth Be Told*

The inside scoop on the greatest show on television. I also have both DVD box sets.

13. David Beresford and Peter Maas, *Ten Men Dead: The Story of the 1981 Irish Hunger Strike*

The run-up to today's power sharing in Ireland.

Wayne Kramer is a songwriter, producer, and composer whose reputation writing music for television and film risks supplanting his legend as one of rock's greatest guitarists. Wayne was the teenage founder and flamboyant lead guitarist of the controversial '60s band the MC5, who are widely recognized as the prototype for punk rock and heavy metal. He spent the '80s in New York City, where he teamed up with the infamous Johnny Thunders for a short-lived but headline-grabbing punk rock supergroup, Gang War. Soon after, he co-wrote the acclaimed R&B musical The Last Words of Dutch Schultz; *then he joined the revolutionary acid funk outfit Was (Not Was). Wayne moved to Los Angeles in 1994,*

*signed with Epitaph Records, and recorded four albums in as
many years. In 2001, Wayne launched MuscleTone Records with
his flagship solo release* Adult World. *He regularly writes with and
produces upstart rock 'n' roll bands, and regularly tours the world
as a musician, speaker, and activist.*

CODY GOODFELLOW'S 10 CYBERPUNK ESSENTIALS

Cyberpunk was a revolutionary school of literature that
brought the worldly, anti-authority DIY aesthetics of punk rock
into the naive nerd's paradise of science fiction, and turned it
out on the street.

1. William S. Burroughs, *Naked Lunch*

First published by France's Olympia Press in 1959, *Naked Lunch*
dropped on America like an atom bomb in 1962 with its release
by Grove Press, and was summarily banned throughout the U.S.
While *Naked Lunch* revels in drugs, pedophilia, fetishism, and
paranoid fantasies, its cut-up structure savaged the very foundation of linear storytelling.

2. Anthony Burgess, *A Clockwork Orange*

Linguist Burgess turned the traditional dystopia on its ear with
his picture of a degraded near-future Britain as a playground for
amoral thug Alec and his vicious yet dapper droogs. Alec's tale
of sin and redemption by brainwashing condemns government
oppression by gleefully celebrating the freedom to commit rape
and murder.

3. Norman Spinrad, *Agent of Chaos*

A seemingly standard throwaway rocket opera, Spinrad's second
novel is less bitingly critical than his later work, but the hero-

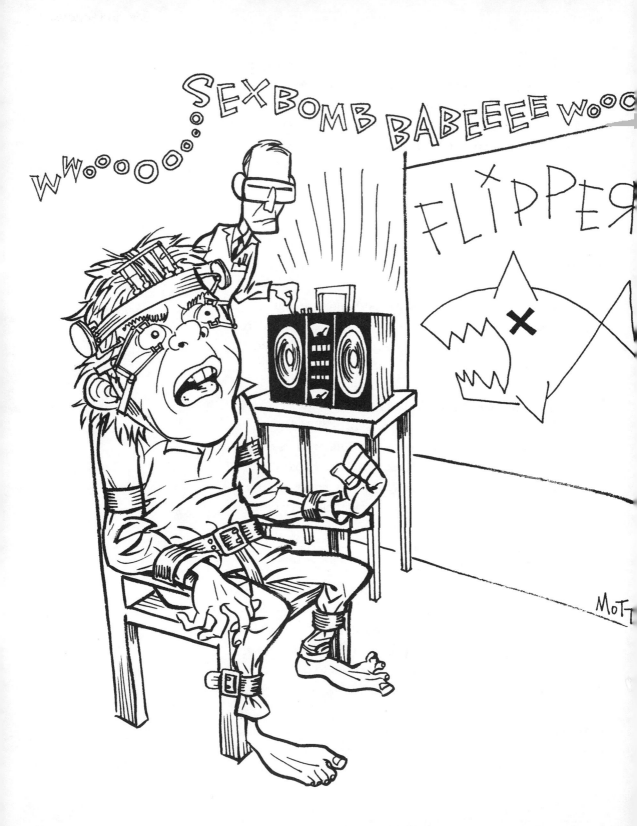

as-anarchist element framed a unique fusion of cynicism and idealism, and introduced the revolution-versus-stasis dynamic that gave cyberpunk its philosophical training wheels.

4. Philip K. Dick, *Do Androids Dream of Electric Sheep?*

The source for the seminal cyberpunk film *Blade Runner*.

5. J. G. Ballard, *Atrocity Exhibition*

Another obscenity milestone, the first U.S. edition of Ballard's most infamous book was printed and immediately shredded by Nelson Doubleday. With audacious vignettes like "Plan for the Assassination of Jacqueline Kennedy" and "Why I Want to Fuck Ronald Reagan," *Atrocity Exhibition* trumped Burroughs' excesses, and held a mirror up to an audience of fetishistic androids.

6. Bruce Sterling, *Artificial Kid*

No one author worked harder or argued more forcibly to legitimize cyberpunk than "Citizen Bruce." With his *Cheap Truth* newsletter and manifestos, convention panel diatribes and a cyberpunk anthology, *Mirrorshades*, Sterling aggressively promoted the cyberpunk word and hacker culture as a model for sci-fi lit and a Big Brother–free future.

7. John Shirley, *City Come A-Walkin'*

The man who put the "punk" in the cyberpunk and splatterpunk movements, Shirley fronted punk bands Obsession and the Panther Moderns. Intimately informed by the realities of outlaw rock-star madness and drug abuse, Shirley's work provided the map of the gutter that later authors cribbed from.

8. K. W. Jeter, *Dr. Adder*

A one-time Dick protégé, Jeter hunted for ten years before finding a publisher for his cult hit about a black-market plastic surgeon who customizes his clients with cybernetic weapons and perverse new sexual organs.

9. Neal Stephenson, *Snow Crash*

Arguably the last word in cyberpunk, *Snow Crash* applied the keyboard skills of a bona fide computer programmer and adroit postmodern fragmentation to what had already become a rote genre formula, to push cyberpunk past the edges of its manifesto and into the realm of black satire. Gray computers between our ears.

10. William Gibson, *Neuromancer*

The crown jewel of cyberpunk, Gibson's debut novel won the Hugo, Nebula and Philip K. Dick awards, and earned critical legitimacy for the cyberpunk school. *Neuromancer* combined Burroughs' hallucinatory prose-poetry and Dick's tight delivery with a Byzantine mosaic of surreal plot devices to perfect the endlessly copied cyberthriller formula. Ironically, Gibson himself did not own a computer, and composed *Neuromancer* on a manual typewriter.

Cody Goodfellow was born in 1970 in San Diego, California. He is the author of the science-fiction/horror epics Ravenous Dusk *and* Radiant Dawn. *As well, his work has appeared in* Cemetery Dance, Hot Blood #13, *and* The Vault of Punk Horror. *He is currently at work on* Perfect Union, *his next novel, and* Seminar, *a feature film.*

JOHN SKIPP'S SPLATTERPUNK LIST-O-RAMA

Also known as "the *other* punk literature"—kind of like "the *other* white meat!"—the subversive hardcore horror fiction called splatterpunk emerged in the mid-1980's to (A) fuck in the punch bowl, (B) dance all night, (C) drape the dining room with loops of intestinal festoonery, (D) stir the soup with whatever dripping socio-political/metaphysical/horny-ass carnographic meat-spoon was closest to hand, and (E) generally degrade the table manners of polite society, while upping the voltage on what could be said and done in the context of modern horror fiction.

This is all bullshit, of course. We were serious writers—stop laughing; we *were!*—out to carefully examine this world of hurt, address the damage, and probe the limits of the imaginable. (If you asked Clive Barker, he'd say, "*There are no limits.*")

We were also havin' waaaaaaay too much fun, in the time-honored shock-art tradition, surfin' on a blood-flume of love and gnosis that runs easily from Shakespeare's *Titus Andronicus* to any given *South Park* episode.

It was all about taking high-art aspirations (like quality and depth) and low-art ambitions (like cheap, filthy entertainment) and then slamming them into each other at 1,000 miles per hour, and seeing what squirts out.

Some of the moist, seminal books in this canon include:

1. Clive Barker, *The Books of Blood*, Vols. 1–6
2. David J. Schow, ed., *Silver Scream*
3. John Skipp and Craig Spector, eds., *Book of the Dead* and *Still Dead*
4. Joe R. Lansdale, *The Drive-In*
5. David J. Schow, *Seeing Red* and *Lost Angels*
6. John Skipp and Craig Spector, *The Light at the End*, *The Cleanup*, and *The Scream*

That's what I'd call the genuine splatterpunk starter kit. It's the shit people were actually reading—and yelling at each other about, in public—by the time Dave Schow came up with the funny word itself.

Sorry I'm on my own dumb list, but there's really no way around it. Plus, it shows what a class act I am!

Wanna fuck in the punch bowl?

ME, TOO!!!

John Skipp remains one of America's most cheerfully perplexing Renaissance mutants: New York Times *best-selling author–turned-filmmaker, satirist, cultural crusader, musical pornographer, splatterpunk poster child, purveyor of cuddly metaphysics, interpretive dancer, and all-around bon vivant. With* The Long Last Call, Conscience, *and the award-winning* Mondo Zombie, *Skipp has returned to the front ranks of modern horror fiction. He lives in Southern California.*

DO THE HAMMERLOCK: HANDSOME DICK MANITOBA'S TOP 24 WRESTLING RULE BREAKERS

1. Fred Blassie

The classy one . . . One of the coolest humans to ever grace God's green Earth . . . Sharpened teeth for biting . . . Bit with the best of 'em . . . Amazing hair, best clothes, BEST RAP EVER!! Matching pastel outfits. Would do anything to win! Had no shame . . . All this at about 5'10" and 215 pounds . . . Was also a great manager of champions . . . Presided at the opening of Manitoba's Bar, January 14, 1999 . . . Made a classic movie with Andy Kaufman (*My Breakfast with Blassie*) . . . Starred in an episode of *The Dick Van Dyke Show* (as himself) . . . Do you need more?

2. Wladek "Killer" Kowalski

"Tore" off Yukon Eric's ear during a match . . . Vicious . . . Savage . . . Wrassled from the '40s through the '70s . . . A crew of Nick Tosches, Richard Meltzer, Scott "Top Ten" Kempner, Mr. Manitoba, and some friends stood and cheered in the early '70s in NY's Madison Square Garden as the Killer beat Bruno Sammartino senseless . . . into a bloody pulp . . . as the other 19,000 people gasped in horror. . . . A highlight of my life . . .

3. The Valiant Bros.

Hair and clothes second only to Blassie's . . . Their rap might have been as good as anybody's . . . EVER! . . . Managed by Captain Lou Albano, these guys were so coooool that Handsome Dick Manitoba "lifted" his name from "Handsome Jimmy Valiant" . . . Luscious Johnny woulda been good too . . . Luscious Dick Manitoba . . . Rock stars parading as wrestlers . . .

4. Mick Foley/Mankind/Cactus Jack

All three personas, all great, credited to the wrasslin' brilliance known as . . . Mick Foley . . . There never was a man who "donated" his body, with as much wrestling abandon, who gave SO FUCKIN' MUCH TO HIS ART/SPORT, as Mick Foley!

5. The Sheik

Although I never saw him wrestle live, the photos, the stories, the history, are what bloody heel (bad guy) legends are made of. You really can't argue if someone claims that the Sheik was the "Baddest of the Bad" . . . Hidden sharpened pencils, razor blades, throwing fire (??!!), and legendary feuds with Fred Blassie and Bobo Brazil were highlights of this evil genius's career. (And Sharky, my editor, LOVES HIM!)

6. Terry Funk

In the same category as Mick Foley and the Sheik. You can flip-flop Nos. 4, 5, and 6. Total abandon . . . Total devotion, total excitement . . . GAVE EVERYTHING to the squared circle. Made some movies. His Japanese barbed-wire death match against Foley is a classic.

7. Dick the Bruiser

8. Reggie "Crusher" Lisowski

9. John "the Maniac" Tolos

10. "Handsome" Harley Race

11. Maurice "Mad Dog" Vachon

12. Johnny Valentine

The last six were guys I always read about as a kid. Never saw 'em live. They were barrel-chested, beer-guzzling, barroom-brawling, nonsteroid legends from other parts of the U.S. of A. Staples in the wrestling magazines I collected. Mythical anti-heroes. Cooler than Dylan. Tolos I actually did see one time at the Garden; he lost to Bruno. When I told Richard Meltzer that I loved John Tolos and wanted to express my feelings for this "heel," Richard, in his infinite wisdom, simply told me to make a REALLY BIG SIGN that just said . . . "JOHN." I did. Tolos, in true bad-guy fashion, hated it!

13. Stan "the Man" Stasiak

Master of the heart punch . . . Managed by the Grand Wizard . . . WWWF champion . . . A favorite of writer Nick Tosches . . . Richard Meltzer wrote his obit.

14. Jerry "the King" Lawler

Hospitalized Andy Kauffman!

15. Stan "the Lariat" Hansen

Broke Bruno's neck!

16. Ric Flair

Did the equivalent of hitting 500 home runs in baseball . . . or winning 300 games . . . Was very, very good, maybe GREAT, for a very long time . . . Takes a bump as good as anyone . . . Sells it in a game where selling it is what it's all about . . . Had good hair and outfits till he modernized too much lately . . . Nevertheless, an all-time great.

17. The Destroyer

The first great masked man, and maybe the greatest one ever. My apologies to Mil Mascaras and Santo . . . Feud with Blassie was the stuff wrestling legend is made of . . . HUGE star in Japan . . . When he stopped off at Manitoba's Bar, years ago, to help celebrate the bar's anniversary, I thought the Japanese kids waiting in line were gonna have a heart attack. . . . THEY WERE BOWING! . . . Had dinner with him . . . He ate dinner with his mask on. . . . Keeps his mask on when going through Japan's airports . . . My kinda guy!

18. Gorgeous George

Babe Ruth, Elvis Presley of heels. Started it all . . . The dyed blond hair, the bragging persona . . . The perfume . . . None cooler . . . We all (heels) owe this man a BIG DEBT OF GRATITUDE. . . . Loved by Bobby Dylan, Muhammad Ali (BIG INFLUENCE), and millions more.

19 & 20. The Grand Wizard/Abdullah Farouk

The greatest two managers ever, and they were the same guy! What a rap . . . What outfits . . . What wrestlers . . .

21. Lou Albano

Managed the Valiant Brothers . . . Was a true rock 'n' roll cat . . .

22. "Wild" Red Berry

A personal fave of mine from my glory years of the '60s . . . Managed the Fabulous Kangaroos and Hans "the Great" Mortier . . . Red would have to use his cane to break Mortier's unbreakable full nelson once it was slapped on a hapless opponent.

23. George "Crybaby" Cannon

Another great manager . . . Inspired Mr. Manitoba's "I Am Right" jacket . . . not to mention the legendary Dictators song . . .

24. Muhammad Ali

Wrestled Antonio Inoki . . . That gets him on the list. . . . A bad guy, in the real world . . . Took Gorgeous George and professional wrestling and incorporated them into life as we know it . . . Took that most cherished American sports institution, the heavyweight championship, and made it pure fun and excitement. Maybe my all-time favorite athlete.

Handsome Dick Manitoba is one of rock 'n' roll's greatest rule breakers.

FROM THE BOWERY TO BROADWAY, SORT OF: JÖRG BUTTGEREIT'S 7 MOST IMPRESSIVE PERSONAL MOMENTS IN PUNK HISTORY

1. In 1980 my friend Arnold and I went to see Throbbing Gristle at the SO36 Club in Kreuzberg, Berlin. Before the gig, Alexander von Borsig of Einstürzende Neubauten intoduced me to Genesis P-Orridge. Before the concert, they screened the Throbbing Gristle film *Cease to Exist*. Arnold fainted during the castration scene.
2. When the Dead Kennedys hit the SO36, the crowd pogoed so hard that the floor broke. The famous German punk girl Jenny went through the floor and her pet rat ran away. After the concert I was arrested for "being a punk rocker."
3. When Black Flag came to Berlin during the *My War* tour, I was totally shocked to see that Henry Rollins looked like a hippie.

4. In the mid-'80s I went to see Psychic TV at the Berlin Atonal Industrial Festival. I had a big camera, and by pretending to be a professional photographer, I was able to get in front of the stage to do some photos. Genesis P-Orridge was kind enough to strip down his pants to show me (and the rest of the audience) his penis with a brand-new cock ring.

5. In the '90s, Glenn Danzig played in the Columbia Club in Berlin. Since the Misfits had never played in Berlin before, this was a big thing. The ridiculous thing was, his majesty Danzig was having a sore throat this evening, and he insisted that this concert be a nonsmoking event. I suppose he was not a punk anymore.

6. In 2005, I directed the German Version of the Ramones musical, *Gabba Gabba Hey!*, in Berlin. Tommy Ramone came over from New York to see my play and he liked it. A lot. Honestly.

7. On January 1, 2006, I went to see Throbbing Gristle again at the Volksbühne in Berlin. Genesis P-Orridge was a woman now. During the last 25 years he/she has never failed to impress me. What's next?

Jörg Buttgereit, born in 1963 in Berlin, is the director and co-screenwriter of the legendary art-house horror movies Nekromantik, Nekromantik 2, Der Todesking, *and* Schramm. *He has also created documentaries and radio dramas, directed music videos and television, and is the author of several books. In 2005, he directed the German version of the Ramones' musical,* Gabba Gabba Hey!

AND WHEN I DIE, AND WHEN I'M GONE: 5 RECORDS MATT PINFIELD WANTS TO BRING WITH HIM TO THE AFTERLIFE

1. Ramones, *Ramones*

I bought it on my 15th birthday. I had just been suspended from junior high for the day for fighting with my archrival over a girl, so we both got sent home. I hitchhiked up to Korvette's and bought the album because it had 14 songs—unlike the latest Yes double album, which only had four.

2. Sex Pistols, *Never Mind the Bollocks*

One day I was sitting at the breakfast table with my parents and my mother mentioned that she was appalled to hear of an English band called the Sex Pistols—on the news it was reported that they were spitting on reporters.

I fell in love immediately.

3. The Clash, *London Calling*

Their finest moment and another defining album in my life. I bought it as an import, and at the time I thought that they had purposely left "Train in Vain" off the credits as a secret track. Later Mick Jones told me it was because they recorded it after the artwork was finished.

4. Elvis Costello, *This Year's Model*

I don't give a fuck what anyone says in the argument about whether EC was punk or new wave, because I was there in the late '70s buying every Elvis Costello single and every punk single that mattered, and this had more venom and spit than every other album that year.

5. Dead Boys, *Young, Loud, and Snotty*

I played this in my high school music appreciation class to introduce my unsuspecting classmates to punk rock, and many ran out of the room with their fingers in their ears.

Throughout the 1990s, Matt Pinfield was the host of MTV's 120 Minutes, *a weekly program that introduced a generation of kids to bands like the Dead Milkmen, Bad Brains, Nirvana, and Jon Spencer Blues Explosion. Pinfield currently hosts the satellite radio programs* Sound Off with Matt Pinfield *and* Matt Pinfield Plays Whatever He Wants.

8 PUNKS, 10 NERVOUS BREAKDOWNS

1. Shane MacGowan (the Pogues), part 1

After a period of drinking and taking a lot of pills, including 100 ml of Valium a day, MacGowan had a breakdown, and suffered from anxiety, depression, and hallucinations. Among his symptoms was seeing Egyptian hieroglyphs on his wall before going to sleep.

MacGowan was put into a drug ward in a London mental hospital. In occupational therapy, he painted terrifying images to scare the other patients, and was allowed to play the guitar, as long as he gave lessons to a schizophrenic girl. As Shane recalled in *A Drink with Shane MacGownan*, "It was very crude and barbaric [in there]. The dragon nurse deloused me, even though I didn't have lice. . . ." He was released after six months, shortly after his eighteenth birthday. "It was fate," he said, "that one of the first bands I should see when I came out was a bunch of people who looked like they ought to be in a loony bin." He was, of course, referring to the Sex Pistols.

2. Joey Ramone (the Ramones)

Joey left high school against his mother's wishes, liberal as she was, and at 19, took some bad acid and wound up in mental hospitals "a few times," according to biographer Everett True. Said his brother Mickey, in *Please Kill Me*, "I guess being in the nuthouse helped Joey, because when he got out, he had made friends with all the people in there, especially with all these chicks." Recalled Dee Dee Ramone, "He always had it better than anyone. Joey . . . always made the best of a bad situation. He was like a pimp. He even got one of these girls to set him up in an apartment."

3. Shane MacGowan (the Pogues), part 2

After having achieved fame, MacGowan experienced his second lockup. "St. John of God's is a kind of loony bin for alcoholic nutters in Dublin," MacGowan explains in *A Drink with Shane MacGowan*. "I was put in there in 1988 because I'd been drinking a lot of *poteen* and I collapsed." He woke up on a stretcher and tried to fight, but was institutionalized by force.

4. Richard Lloyd (Television)

Lloyd reported in *Please Kill Me*, "After I was hospitalized a number of times, in increments of nine months to a year, I would go insane." Lloyd's parents would not sign for electroshock therapy, and their son was given what he described as "chemical shock therapy, which consisted of them giving you a drug that puts you to sleep . . . every four hours, by injection." Then Lloyd was taken off that drug, and the doctors would administer its opposite, "a high-powered speed—and let it wring you out like a sponge." After this treatment he was put in a rubber room, where doctors observed him through a small window. Afterward, said Terry Ork, "He said that he sensed that he couldn't connect in the same ways anymore, and that he was a little crazy."

5. Lou Reed (the Velvet Underground)

In *Please Kill Me*, Sterling Morrison states that "Lou Reed's parents hated the fact that Lou was making music and hanging around with undesirables. . . . [T]here was always this constant threat of them seizing Lou and having him thrown in the nuthouse. . . . Every time Lou got hepatitis, his parents were waiting to seize him and lock him up." After a violent episode in school, Reed was given extensive electroshock treatment. The Velvets' guitarist, Bob Quine, said that Reed's doctors showed him "pictures of naked men, and if he got a hard-on he would get zapped with this electric pulse." Reed never forgave his parents for their "treachery" in subjecting him to these treatments, which he wrote about in the song "Kill Your Sons." Not surprisingly, the shock treatments were one of the pivotal events in Reed's life. He has said that they taught him the power of electricity, but at the same time they wiped out so much of his memory he despaired of ever becoming a writer.

6. Shane MacGowan (the Pogues), part 3

MacGowan was drunk in the Dublin airport and slipped, crashing into a woman, sending her luggage flying. She pressed charges, and Shane went back to St. John of God's. The woman dropped charges, but this time MacGowan was certified insane and kept in. He was made to attend group therapy meetings, which he later described as "whinging competitions, who's the biggest wanker competitions," adding, "I don't need to go to a meeting to ask God to help me—I can do that by myself."

7. Rat Scabies (the Damned)

In Clinton Heylin's *Babylon's Burning*, Brian James of the Damned had this to say about band member Rat Scabies: "Rat had something of a nervous breakdown. It was [the] 24-hour-partying. In France, he set up a little campfire in the middle of his hotel room, downed a couple of bottles of brandy, and tried to jump out of the window." Scabies told the music press he was "fed up with the John Wayne syndrome—people poking you in bars, trying to prove how hard they are. But more than anything, it was the pressures of being with four people in a year." During this period he wrote the memorable tune "Stretcher Case Baby." Rat soon left the band.

8. Emmett Jefferson "Patrick" Murphy III, a.k.a. "Murph" of Dinaosaur Jr.

In *Our Band Could Be Your Life*, Dinosaur bassman Lou Barlow tells the tale: "Mascis tossed some offhand barb at Murph. And Murph just yells at him, 'You should be raped by a bald black man!' And J goes, 'And that would be you, Murph?'" With wicked precision, the remark hit on both Murph's sexual insecurities and the fact that his hairline was prematurely receding. "And Murph," says Barlow, "just had a total breakdown. Murph hurled a table, a suitcase, and a lamp across the room and began crying and saying, 'I can't take it, I just can't take it!' . . . Hours later Murph was still weeping and pacing around. . . . Mascis was sound asleep in bed."

9. Brody Dalle (the Distillers)

Not a full-tilt nervous breakdown, Dalle only suffered from cultural meltdown, as recounted in *My So-Called Punk*. After immigrating to the U.S. from her native Australia, she had a severe anxiety attack in the supermarket. "I couldn't stand how many options I was given when I went to the grocery. I literally cried when I went to the store because I had to pick fucking cereals and I was faced with, like, 30 options. I'm standing there just devastated in the aisle, torn between Captain Crunch or Lucky Charms. Which one, y'know?"

10. Poly Styrene (X-ray Spex)

Styrene's breakdown came during the period her song "Identity" was in the Top 30 in Britain. The 21-year-old Poly was on tour when one night, at 3 A.M., she saw a luminous disc whose "radiation effect hit my body. . . . I don't know why I'd seen this thing," she said. "It hit me so much as an omen that I didn't want to play music anymore. It was horrible: I had a kind of breakdown. I wanted to take a break and rethink what I was doing. . . .

I [knew] I shouldn't continue. The only way I could resolve it was through mysticism, and that took some time." Styrene had a second breakdown one night at John Lydon's Gunter Grove house, hacking off her hair, convinced that a black magic ritual was taking place at the house.

11-STEP PROGRAM: HOW TO DANCE PUNK

1. The Pogo

The first official punk dance was the pogo, and all agree that Sid Vicious started it, though there are a variety of tales about how it happened. Sid was tall, but according to one version, he was in the back of a club and put his hands on the shoulders of the person in front of him to leap up and get a better view. And thus a dance craze was born. Sid claimed to have started it at early Sex Pistols concerts, since they "were the only group I wanted to see. I didn't know how to dance, so I just jumped up and down and bashed people. Then everybody else started doing it, but they didn't get it right, so I quit."

2. Slamming, Pushing, and Shoving

Says Shane MacGowan in *A Drink with* . . .: "The other big punk dance apart from pogoing was pushing and shoving, you know, 'slam dancing' they called it later. . . . But it was known as push-ing and shoving. There's a song, 'No Lip' by Dave Berry & the Cruisers, and it goes, 'Won't get none of my sweet sweet lovin', if you don't stop pushin' and shovin', pushin' and shovin' . . . and everybody would start pushing and shoving each other, and throwing each other onto the stage. . . . Then if anyone landed on the stage, one of the Pistols would boot him in the head and then try to fling him back into the audience. He'd disappear into the audience and get trampled. . . . He'd love every minute of it, y'know. He'd been beaten up by the Pistols." *[Author's note: Sorry to quote so much from this book, but it's the née plus ultra of punk memoirs. Lydon's is the other good one. I wish Joey R. had written one like these!—A.W.]*

3. The Worm

This was a favorite of Johnny Rotten's. It involved lying on your back and squirming.

4. The Robot

An early punk dance, popularized by Herr Rotten, the Robot involved jerky, machinelike movements, a kind of antidance dance.

5. Skanking

This one almost looks like a dance. It involves raising the right elbow to meet the uplifted left knee, and doing the same in reverse. Skanking originated in the 1950s at Jamaican dance halls and was later revived by punks. See D.R.I.'s (Dirty Rotten Imbeciles) indelible logo for proper form.

6. Stage Diving

Not quite dancing, but ditto a laudable form of self-expression. Be careful you don't land on your face.

7. Crowd Surfing

What follows a successful stage dive.

8. The Wall of Death, a.k.a. the Braveheart

The audience divides into two sections, with a gap of about ten yards between them. The two groups then run into one another, violently, and at top speed. Not dangerous at all.

9. The D.O.D., or "Dance of Death"

Steve Blush, author of *American Hardcore*, wrote, "Guy and Brendan of Insurrection were the D.O.D. boys—when kids slam danced, the two of them rolled around on the floor. If you did the D.O.D. now, you'd be killed."

10. Punk Rock Yoga

Yeah, really. Punk Yoga was started in 2003 by a yoga instructor who found traditional classes rigid and cliquish. Founder Kimberlee Jensen Stedl said, "I see Punk Rock Yoga teachers as rebelling against a broken yoga establishment. As an example, in my classes we practice 'mantra anarchy' . . . the students all consider a conception—such as determination—and then we all simultaneously chant our own word that embodies that concept. It makes for a beautiful cacophony."

11. Punk Rock Aerobics

Maura Jasper, a graphic artist, and Hilken Mancini, of the rock 'n' roll band Fuzzy, were bopping in their living room to fave punk rock tunes. The worked up quite a sweat while having fun! They went through all the necessary red tape, hired a dance club, and scheduled classes in Boston. The classes took off, attracting the likes of Evan Dando of the Lemonheads and J Mascis of Dinosaur Jr. Music includes the Buzzcocks, the Sex Pistols, and the Ramones. The beginning stretch is done to Fugazi, and the cool-down is done to Kraftwerk. Workout moves have names like "Beat on the Brat" and "Iggy's Pop." If a student doesn't have free weights, they're given a brick. And of course there's a shortage of Lycra and a lot of fishnets, and the air smells of stale beer and cigarettes. A piece of advice: "If spitting while pogoing, make sure you drink plenty of water to avoid dehydration." Plans for a franchise and a workout video are in the works.

7 TIPS FOR MOSH PIT FASHION, ETIQUETTE, AND SAFETY

This list is based on an excellent Internet article by Antigone, which can be found at www.gothpunk.com/howtos/ how-to-dancepunk.html.

1. Danger!

Remove dangling jewelry, earrings, and piercings. Writes Antigone, "Having your earlobe ripped in half is kind of cool when it happens, but you'll be pissed off for weeks afterward." If you don't want to remove your nipple piercings, wear a vest.

2. Don't . . .

Please don't bring cigarettes or glasses into the pit. In general, keep beverages out; the floor will lose traction if wet, and it will be your fault when everyone goes ass-over-teakettle and the hard-core moshers turn into Keystone Cops. Most discourteous.

3. Be a Gentleman . . . or a Lady

If somebody falls, on the edge of the pit or inside, please be a sport and give them a hand up.

4. Size Matters

If you're huge, don't mosh the skinny kids. And if you're tall, watch out for short people—you might fuck with their heads by accident, and in return they might fuck with your ribs or kidneys.

5. Arms and Legs

Flying leaps are dangerous. Keep your arms still, don't flail. You're not there to actually hurt people, even if you are practicing for a lifetime of crime.

6. Safety Tip

Learn how to fall, preferably from a martial artist. Or ask someone younger than you.

7. Finally . . .

Don't be an asshole. You know what we mean.

ERIC FRIEDL'S 10 THINGS THAT MADE MEMPHIS PUNK

Memphis, for all its legend as a blues mecca, is a pretty ornery place—some crossroads of magic and dirt, charlatans and day laborers. Folks here just believe that they can do it better, differently. This is true for Sam Phillips and Ike Turner and of Tav Falco, the Grifters, and modern punk rock. While lots of folks have played up the revolutionary aspects of Elvis, Jerry Lee Lewis, and Sam Phillips's Sun Studio, here are a few underappreciated punk moments from the Bluff City.

1. "Skin," Dan Penn

Known more for his epochal soul sides written for geniuses like Aretha, Otis, the tortured James Carr, and even popsters the Box Tops, here the white soul master turns guitars into bizarre washes of strings in a rambling, psychedelic but damn real meditation on racism and injustice. Available on his *Nobody's Fool* EP and also, bizarrely, on 45.

2. Tav Falco on Marge Thrasher's TV Show

Playing "Train Kept A-Rollin'" with a band versed in the use of chainsaw, video camera, and other ridiculous instruments, Tav Falco summoned music out of nothing more than appreciation of the odd and great, and (mostly, at this point, at least) sheer will. His donkey voice has never sounded so much like "ringing the bell" as he took on the truly bourgeois Mrs. Thrasher and all of Memphis society with his wild new art.

MARGE THRASHER: That may be the worst sound I've ever heard come out on television.
Tav Falco: Thank you very much.

3. "Cadillac Man," the Jesters

Legendarily sly session man/producer Jim Dickinson sneaks onto the Sun label and unleashes a bleating rock 'n' roll number with all of Jerry Lee's fury and none of his finesse. Beautiful.

4. "Mama, Look at Sis," Uncle Ben & His Nephews

Recorded live on Beale Street in the middle of the 1980s, featuring a guitarist/vocalist, perhaps a bassist nephew, and a drum machine. This unlikely combo creates simple, hypnotic blues out of nowhere, captured and released on Dr. David Evans' Memphis-based state-funded High Water label. DIY perfection undaunted by "appropriate" instrumentation.

5. "Did You," Copout

Memphis hardcore had a bigger run with the kids in the briefly popular hardline punk movement (straight edge gone ultrapuritan, until it became obvious that the leaders couldn't walk such a straight line—sound familiar?), but for straight old-school "I wanna punch your guts out" fury, Copout couldn't be beat. Ragged but tight, the band played through huge amps, screamed in pre–Cookie Monster style, and were very intense and ultimately very influential. Band members have gone on to Tragedy, His Hero Is Gone, War Cry, Severed Head of State, Talk Is Poison, and others. At some point, basically, they went on tour and never came back.

6. "Man With Gun Lives Here" Graffiti

Man with Gun were pretty interesting drunk/spastic panic protest punks, and included future His Hero Is Gone bassist Carl Auge and now–NYC dweller Mike Federline. In the 1990s, the band performed alongside other truly underground and independent Memphis punk bands, among them Taint Skins and Koma Toast. What was more impressive overall, though, was their citywide graffiti, a triangle with arms that was the hobo's sign for their band's name—"Man with Gun lives here." Like Missing Foundation's upside-down cocktail glass, which could be found all over the Lower East Side in the late 1980s/early 1990s, the Man with Gun symbol was *everywhere* in Memphis while this band was playing, and persisted (and seemed to keep multiplying) even after they'd disbanded. I'm sure, a decade later, there are still some symbols left, testament to a scene that thrived for those who knew and cared about it and only offered obscure signs of underground activity to those who didn't. Great.

7. "Superman Damn Fool" Graffiti

This is also gone, but during the early 1990s, this phrase was spread huge across the brick side of a building in white house paint on high-visibility Poplar Avenue as you left downtown, maybe leaving the courts as either lawyer or convict. A greater statement of punk underdog aesthetics I cannot fathom.

8. Little Jimmy King, live at Dwayne Burnside's Club, March 14, 1998

Guitar Wolf volume plus Gale family upside left-handed guitar chops assisted by unknown quantities of unknown substances. Riffing with only his right hand on the guitar neck, Jimmy bends over and slowly turns up his distortion pedal, staring into the crowd with a sinister smile, as the room is enveloped in pure noise. The cement walls screamed, the band was completely drowned out, and everything seemed perfect. Ears are still ringing. The club didn't last long, and by 2002, Jimmy was dead at 34, much too young. R.I.P.

9. Wattstax

Serving as soul missionaries, Memphis' finest takes on post-Watts riot L.A. anarchy. Rufus Thomas' crowd-control technique (not to mention his hot pants) cannot be topped. But the highlight for me is the post–plane crash Bar-Kays, an almost-completely new band now freaked out with bleached afros and wild outfits, launching into "Son of Shaft" with the classic "I'm the son of a BAAAD...." Pure adrenaline as the funk drops like any great Black Flag attack.

10. Punk Comes to Memphis

New York Dolls/the Stooges, Auditorium South Hall, 1973;
Sex Pistols, Talysen Ballroom, 1978; and
GG Allin, Antenna Club, 1991

These shows served as focal points for the confrontation of Memphis and midsouth punks versus nonpunks, and even what "punk" means to the punkers, not to mention punk versus rock "tradition." The location of the Sex Pistols show is now a Taco Bell. GG played the second-longest-running punk club in the U.S. (after CBGB), which is now a lesbian bar. New York Doll David Johansen fared the worst, arrested for either inciting a riot (according to newspaper reports) or, by his account, female impersonation. The Sex Pistols apparently survived unscathed. GG was reportedly later stabbed by a less-than-pleased female fan, but completed his "show"/defecation/nudist display before the police showed up to shut him down.

Bonus: 1910 Fruitgum Company's Bubblegum Riot

Those punk shows seem rather tame compared to this account from Memphis historian Jim Cole: "My number one punk rock moment was the first show I ever went to. I was in fifth grade and my two faves were at the Mid-South Coliseum—Tommy James & the Shondells and Tommy Roe! Also on the bill was a band called the 1910 Fruitgum Co. The 1910 Fruitgum Co. went nuts with a couple of members running up and down the aisles of the coliseum during their set. The MC came out and tried to get them to leave, but they kept playing. A security guard came onstage and the lead singer took a swing at him. A scuffle broke out and a dozen cops rushed the stage to physically drag them away. It was damn near a bubblegum rock 'n' roll riot! Well, so it seemed at the time.

"Memphis will do that to even the most tame of the bubblegummers! Memphis is, and will forever be, *punk*!"

Eric Friedl was taught the rudiments of punk rock guitar by Greg Cartwright and Jack Yarber and traveled the globe as Eric Oblivian in the Memphis garage punk band the Oblivians, performing such favorites as "Guitar Shop Asshole," "And Then I Fucked Her," and "Memphis Creep." He currently co-owns the Goner Records record store and label in Memphis, TN, and performs irregularly with True Sons of Thunder. He loves pelicans, Clint Howard, and vocoders.

ERIC DAVIDSON'S UNSUNG PUNK HOTBEDS OF THE 1990S

1. Green Bay, Wisconsin

Some gregarious goof named Time Bomb Tom threw a million great all-ages gigs at a crappy ex–bowling alley (Concert Café) right next to a dive called the Speakeasy (with the best punk CD jukebox in America) that might actually have been a speakeasy in this town where folks feel the constant need to get more drunk than Prohibition-era priests. The right Reverend Nørb presided over the pit, and a sense of humor was always rated miles above fashion, politics, and the usual bringdowns.

2. Groningen, the Netherlands

Any band that has played at the Vera club can attest to its ridiculous awesomeness. Free food and booze, backstage lined with old flyers and promo pix, they filmed every show, built four swanky apartments in the back for the bands, screen-printed their own fanzine and boss show posters upstairs, and the shows were always bawdy blasts, with a cavernous club in the basement for postshow shenanigans. Great record store right down the street. Lots of rich German tourists to make fun of.

3. Columbus, Ohio

Cheap rent; 25-cent beer nights at a bar right across the street from Stache's (a small joint that booked every '90s band you can name); two other punk clubs within stumbling distance; amazing record stores; three active indie labels; loads of noisy local bands; and about 40,000 frat guys to get pissed off at.

4. Austin, Texas

Though the city isn't exactly "unsung" for all the SXSW hoopla, the best shows were usually spewed out on a Wednesday in the middle of October by the Sons of Hercules, the Motards, the Cryin' Out Louds, Jack o' Fire, and others in an especially sweaty garage punk scene

5. Toronto, Canada

Lee's Palace was maybe the only big-ass club (and big-ass for punk is like 500 capacity) that was actually suitably dingy and suds-stained for the garbage rock set. There was shit going on in Montreal, too, but all the bands, zines, fans, and fights seemed to matriculate around this metropolis. Plus, it's close to . . .

6. Detroit, Michigan

Bandwagoners-come-lately cooed about the White Stripes five years after Detroit had been burning anew with post-Gories trash-stomp (Bantam Rooster, Chinese Millionaires, Dirtbombs, Dirtys, Clone Defects). Cool dives, good record stores, loads of unemployed drunks, decrepit industrial ghost buildings, incredibly dangerous dark alleys—all the good stuff.

7. Bloomington-Normal, Illinois
Great loser bands who never released much (Guilty Pleasures, Defilers), loosey-goosey backwash gigs from Chicago, and the great Mother Murphy's record store.

8. Solingen, Germany
If only for the hilarious goof-punk of the Jet Bumpers alone, this town would rank up there because how many fun punk bands are there from Germany . . . ever? Okay, the Steve McQueens. Anyway, the thing is, any band touring through Europe in the '90s had to go through Germany whether they wanted to or not, as German clubs had more moola and dedicated fans than you'd think, and this town was as active as any of them in the crazed punk show department. Runner-up: Münster, Germany.

9. Ponferrada, Spain
The whole country houses some of *the* most insane music fans. But this tiny outpost added a small after-show gathering hole (can't remember the name; gee, I wonder why?) that had—get this—a Lazy Cowgirls mural!! So tiny you couldn't help but take on the sweat stink of the greaseball next to you as he screamed at the bar keep for more Devil Dogs and Misfits tunes. I calmly asked the bartender for a screwdriver: BAM!—bottle of OJ; BAM!—bottle of vodka. 'Nuff said.

10. Regina, Saskatchewan, Canada
Actually, it wasn't much of a scene. It's just fun to make puns with the word Regina while stuck in the middle of Canada on tour.

Eric Davidson currently staves off creditors with his wit and minimum monthly payments whilst working as an associate editor at CMJ *magazine. But for the majority of his formative years, he was the singer for Columbus, Ohio, cad-punk band New Bomb Turks, who released numerous platters on Crypt, Gearhead, and Epitaph Records, among others, and toured the world and elsewhere.*

29 GRAFFITI MESSAGES FROM THE MASQUE CLUB

L.A.'s legendary punk rock club the Masque was started and run by Brendan Mullen. With Germs drummer Don Bolles and Feral House publisher Adam Parfrey, he wrote *Lexicon Devil: The Fast Times and Short Life of Darby Crash and the Germs.* The book features a long list of Masque graffiti. Here are our picks:

1. KILL GOD!
2. Eraserhead—ALRIGHT!
3. White Dopes On Punk
4. "The only way to escape horror is to bury yourself in it." —Jean Genet
5. Not all fags are wimps
6. DIE, NAZIS! Nope, not so simple
7. Crickets make nasty snacks for reptiles
8. The Germs steal stuff
9. I Knew This Would Happen
10. Get Right With God
11. Anarchy = Peace
12. Let All the Poison that Lurks in the Mud pass out
13. Blow God
14. Suicide Pole—Hit Head Here 50 MPH
15. Punks Rule—fuck disco
16. Kill the 70's
17. Everything is wrong
18. Kill yourself
19. Kill Hippies!
20. Long Hair Forever!
21. Bong Ludes!
22. No! No! No!
23. No Drugs No Pussy No Future No Bags
24. Who Cares About Cows
25. Barry Manilow was here
26. Cal Worthington Was Here—He's a Commie!

27. Quoth the Raven, "Nevermore!"
28. Pussy Power
29. Fuck the Whisky the Masque is Alive

THERESA KEREAKES' 5 SUREFIRE WAYS TO GET THROWN OUT OF THE WHISKY, 5 SUREFIRE WAYS TO SNEAK INTO THE WHISKY (OR OTHERWISE GET IN FREE), 5 SUREFIRE WAYS TO GET BOOKED AT THE WHISKY, AND 5 SUREFIRE WAYS TO NEVER GET BOOKED AT THE WHISKY (OR INVITED BACK)

5 Surefire Ways to Get Thrown Out of the Whisky

1. Let the stealth security guys hear you brag about sneaking in without paying.
2. Smuggle in your own booze or beer. (That's worse than sneaking into the club! This is where we make our money.)
3. Steal the Dead Boys' street clothes from the dressing room. (True story! That kid got his ass kicked by the world's most loyal and hardworking roadie, the Runaways' Kent Smythe.)
4. Jump up onstage when a major label band is playing and start singing Germs songs.
5. Grab Freddie the hot waitress's ass without her permission.

5 Surefire Ways to Sneak Into the Whisky (or Otherwise Get in Free)

1. Tell the box-office girl, "I'm the Germs' new drummer." (True story: this happened regularly before Don Bolles joined as a permanent drummer.)
2. Hide in the bathroom in between sound check and the show.

3. Deliver drugs to the backstage entrance.

4. Tag along with Rodney Bingenheimer (chances of being able to do so were highly increased if you are a young lady).

5. Bum rush the door.

5 Surefire Ways to Get Booked at the Whisky

1. When the booker is raging drunk at the end of any given show, offer to drive her home. On the way, take her to Canter's, buy her pastries for her next day's breakfast, then go to the 24-hour Rock 'n' Roll Ralphs and buy her a liter of water and some aspirin. Make sure she drinks half the bottle and takes two aspirin before she gets out of your car. If she pukes, hold her hair. Leave a cassette of your band with her, and call her the next day to ask if she's feeling all right.

2. Make sure your band has a reputation for attracting a heavy-drinking crowd. We sell more beer!

3. Agree to open for the most heinous major-label band on a Monday night for bad money.

4. Get discovered by Kim Fowley and let him create a show around your band.

5. Socks on cocks! (See below.)

5 Surefire Ways to Never Get Booked at the Whisky (or Invited Back)

1. Call up and say, "We're taking an ad out in the Weekly for all our gigs and want to make sure we include the Whisky on the list." AS IF! (True story: in 1980, Mötley Crüe's Nikki Sixx said this to me over the phone. I turned him down. But that's because he was my downstairs neighbor and the Crüe kept me up till all hours with their wanna-be rock-star antics.)

2. Take all your clothes off onstage, cause a riot, and then call up the next day asking for another gig. (True story. I

overheard Dee Dee, the owner's right-hand gal, talking with Anthony Kiedis on the phone. She said, "Well, then, put a sock on it!" Red Hot Chili Peppers did get invited back. Socks on cocks.)

3. Tell the booker you just played at the Starwood or Country Club. (Because you'll have to wait at least a month before we even think about booking you. Traitor!)

4. Drink more "free" beer than your rider allows, and have more people on your guest list than the headliner . . . and stiff your waitress on her tip.

5. Your band sucks, your agent's a dick, your audience trashes the club and sneaks in their own beer. You got nothing to offer.

Theresa Kereakes worked at the Whisky a Go Go during the Golden Age of L.A. Punk (1976–80) until the club closed in 1982. During that time, she was the photographer for seminal L.A. punk fanzine Lobotomy, the Brainless Magazine; *among her other credits is the photo on the cover of the Germs single "Forming."*

CLEM BURKE'S TOP 10 OF CBGB'S JUKEBOX'S GREATEST HITS

In all the years of doing this, I'd have to say that hearing our first single, 'X Offender,' for indie label Private Stock, for the first time on the CBGB jukebox was one of my biggest thrills. The feeling of knowing someone actually chose to hear it was very gratifying—I felt levitated.

1. Patti Smith, "Piss Factory"

The sound of rock 'n' roll poetry. A Patti Smith performance in 1975 was a life-changing experience. Here it is come to life on a

45-rpm record: Patti, Lenny, and Richard in all their ragged glory. Thank you, Robert Mapplethorpe.

2. Television, "Little Johnny Jewel"

Television is one of the greatest guitar bands of all time. This first single was so not "punk rock" and brilliant. Richard Lloyd takes a bow, and Billy Ficca channels Elvin Jones on Bleecker and Bowery (now Joey Ramone Place).

3. The Ramones, "Blitzkrieg Bop"

If CBGB was our Cavern, guess who were our Beatles? The first single on Sire Records was more then a little inspired by the Bay City Rollers, the '70s Beatles. "Hey, ho, let's go."

4. Richard Hell & the Voidoids, "Blank Generation"

Originally released on Jake Riviera's Stiff Records, this song owes more than a little to the Ray Charles classic "Hit the Road, Jack," and features the late, great Robert Quine on guitar and future Ramones drummer Mark Bell. An anthem.

5. Count Five, "Psychotic Reaction"

A '60s garage rock classic with a great Yardbirds-inspired rave-up. The song was even more frantic when covered by Television at CBGB. Was that you who chose that, Tom?

6. The Stooges, "I Wanna Be Your Dog"

Sometime in '76, Iggy showed up at CB's. Talk about the return of the Messiah. There are some great photos from that night of Ig and the Ramones together. This is PUNK ROCK!

7. Dead Boys, "Sonic Reducer"

A great record. The Dead Boys were managed by CB's owner Hilly Kristal and played there constantly. They also probably played this song all the time on the jukebox. We all played a benefit for drummer Johnny Blitz when he was stabbed on Second Ave. R.I.P. Stiv Bators.

8. New York Dolls, "Trash"

First there was the Velvets, then the Dolls, "the Kings of NY," or should I say Queens? But seriously, folks, we all worshiped this band, a major influence on everyone on the scene. Too bad the original Dolls had split up just as CB's got going, but this track, the first single from their second album, *Too Much Too Soon*, always sounded great on the jukebox. David Jo, Syl, Arthur, Jerry, Johnny—thank you.

9. The Heartbreakers, "Chinese Rocks"

Was this song written by Thunders or Hell or Dee Dee Ramone? It seems as though at the time there was a lot of confusion about that. It was later covered by the Ramones and also credited to them as writers, so I guess Dee Dee wins. A great song by one of the greatest rock 'n' roll bands ever. I saw many Heartbreakers shows at CB's, and they were always rockin'. Thunders really knew how to turn it on. When the Dolls split, we got the Heartbreakers—not bad.

10. Blondie, "X Offender"

All right, I'll admit I spent a few quarters playing this one at the club. Call it self-promotion. As I said, in the beginning it was always a thrill to be standing at the bar or talking to somebody when all of a sudden, there it was, your band's song being played on the jukebox. By the way, where is that jukebox today? What about all those original 45s? This is the song that led to our album deal and showed the world that we could make a good recording. Thank you, Richard, Craig, and Marty.

Clem Burke is the drummer for Blondie and has played with the Ramones (as Elvis Ramone), Dramarama, Chequered Past, the Romantics, and Iggy Pop, among many other punk rock luminaries; he has also played with Bob Dylan.

Rodney Bingenheimer's

"10 Punk Songs I Played First ... on KROQ"

1. "Blitzkrieg Bop"—the Ramones
2. "In the Sun"—Blondie
3. "Janie Jones"—the Clash
4. "New Rose"—the Damned
5. "Sonic Reducer"—Dead Boys
6. "(I'm) Stranded"—the Saints
7. "12XU"—Wire
8. "Johnny Hit and Run Pauline"—X
9. "In the City"—the Jam
10. "Orgasm Addict"—Buzzcocks

Rodney Bingenheimer vaulted into radio in late 1976 on KROQ, 106.7 in Los Angeles and launched punk rock on that very station, where Rodney still rules today. Mr. Bingenheimer has a star on the legendary Walk of Fame in Hollywood and has appeared in the movies Up in Smoke, Back to the Beach, *and* Rock and Roll High School. *He currently resides in Hollywood, where he can be seen riding up and down the strip in his Blue '67 GTO.*

A SEX PISTOL'S TOUR OF LONDON: 7 PLACES TO CONSIDER ERECTING STATUES, POSTING PLAQUES, OR JUST BLOWING UP

1. 430 Kings Road, SW10

This was the site of Malcolm McLaren and Vivienne Westwood's SEX Boutique, the epicenter of the punk revolution, where the look (spiky hair, clothes ripped or held together by safety pins) was created and where the Sex Pistols were formed, initially to promote the shop. Chrissie Hynde of the Pretenders was one of several future punk stars who worked at SEX.

2. Central St. Martins College of Art and Design, Charing Cross Road, WC2

The Sex Pistols had their first gig here in November 1975, supporting a band called Bazooka Joe. (Stuart Goddard, later Adam Ant, was a member of the headlining band.) At the time, several of the Pistols were living in an attic flat on Denmark Street, only a couple of hundred yards from the college, so they had only a little distance to travel to the gig, an important consideration for McLaren, whose earlier attempts to get all the band together at the same time had often ended in fiasco.

3. The 100 Club, Oxford Street, W1

This long-established music venue at 100 Oxford Street (it dates back to World War II) was the scene of a two-day punk festival, organized by Malcolm McLaren, on September 20–21, 1976. Many later-to-be-famous bands, including the Damned, the Clash, the Buzzcocks and the Sex Pistols, played during the two days. Sid Vicious, not yet a member of the Pistols, lived up to his name by attacking music journalist Nick Kent with a bicycle chain.

4. Thames TV, Euston Road, NW1

Studio 5 was the scene of the December 1976 confrontation between the Sex Pistols, attended by friends like Siouxsie Sioux, and the TV presenter Bill Grundy. Goaded by Grundy and encouraged to "say something outrageous," the band duly obliged with a volley of four-letter words of the kind not usually heard on television in the 1970s. Grundy also made a disastrously misjudged attempt to flirt with Siouxsie Sioux and was accused of being "a dirty old man."

5. 181 Marylebone Road, NW1

The Marylebone Magistrates Court at this address was where Sid Vicious and his girlfriend Nancy Spungen appeared on drugs charges in May 1978. Sid made faces at the court officers, fell asleep during the proceedings, and then attacked one of the photographers waiting outside the building to snap the couple as they left.

6. Buckingham Palace, SW1

The short-lived signing of the Sex Pistols to A&M Records took place on a table set up outside the gates of Buckingham Palace.

7. Lansdowne Studios, Lansdowne Road, W11

Here was where the Sex Pistols' first single, "Anarchy in the U.K.," was recorded. The anarchy was not restricted to the lyrics of the song. Both EMI and Polydor were under the impression that they had booked the group to record, and representatives of both labels squabbled among themselves while the band members and their entourage, none of whom had any idea how to make a record, spend two weekends of studio time producing endless, unusable tape.

This is from The Book of Lists—London *by Nick Rennison, first published in Great Britain by Canongate Books, Ltd., 14 High Street, Edinburgh, EH1 1TE.*

3 ABSURD PUNK ROCK ARRESTS AND LAWSUITS

1. Female Impersonation

In September 1976, the New York Dolls were touring the deep American South. Conservative rabble-rousers (not the Frank Zappa fan club) Mothers of Memphis were up in arms against the degenerate rockers. Co-headliner Iggy Pop performed without incident, but things went awry when the Dolls went on. A fan jumped onstage to kiss David Johansen, and the cops started beating the crowd with nightsticks. The singer was jailed, accused of starting a riot, and with female impersonation, for wearing pumps. Said Johansen, "I'm not impersonating anybody. I'm perfectly satisfied with what I am."

2. Politically Correctable?

In 1985, the Dead Kennedys were charged with distributing porn to minors when an 11-year-old girl bought a copy of their album, *Frankenchrist*, which included an insert by artist H. R. Giger known as *Penis Landscape*. The DKs were eventually acquitted, but the trial took a heavy toll: their record company went bankrupt, and the band was falling apart. Lead singer Jello Biafra got into hot water again when former bandmates East Bay Ray, D. H. Peligro, and Klaus Flouride discovered that Jello, generally known as a man of the people, had defrauded the band to the tune of $80,000 in back royalties. Jello's attempts to cover up the situation only worsened matters, and eventually the three band members filed a lawsuit alleging fraudulent conduct on the part of Biafra and his label, Alternative Tentacles. "We ain't gonna work on Biafra's farm no more," said guitarist East Bay Ray, accusing Jello of perpetrating the exact corporate evil against which he had spent his entire career preaching. Biafra was found guilty and ordered to pay his former bandmates their due, a decision upheld by an appellate court in 2004. When all was said and done the courts awarded the remaining Dead Kennedys in excess of $225,000 in damages. The Dead Kennedys continue to soldier on, performing with various singers filling in for Biafra.

NOSY . . .

MOTT

3. If It's on TV, Then It Must Be True

In 1997, John Rotten, née Lydon, took his troubles to daytime television courtroom show *Judge Judy* to bring his case against ex-PiL drummer Robbie Williams, who was suing Rotten for unpaid fees. Judge Judy found for Lydon, but not before telling him to control himself, and calling Williams a "nudnik." After the trial, Lydon exclaimed, "I love this country!"

13+ THINGS STOLEN BY SEX PISTOL STEVE JONES

Steve Jones was a kleptomaniac, with a passion for fine musical equipment. To start a group called the Strand (after the Roxy Music song), Jones, Paul Cook, and Warwick Nightingale lifted an amazing amount of gear, some of which wound up in the possession of the soon-to-be-formed Sex Pistols. Jones had many convictions for breaking and entering, theft, etc., and claims it was being in the Pistols that saved him from a life in the Big House. At an early Pistols gig, an audience member observed, "They didn't know how to play, and their equipment looked expensive, like it didn't belong to them." The following details are from Jon Savage's *England's Dreaming*.

1. Trendy Clothes

Because Jones wanted to wear the same clothes as Rod Stewart, he nicked stuff from the famous Kings Road Shop Granny Takes a Trip, among others.

2. A Car

The gang of friends stole a Jaguar and drove down Kings Road in their new duds.

3. Ronnie Wood's Fur Coat

In the winter of 1972–73, Jones' breaking and entering grew more adventurous. From Ronnie Wood's Richmond Hill mansion came a fur coat.

4. Keith Richard's Color TV

Richard's house on the fashionable Cheyne Walk yielded a color TV and more hip clothes.

5. A Drum Kit

Some of a Premier Drum Kit was liberated from the Shepherds Bush BBC studios. Paul Cook was the only one of the lads with a job, and he bought the odds and ends to make a full kit.

6. A PA System

Most of the Strand's PA was lifted from a van parked near the river in Hammersmith: it belonged to a cabaret group.

7 & 8. Two Columns and an Amp

Stolen from a reggae group in Watford.

9. A Fender Bass

This lovely guitar was "walked" from a van in Acton.

10. A Strobe Tuner

Stolen from a Roxy Music concert.

11 & 12. Two Guitars

One of the guitars was a genuine Les Paul, taken from Rod Stewart's mansion in Windsor.

13. David Bowie's PA and Miscellaneous Expensive Gear

Wrote Jon Savage, "The gang's greatest coup came in July 1973." David Bowie was playing a big concert at the Hammersmith

Odeon, to be filmed by D. A. Pennebaker. The boys slipped in easily since it was their local, and hid until nighttime. "There was a security guard asleep," said Warwick. "We walked onstage with a pair of pliers, snipping the wires. We took the whole PA, every single one of their microphones. RCA were recording it, so they were Neuman microphones, about five hundred pounds apiece. Prior to that, Steve had gone out and nicked a minivan to cart the stuff away in. It was me and Steve: Paul didn't want to go."

HENRY ROLLINS' LIST OF THE BEGINNINGS OF WHAT COULD HAVE BEEN GOOD LISTS

1. Worst thing man says to woman on television show, before they tear each other's clothes off ("We've been dancing around each other for a long time now. . . .")
2. Tip-offs that it's going to be a bad action film (when a man is surprised by another man in a scene, he says very audibly, "What the—!")
3. Top ten places where LSD will enhance your experience (e.g.,the Creation Museum)
4. List of things Pat Robertson may have yelled when he still had orgasms ("Jerry!")
5. A list of people whose hides will make a good coat after they're gone (e.g., George Hamilton)
6. A list of things George H. W. Bush fears more than his wife (????)

Henry Rollins is a musician, writer, speaker, and witness to the last days of a crumbling empire.

CHOSEN FROM THOUSANDS, 12 RANDOM PUNK ROCK QUOTES

1. Jim Carroll on the Roots of Punk

"I love the rituals of Catholicism. I hate the fucking politics, and the pope and shit, but the rituals of it are magic. I mean, the mass is a magic ritual for God's sake, it's a transubstantiation, and the stations of the cross—I mean, a crown of thorns? Getting whipped! Its punk rock."

2. William Burroughs on the Origin of the Word "Punk"

"I always thought that a punk was somebody that took it up the ass."

3. Marty Thau on the Invention of "New Wave"

"Seymour [Stein] . . . coined the phrase 'New Wave' because 'punk' was too tough to digest as a word for the record industry in conservative America, because of the connotation of 'punk.' It was a '30s, '40s prison term. If you were a punk in prison, you were the girlfriend of someone in Cell Block Five."

4. Writer Gordon Lamb on Punk, Then and Now

"There are pretty much two types of punks left in the world: those who act like it's 1977 and drape themselves in leather and studs—speaking vaguely on anarchy between sips of malt liquor; and those who won't wear leather at all, couldn't care less about 1970s punk rock, and speak seriously about anarchy during vegan potlucks."

5. Grant Hart (Hüsker Dü) on the Architecture of Punk

"You know the whole deal with tearing down the old to make room for the new? Well, music isn't city planning."

6. Darryl Jenifer (Bad Brains) on the Importance of Being Crucial

"My man [Bad Brains front man] HR started to realize more the crucialness of Rasta and started to act more crucial—which he still does. That's all that's about, crucialness."

7. Writer John Holmstrom on the Sex Pistols

"It's unbelievable that a rock group that played no more than 100 live performances and existed for only 27 months could become so internationally disliked as the Sex Pistols were."

8. Genesis P-Orridge (Throbbing Gristle) on Darby and Sid

"I knew Darby Crash was doomed the same way I knew Sid Vicious was doomed the first time I met him. I actually shivered. Like Sid's, Darby's life became an absolute commitment to recklessness . . . he had no choice. Some people are like that. They're here for a very specific catalytic reason, and their body and soul are here temporarily to perform a function on behalf of the psychic hygiene of the species and then they go. And they should be honored for that."

9. John Lydon (Sex Pistols, PiL) on Being Famous

A *Rolling Stone* reporter wrote in 2007, "Sid used to tease John, 'You'll spend the rest of your life with people coming up to you and saying, 'Weren't you Johnny Rotten once?' But in the end this proved wrong. Instead, Lydon said, 'I've had people ask me, "Are you the one who died?" And my answer is always yes.'"

10. Shane MacGowan on "The Last True Punks"

From John Lydon's *Tales of Johnny*: "Shane MacGowan, when asked if he and [Johnny] Rotten were the last true punks standing, wheezed, 'I didn't know he was still standing. I thought he was kneeling down giving me a blow job. He's only a little feller . . . But he's all right.'"

11. Joe Strummer (the Clash) on Conflict Resolution

"If you're having an argument which won't resolve itself . . . there's nothing better . . . than smashing someone's face in."

12. Black Randy (Black Randy & the Metrosquad) on How to Get Out of Jury Duty

"You get a big, black felt pen and you write in big letters across the form VIVA LA ANGEL DUST and you send it back in. They'll never bother you again."

BIBLIOGRAPHY

Antonia, Nina, *Johnny Thunders . . . In Cold Blood* (Jungle Books/Cherry Red Books, 2000).

Azerrad, Michael, *Our Band Could Be Your Life: Scenes from the American Indie Underground 1981–1991* (Little, Brown; Back Bay Books, 2001).

Berber, Steven Lee, *The Heebie-Jeebies at CBGB's: A Secret History of Jewish Punk* (Chicago Review Press, Inc., 2006).

Blush, Steven, *American Hardcore: A Tribal History* (Feral House, 2001).

Colegrave, Stephen, and Chris Sullivan, *Punk: The Definitive Record of a Revolution* (Thunder's Mouth Press; Avalon Pub. Group Inc.; and Cassell & Co., 2004).

Diehl, Matt, *My So-Called Punk* (St. Martin's Press, 2007).

Edwards, Gavin, *Is Tiny Dancer Really Elton's Little John? Music's Most Enduring Mysteries, Myths, and Rumors Revealed* (Three Rivers Press, 2006).

Heylin, Clinton, *Babylon's Burning: From Punk to Grunge* (Canongate, 2007).

Heylin, Clinton, *From the Velvets to the Voidoids: The Birth of American Punk Rock* (A Cappella Books, Chicago Review Press, Inc.).

Hogshire, Jim, *Pills-A-Go-Go: A Fiendish Investigation into Pill Marketing, Art, History & Consumption* (Feral House, 1999).

Johnstone, Rob, ed., *John Lydon: Stories of Johnny—A Compendium of Thoughts on the Icon of an Era* (Chrome Dreams, 2006).

Jovanovic, Rob, *Big Star: The Short Life, Painful Death and Unexpected Resurrection of the Kings of Power Pop* (A Cappella Books; Chicago Review Press, Inc.; and HarperCollins, 2005).

Lydon, John, with Keith and Kent Zimmerman, *Rotten: No Irish, No Blacks, No Dogs* (Picador/St. Martin's Press, 1994).

MacGowan, Shane, and Victoria Mary Clarke, *A Drink with Shane MacGowan* (Grove Press, 2001).

Marcus, Greil, *Lipstick Traces: A Secret History of the Twentieth Century* (Harvard University Press, 1989).

McNeil, Legs, and Gillian McCain, *Please Kill Me: The Uncensored Oral History of Punk* (Grove Press, 2006).

Mullen, Brendan; Don Bolles; and Adam Parfrey. *Lexicon Devil: The Fast Times and Short Life of Darby Crash and the Germs* (Feral House, 2002).

Mullen, Brendan, and Marc Spitz, *We Got the Neutron Bomb: The Untold Story of L.A. Punk* (Three Rivers Press, 2001).

Needs, Kris, and Dick Porter, *Trash! The Complete New York Dolls* (Plexus Publishing Ltd., 2006).

Porter, Dick, *Ramones: The Complete Twisted History* (Plexus Publishing Ltd., 2004).

Porter, Dick, *The Cramps: A Short History of Rock 'n' Roll Psychosis* (Plexus Publishing Ltd., 2007).

Reynolds, Tom, *I Hate Myself and Want To Die: The 52 Most Depressing Songs You've Ever Heard* (Hyperion, 2006).

Savage, Jon, *England's Dreaming: Anarchy, Sex Pistols, Punk Rock, and Beyond* (St. Martin's Griffin, 2001).

Stark, James, *Punk '77: An Inside Look at the San Francisco Scene Rock n' Roll Scene 1977* (RE/SEARCH Publications, 2006).

Thompson, Steven, and the Onion AV Club, *The Tenacity of the Cockroach: Conversations with Entertainment's Most Enduring Outsiders* (The Onion, Inc; Three Rivers Press, 2002).

Thomson, Graeme, *Complicated Shadows: The Life and Music of Elvis Costello* (Canongate, 2004).

True, Everett, *Hey Ho Let's Go: The Story of the Ramones* (Omnibus Press, 2005).

We Owe You Nothing: Punk Planet—The Collected Interviews (Akashic Books, 2001).

Wells, Steven, *Punk: Young, Loud & Snotty—The Stories Behind the Songs* (Thunder's Mouth Press; Avalon Publishing Group, Inc.; and Carlton Books, Ltd., 2004).

ACKNOWLEDGMENTS

AMY WALLACE

First and foremost to my brother David and the memory of our father, Irving Wallace, without whom the *Book of Lists* phenomena would never have exploded. To my original coauthor, Oe Warner, and her bitchin' interview with Dee Dee and Johnny. To Robert Nacey. To my current coauthor, Handsome Dick Manitoba, and his mighty fine wit and spectacular wife, Zoe; to Mike "the Shark" Edison, editor par excellence, without whom, and so on, and so forth, etc., and love. With gratitude to the wonderful Cliff Mott. To my agent, Ming Russell, Go Girl! Thank you. The list of friends old and new who breathed the air of the gods into this book is long: I'll keep it truncated. Mr. Tom O'Connor, master of the arcane, who helped me get this thing sold; to Emily Bradley, as fine a consultant and gal pal as ever there was; to Allison Berry—aw shucks, there just ain't words for you, you so fine; to Jonathan Richman, who never was a punk but somehow got lumped in with the population—a dear old friend and an inspiration to many: thanks for getting me to go see Van Morrison—let's keep dancing when we're in our walkers; to Ned Claflin: bard, baritone, and as true a friend as they make 'em (the world can't be all bad if there's a Ned in it); to maestro Adam Parfrey and his elfin muse, Jodi Willie; to beloved Sophie Duriez, who is forever; great big heap of thanks to Dr. Michelle Ware, who gave so much inspiration (more than she knows, I'll bet); to Sean "the Captain" Carasob—it was an honor to meet you and to have insider help. To my dearest Irene Miracle, who has the rare gift of being happy for others—thanks for so much help. Enormous thanks to Richard Stanley. Beloved thanks 4-ever to BadAss Will Houston. Chester Simpson—next book! Michael Loftus, Franz Rodenkirchen, Chris Miller, and Mark Levinthal—deadline was too short: next book, and a round on me. Paul McConnell, generous, sultry friend—thank you. Will Huston, you dawg. Carol McArthur (next book, ahoy!) And to Charles Hauther, Kerry Slattery, Sophia the Great, Courtney, Emily, Darin, Lucy, and all my dear friends at Skylight Books—too many to name—bless your bizarre, bookworm hearts. Thanks for feeding me pickles throughout this book's pregnancy. And a few fond punk memories of the class of 1975–80, the Fab Mab, that iconic last gig at Winterland, smoking opium and reading tarot cards with Nick Knox of the Cramps—a tip of the hat to Alex Chilton, and delightful meetings; a clink of the highball glass to Paul Westerberg, who I hope to meet someday. To Bob Bassing, best of friends, finest of writers and confidants. To Jeff Scott and Josef Marc—keep on provin' it. To all the punk writers, cashiers, check-outers, and barflies—lets go out on a wing and a prayer.

—A.W.

HANDSOME DICK MANITOBA

Thank you so much to my cowriter and tireless coworker, Amy Wallace . . . my wife and partner, Zoe, for saying, "Do the book!" . . . my editor, Mike "Sharky" Edison, the Grand Wizard of Publishing, for guiding me to the belt . . . my favorite illustrator (after Steve Ditko and Jack Kirby, of course), the "Sensational" Cliff Mott . . . my Main Mensch, Danny Fields . . . Mr. Manitoba's favorite lawyer in the world, David Zensky (Akin Gump) . . . Tony "Buzzcock" Barber (whatta pal!) . . . and all the cats and chicks that I call *friends*, who responded in kind with a list . . . and thank ME, (shades of Dee Dee Ramone!) for keeping my shit together, creating a value for my services out of the fuckin' ashes, workin' my ass off, and showin' up for life!

—H.D.M.

Amy and Richard would also like to thank the extended team of punks: Theresa Kereakes, Eric Davidson, Aaron Lefkove, Jenna Young, Polly Watson, Steve Ramirez, Clare Cerullo, and the punkest of the punk, Sheena Armstrong, all of whom left their mark on *The Official Punk Rock Book of Lists*.

ABOUT THE AUTHORS

Amy Wallace is the author and coauthor of 15 books, among them the No. 1 *New York Times* best seller *The Book of Lists*, written with her father, the late Irving Wallace, and her brother David Wallechinsky. She is the author of the acclaimed erotic novel *Desire* and of the groundbreaking *The Prodigy: A Biography of William James Sidis, America's Greatest Child Prodigy*. In print for 30 years is *The Psychic Healing Book*, coauthored with William Henkin; the highly controversial *Sorcerer's Apprentice: My Life with Carlos Castaneda*; and *The New Book of Lists*. She is coauthor of two upcoming books: *The Horror Book of Lists,* with Scott Bradley and Del Howison, to be released on Halloween, 2008; and the updated *Sex Lives of Famous People*, a Wallace family book, to be released in spring 2008. She lives in Los Angeles with her feline muses, Hank da Tank and Bella.

Handsome Dick Manitoba, born Richard Blum in Manhattan, grew up in the Bronx . . . failed college music class . . . dropped out soon after . . . kicked heroin and alcohol's ass . . . has been since 1974 lead singer of NYC punk legends the Dictators . . . is occasional lead singer with the MC5 (DKT/MC5) . . . is the proprietor of the "World's Greatest Rock and Roll Neighborhood Tavern," Manitoba's, Ave. B . . . is the NYC star of *The Handsome Dick Manitoba Radio Program*, in Little Steven's Underground Garage, on Sirius Satellite Radio . . . lives happily ever after, in the East Village, NYC, with his beautiful wife, Zoe, and his perfect boy, Jake Koufax Manitoba.

Drawing inspiration from liberal doses of *Mad* magazine and the Ramones, **Cliff Mott** applied his irreverent and DIY sensibilities as art director of *Cracked* magazine, working with such artists as Don Martin, John Severin, and Steve Ditko. Not content to limit his vision to the guts of a humor mag, he has punked it up plenty with pen and ink for such luminary reprobates as the Devil Dogs, Boss Hog, Jon Spencer Blues Explosion, the New York Dolls, the Hellacopters, and the Dictators, not to mention hot rod hero Ed "Big Daddy" Roth.